CHRONICLES OF THE

# Vikings

There have been many books about the Vikings but few that see them from their own point of view. Most books rely heavily on the records of prejudiced observers (who saw the Vikings only as savage and unscrupulous raiders and invaders) or on the archaeological record which tells us much about the material culture of these peoples but little about their values and ways of thinking. This book brings the Vikings to life, showing them as they saw themselves, portrayed in their own writings or in the reports of people who knew them closely. It comprises a series of new translations from primary sources: runic inscriptions left behind by the Vikings, poems of their official skalds, literary works that entertained them, the few prose historical accounts that derive direct from Vikings, and eyewitness reports of how the northern peoples lived.

It defines the social values of the Viking Age, their heroic view of life which sometimes contrasts with a much more down to earth way of looking at things. It looks at the problems they encountered in discovering, populating and cultivating new lands, the difficulties of keeping law and order and the solutions they tried. It shows how they coped with famine and other natural disasters, travel and its perils, something of their popular culture, proverbs and aphorisms, and their sometimes irreverent approach to their gods and goddesses, the supernatural, magic and charms. Both at home and overseas, the Vikings live in this book.

To understand the primary sources it is essential to have some idea of how they came into being and how they were preserved. In his extensive introduction, Professor Page discusses the problems involved in using writings of this sort and looks at the information that is preserved solely in these primary sources.

Professor R. I. Page is Emeritus Elrington and Bosworth Professor of Anglo-Saxon at the University of Cambridge, a Fellow of Corpus Christi College and Special Professor of Anglo-Saxon Studies at the University of Nottingham.

CHRONICLES OF THE

# Vikings

*Records, Memorials and Myths*

R. I. Page

University of Toronto Press
Toronto Buffalo

© 1995 R. I. Page

Published by British Museum Press
First published in North America by
University of Toronto Press Incorporated
Toronto Buffalo

R. I. Page has asserted his right to be identified as the author of this work.

ISBN 0–8020–0803–8 (cloth)
ISBN 0–8020–7165–1 (paper)

Canadian Cataloguing in Publication Data
Page, R. I. (Raymond Ian)
Chronicles of the Vikings

Includes index.
ISBN 0–8020–0803–8 (bound)
ISBN 0–8020–7165–1 (pbk.)

1. Vikings – History – Sources.   I. Title.
DL65.P34   1995      948'.022      C95–931684–1

Designed by Andrew Shoolbred
Typeset by Create Publishing Services Ltd, Bath, Avon
Printed in Great Britain by The Bath Press, Avon

# Contents

# Preface

This is both a book about Vikings and a book by Vikings. It shows how they portrayed themselves, giving translations of written sources that come from Viking Age Scandinavia either immediately or indirectly. In general, then, it makes use of sources that derive from the Vikings or from people who observed their practices, values and activities at first hand. It makes no attempt at a formal history of these northern nations – only marginally does it treat of political and economic effects of Scandinavian aggression against the kingdoms and peoples of Western and Eastern Europe in what is called the Viking Age.

The Viking Age is variously dated, according as scholars wish to present their own particular theses about it, but generally accepted limits are *c*.800–1100 AD. In a period of three centuries there are bound to be changes in ways of behaving and thinking; and in the several countries that constitute Viking Scandinavia there are likely to be local variations. Because of our lack of primary source material from diverse places and times, these can only be hinted at here. Instead I present a broad account of aspects of Viking society – distinctions of class, of occupation, of values, of beliefs. I record farmers, fishermen, merchants and mercenaries (though these are not necessarily different people); pagans and Christians and magicians; kings and courtiers, poets and peasants; strong-minded men and strong-minded women; Vikings abroad and Vikings at home; how they made money and what they spent it on. Or at least what they were prepared to admit publicly about all these things.

Many of the best and best-known tales of Vikings are preserved in questionable sources – most obviously in the splendid Sagas of Kings and Sagas of

Icelanders that give a latter-day picture of Vikings. These I have not used, save as secondary, explanatory, material, since the rigorous historian must look at them with suspicion. Instead I try to present primary sources in as close translation as I can achieve with any degree of felicity, and always with the reminder that a translation must not be accorded the respect of an original. This problem of how to use the written evidence I discuss in some detail in my first chapter. The choice of extracts for translation is my own and some will disagree with what I have picked, what I left out; here I have had valuable suggestions and advice from Dr Lesley Abrams of Cambridge University, Dr Judith Jesch of Nottingham University, and Professor Jan Ragnar Hagland of the University of Trondheim, Norway. On matters of detail I have had the botanical advice of Dr Oliver Rackham of Corpus Christi College, Cambridge, and of Dr K. D. Bennett of the Subdepartment of Quaternary Research, Cambridge; while Mr Geoffrey Styler, also of Corpus Christi, has supported my failing footsteps through the Greek texts.

In the presentation I have distinguished between primary and secondary sources and my own comments. Extended translations are indented, to distinguish them from my own comments which are not. Where an original text is post-Viking Age, I have differentiated it by putting a dagger † at the beginning and end. Within texts my own explanatory comments and additions are enclosed in square brackets [   ]. Shorter quotations are set within my text, distinguished by single inverted commas if they are contemporary with the Viking Age, by daggers if they are later. In inscriptions square brackets denote words no longer visible but recorded in earlier drawings, while diagonal brackets ⟨   ⟩ indicate words and phrases implied but which need to be added to a text to make up the sense in English.

Inevitably there are problems in quoting Viking words and name forms. During the Viking Age the languages of Norway, Sweden, Denmark and their colonies were closely alike; yet there were some differences, notably between East Norse (Danish and Swedish) and West Norse (Norwegian and Icelandic). All were different from what students tend to think of as 'standard Old Norse', which is an artificial form of the rather later medieval Icelandic tongue, generally used in editions of the sagas. Quotations in *italics* commonly use this latter version of the language. Transliterations of runic Norse are given, as is standard practice, in **bold**. Name forms always cause problems. I have usually tried to normalise these by removing inflexional endings, accent marks and peculiar Norse characters, so that, for instance, the personal name *Þorlákr* will appear as Thorlak, the place-name *Breiðafjörðr* as Breidafiord. Where there is a commonly-known English form, however, I have tended to use that – it would be pedantic to call Iceland *Ísland*. There are, of course, uncertainties here. How do we name the great Dano-English king whom we have learnt to call Canute: Cnut (as the Anglo-Saxons, and Anglo-Saxon historians use) or Knut (= Old Norse *Knútr*)? (I have tended to call him Cnut in an English context, Knut in a Scandinavian one, but these cannot always be distinguished). My colleagues will have differing opinions as to what should be done, and that will affect in particular the rendering of name forms found in runic texts.

In general a Viking had only one name. To distinguish him (or her) from others with the same name there could be added some byname which could refer to i) father (or sometimes mother) as Olaf Tryggvason, Svein Estridsson; ii) dwelling-place, as Lon-Einar to distinguish him from Einar Sigmundarson who lived nearby; iii) a nickname that might define some characteristic or achievement. Such nicknames are tricky for the translator. Some are clear enough, as *Helgi magri*, Helgi the Skinny who had suffered from undernourishment as a child, or *Þuríðr sundafyllir*, Thurid 'sound-filler', whose strange byname the historian feels impelled to explain (p. 66 above). In such cases I have usually translated the nickname. In others, however, the byname is opaque or at least in dispute, and here I give an anglicised form of the Old Norse without explanation. Critics will doubtless find fault with my varied practices. I hope I shall be judged 'constant, if only in inconstancy'.

Such a book as this has not been easy to process, and I should like to thank those in the British Museum Press who have been so helpful: Celia Clear, who first accepted the idea of this book and commented on an early draft, and her colleagues, Sarah Derry, Teresa Francis and Julie Young, who have seen it through the press with a commendable appearance of patience.

R. I. PAGE
March 1995

# CHAPTER 1

# Getting to know the Vikings

The Vikings were not famed for their literacy. In the usual sense of the word medieval peoples became literate when they became Christians, for Christianity was the religion of the Book and of books. So it was not until their conversion to the new religion (quite late in the Viking Age) that Norsemen learned the roman alphabet and the practice of reading and perhaps writing. That, at least, is what is commonly believed. In fact, the Vikings had an earlier if restricted form of literacy; they produced texts in a script called runic, one designed not for writing on parchment but for engraving on wood, bone, metal and stone. It is only in these inscriptions that the Vikings speak directly to us, without intermediary; but though they speak, they do not say much. Little of what they once inscribed has survived. Wood perishes quickly. Metal corrodes, or if it is precious is likely to go to the melting pot. Stone weathers and wears, or is re-used in buildings or roads. Thus, many Viking Age inscriptions have gone; others survive only in part. Inscriptions are unlikely to be long, so they record only snippets of information that have to be supplied from other sources.

The runic alphabets the Vikings used were not ideal for expressing the Northern languages of the early Middle Ages. Until the later part of the Viking Age each *futhark* (as the rune-rows were called) had only sixteen distinct letters. Four were vowel symbols (for part of the time there were no distinct graphs for the common vowels *e* and *o*). The other twelve were consonant symbols, and twelve was not nearly enough. There were no specific letters to cover the sounds usually represented by *d, g, p, v/w*. Thus runic spelling had to be approximate, with *d* given by the related **t**; *g* by **k**; *p* by **b**; *v* by **u**. There were two symbols representing *r* sounds, sounds which were distinct at the beginning of the Viking Age though they fell together by its end. Thus spelling could not reflect pronunciation closely, and there was no standard spelling tradition. There was no consistent punctuation or word separation. Such a word as Old Norse *eftir* (which means 'after', 'in memory of', and so is common in memorial inscriptions) can be spelled **aftir**, **aftiʀ** (with the variant *r*-rune), **iftiʀ**, **aiftiʀ**, **auftiʀ**, **uftiʀ**, **huftiʀ** and in other ways too. Doubled letters were usually cut singly, even if they occurred in successive words. A Swedish Viking, wanting to record that 'he took danegeld from Cnut in England' (*hann tók Knúts giald á Englandi*), cut **hantuknuts | kialtænklanti**. From this readers should conclude that interpreting Viking Age inscriptions is a matter for specialists, and they must regret that specialists often disagree about both form and meaning of a text.

Though runic inscriptions have their problems of interpretation, yet they are a primary and valuable source of information on the Viking Age. Many of them are epitaphs, cut on the great stones that can still be seen dotted about the Swedish landscape, or more sparsely in museums and churches in Denmark and Norway and in Viking-settled lands overseas. They record activities, adventures, exploits; property holding and inheritance; personal and public relationships; social ranks; political activity; devotion to a god; acts of social charity; and so on. We are of course faced with the obvious fact that epitaphs do not always tell the truth about the dead and certainly not the whole truth. Yet though such inscriptions may not always give us the facts about what Vikings did, were and believed, at least they show what were the public values of the Viking Age, how Vikings thought they ought to behave, what qualities they admired and what despised. They may give historical information inadequately reported in other sources: that Swedes took part in the Danish attacks on England; that Norsemen intermarried with Celtic settlers on the Isle of Man; that the Viking settlement in Novgorod, Russia, lasted long enough into Christian times for them to set up a church there; that a Danish force under a King Svein besieged the important market town of Hedeby (Haddeby, Schleswig: **haiþa bu** in runic spelling); that fighting-men from Skåne, in the south of modern Sweden, took part in a great battle at far-away Uppsala.

Like all 'written' sources the rune-stones need interpretation. What we get in this book are translations of the inscriptions, but it should be remembered that there are two stages before translation. The inscription must be transliterated: that is, its text must be transferred from the original runes to a form of roman script to make it accessible to the reader who is more concerned with its content than its form. It must then be transcribed: the transliterated text put into a 'standard form' of the language, Old Norse, that the Vikings spoke, to remove individual peculiarities of runic spelling and sentence form. Each of these practices increases the distance between the modern reader and the early medieval rune-cutter. For instance, at Sövestad, Skåne, Sweden, is a stone with the text (transliterated): x **tuna** x **sati** x **stain** x **þansi** x **aftiʀ** x **bram** x **bunta** : **sin** x **auk** x **askutr** x **sunʀ** x **hans** x **han** x **uaʀ** x **bastr** x **bumana** x **auk** x | x **miltastr** x **mataʀ**. It is quite an easy text because it happens to be divided into its individual words (which does not always happen in runic texts). Transcribed into a 'standard' form it becomes *Tonna setti stein þensi eftir Bram bónda sinn ok Ásgautr sonr hans. Hann var beztr búmanna ok mildastr matar.* Translated this becomes: 'Tonna (and Bram's son Asgaut) set this stone in memory of her husband Bram. He was the best of *búmenn* and most liberal of food.' The word order has to be changed for modern English because we have no formal way, as Old Norse has, of signalling that Asgaut also was the subject of the verb *setti*. We indicate this by word order whereas Norse adds the appropriate masculine case ending *–r* to the name. I have left the word *búmenn* because we are uncertain of its precise meaning. Literally, the word (singular *búmaðr*) means 'farmer, man of the farm', but it is possible that here it defines some sort of office, 'bailiff'. A translation has to choose arbitrarily one of the two meanings, and to that extent may mislead. The phrase 'most liberal of food' is a literal one and its implications for Norse behaviour are important. Hospitality was much admired. It was also a necessary feature of country life in an early society without a formal road and inn structure. Or the phrase here may indicate that Bram was generous enough to feed his servants and retainers well, so he could count on their loyalty if he were in trouble.

Runic inscriptions are not uniformly distributed throughout Scandinavia or throughout the Viking Age. There are favoured regions and times. Sweden has far more rune-stones than Norway and Denmark, and in certain districts of Sweden they are particularly common, in Uppland, Södermanland, Gotland, Öland, Öster- and Västergötland. The eleventh century is a peculiarly rich period for Swedish runes. In the Norse colonies overseas the tiny Isle of Man has a surprisingly large collection of rune-stones, mainly from the tenth century; whereas Iceland, settled almost exclusively by people of Norse stock, has no Viking Age runes. Why such disparity should be is unknown. Some distribution patterns may represent population density; but things like social rank, settlement and inheritance patterns, ethical ideas, cultural influences may also have their effects on the production and distribution of rune-stones. Wealth must have played a part too, for an elaborate rune-stone would presumably be an expensive luxury. Thus rune-stone inscriptions cannot be taken as documents typical of the Viking Age as a whole.

Rune-stones are public documents intended to be widely read or at least widely understood. Their statements may be significant in the public domain. They may serve as death certificates and so as statements of inheritance, of claim to land or property; something needed in an age that had no tradition of written documents to do the job. They may record the local fame of an individual or assert a family's prestige. That is why they are often erected on public sites: by the side of a main road, at a bridge-point over a watercourse, on a field where legal moots were held. Also why they sometimes form one part of a complex and eye-catching monument that may have other, uninscribed, standing stones. Or are carved on a cliff-face or natural boulder with the highway passing just by. In many cases it seems the runes were brightly coloured to throw the text into prominence, though the colouring has vanished with time.

In contrast, the runic inscriptions on other objects are private documents and often trivial in information; trivial but not negligible. For example, from somewhere in Norway comes a house-shaped wooden reliquary shrine covered with metal plates with copper-alloy fittings; it has, cut into its base, a group of decorative patterns, some based on Viking ship stems, and the text *Rannveig á kistu þessa*, 'Rannveig owns this box'. The runes are of a type tentatively dated *c*.1000, perhaps from west Norway. The box is of

Celtic design. Apparently this is part of booty stolen from Scotland by a Norwegian Viking and given to his woman. Though the text is trivial – an ownership formula – its implications are not. Again, at Timans in Gotland, Sweden, was found a small sandstone implement, part cut out to form a mould for casting metal. On the opposite flat side is engraved an inscription in runes that have been dated to the eleventh century. They read: :ormiga:ulfuair:krikiaʀ:iaursaliʀ:islat:serklat, two unusual personal names followed by four names of peoples or places: krikiaʀ, *Grikkiar*, 'Greeks', usually used of the peoples of the Byzantine Empire; iaursaliʀ, *Iórsalir*, 'Jerusalem'; islat, *Ísland*, 'Iceland'; serklat, *Serkland*, an eastern country occupied by dark-skinned peoples. The stone then records four regions where Vikings were active for different purposes: Byzantium for trade, Jerusalem for pilgrimage, Iceland for settlement, the Middle East for adventure. Why this inscription was cut is unknown, but it summarises the outgoing nature of the Viking Age.

Minimally literate though the Vikings were, yet they had a literature. Poetry flourished among them but could not be extensively written down in Viking times. It was preserved in memory and performed orally, and was not formally recorded – save for small samples in runic texts – until the Scandinavian peoples encountered Christianity and took up its writing systems. Thus this literature does not come to us direct from the Viking Age, but through the intermediary of later medieval times, and that can cause difficulties. There are two major sorts of verse, Eddic (or, as some say, Eddaic) and skaldic. The division is not absolute – some skaldic verse had characteristics appropriate to Eddic – but the distinction is a convenient one.

Most of the Eddic verse is preserved in two manuscript books of the thirteenth century (which is a couple of hundred years after the end of the Viking Age). The primary manuscript is that called the Codex Regius, the Royal Manuscript, since it was kept for three centuries in the Royal Library, Copenhagen (where it had the press-mark GkS 2365 4°), before being returned to Iceland in 1971 under an agreement between Danish and Icelandic governments. It is undistinguished in appearance but invaluable in content, for it contains twenty-nine poems, complete or fragmentary (a gathering of eight leaves is lost in the middle). A second, somewhat later, book numbered AM 748 4° in the Arnamagnean Institute, Copenhagen, has seven poems, one of which is not in the Codex Regius. A few more poems showing similar characteristics survive in other manuscripts; or fragments of verse are quoted in later prose texts, suggesting an extensive literature largely lost. This whole group of poems is known under the title of the *Elder* or *Poetic Edda*.

The Eddic poems preserve indirect evidence of the nature of the Viking Age. They do not tell of Vikings as such, but relate religious myths and traditional ways of thinking, and tales of ancient heroes. So they are primary sources of information on early Scandinavian religious belief and attitudes, on modes of thought; while the adventures of the great warriors and princes of the Germanic past that entertained Norsemen give some clue to the values they accepted and to the tenor of life in the Viking Age. But of course, the Eddic poems are not as easy to use as that. In the first place, it is hard to date their composition, though it is generally thought that some of them are from the Viking Age and others later, perhaps as late as the twelfth century. In the second, it is hard to localise their composition, to establish which parts of the Viking world they were written – or even preserved – in. In their present form the texts of the two major manuscripts, which are both Icelandic, derive from a common early-thirteenth-century original and these are about the only facts known concerning the background of the Eddic poems. Thus they can only be used in the present book with caution, as peripheral illustration of manners, beliefs and modes of thinking. Yet they must be used. Without them our knowledge of early Norse religion and our under-standing of the heroic code of the Vikings would be immensely impoverished.

Verse forms of the Eddic poems are comparatively simple. The poems are stanzaic. Their metres are quite elementary. There is no, or little, rhyme; in its place is alliteration, the practice of beginning important syllables in a line with the same sound. As an example, here is the opening of the first poem of the Codex Regius, a summing up of pagan mythology known as *Völuspá*, 'The wise woman's prophecy'. I give an edited form (not an exact copy of the manuscript) for convenience, dividing the text into its poetic lines and indicating alliteration in **bold**.

| | |
|---|---|
| **H**lióðs bið ec allar | **h**elgar kindir, |
| **m**eiri oc **m**inni, | **m**ögo Heimdalar; |
| **v**ildo, at ec, **V**alföðr, | **v**el fyrtelia |
| **f**orn spiöll **f**ira, | þau er **f**remst um man. |

The story line of an Eddic poem is usually fairly simple too. Straightforward narrative, or dialogue, or dialogue interspersed with narrative (perhaps supplemented by a prose explanation), or straightforward monologue. There are difficulties, of course. Some words and phrases are uninterpreted, perhaps corrupt. There are allusions that a contemporary audience would pick up without difficulty but which are dark to a less informed readership like us. There are gaps in the texts here and there, and perhaps wrong verse order - something that might result from oral telling or may have arisen during transfer to the written page. But on the whole the Eddic poems present comparatively few problems of reading.

Not so the bulk of the skaldic poems. These are often ferociously difficult in vocabulary, word order, sentence structure, allusion. They were created for trained audiences who knew what formal qualities to expect in such poems. They were also composed for specific occasions. Whereas the Eddic poems are anonymous, the skaldic verses are often attributed to professional poets whose names, dates and political allegiances are known. Thus many of the skaldic verses can be dated, either precisely or approximately; they can be referred to specific events in Viking history; they record contemporary reaction to the facts or fictions of Viking life. They are the abstracts and brief chronicles of the time, but they need a lot of work by the modern reader to make them so.

The word 'skaldic' derives from Old Norse *skáld*, 'poet'. As borrowed into modern English the word implies a special sort of professional, the court poet of the Viking Age, attached to the entourage of a king, earl or other great leader. Such a poet had a trained and captive audience and in them he could assume a primary education in poetic conventions. In consequence, the poetry he wrote for the court was commonly highly stylised. It had an artificial diction and sentence structure, an elaborate combination of verse forms, rhymes and alliterations, an appeal to abstruse references, often to details of the ancient mythology of the Scandinavian peoples. At its most complex it must have been hard indeed for anyone to follow at first hearing. It was also hard for later scribes to copy accurately and hence for modern scholars to edit. It is certainly so for modern readers to understand.

It is best to begin with an example of a single verse of skaldic poetry. I take the most common of the stanza forms, that known as *dróttkvætt*, 'court metre', though this has numbers of variants. The basic form looks like this:

| | | |
|---|---|---|
| 1. | fekk **m**eira lið **m**iklu | 2. |
| | **m**ildr en gløggr til hildar, | |
| | **h**irð þás **h**ugði forðask | |
| | **h**eið þióðkonungs reiði; | |
| | en **v**inlausum **v**ísa | |
| | **v**arð, þeim es fé sparði, | |
| | – **h**áðisk víg fyr **v**íðum | |
| | **v**angi – þunt of stangir. | |

2.
fekk meira lið **mik**lu
**mild**r en gløggr til **hild**ar,
hirð þás hugði forðask
h**eið** þióðkonungs r**eið**i;
en vin**laus**um vísa
v**arð**, þeim es fé sp**arð**i,
– háðisk víg fyr víðum
v**angi** – þunt of st**angi**r.

The eight-lined verse has a division of sense after the fourth line. Each line has six syllables, three stressed and three (often endings) unstressed. Each half-stanza consists of two couplets. The first line of each couplet has two stressed syllables that begin with the same sound, which is also the same sound as begins the first stressed syllable of the couplet's second line (the alliterating opening letters are given in **bold** in 1 above). The other stressed syllables in the lines must not alliterate. In addition, the first line of each couplet has a pair of its stressed syllables that 'half-rhyme' together: they end with the same consonant but have different vowels. The second line of each couplet has its first stressed syllable rhyming fully with another stressed syllable in the line (half-rhymes in *fekk* and *miklu*, full rhymes in *mildr* and *hildar*, etc., given in **bold** in 2).

In this example, both sentence structure and diction are simple. The word order is not that of prose, but this presents less difficulty in Old Norse than it would in English since Norse is an inflected language, that is, it expresses much of its syntax, its meaning, by the endings it puts on nouns, adjectives and verbs rather than relying on word order as we do. Putting the stanza into prose form it would be: *mildr fekk miklu meira lið til hildar en gløggr, þás heið hirð hugði forðask þióðkonungs reiði; en vinlausum vísa, þeim es sparði fé, varð þunt of stangir. Víg háðisk fyr víðum vangi.* 'The generous (prince) got much greater support in battle than the stingy one when the bright host sought to escape the great king's wrath. But for the friendless leader who had been holding on to his wealth, there were few round the war-standards. Battle raged off the wide land.' The only peculiarity – and it is a common feature of skaldic syntax – is that in the second half-stanza one sentence, *víg háðisk fyr víðum vangi*, is enclosed within another. The sense is clear. The scene of the action is a sea-battle between two Viking leaders, and the only point of historical interest is the statement of social obligation; that a leader must be generous to his retinue so that they repay him with their loyal service.

The verse features – alliteration, rhyme – serve as aids to memory for anyone who wants to learn the poem for future repetition (and also give clues to the modern scholar as to how a badly corrupted verse can be amended). The poet prevents the rhythm of his verse becoming monotonous by varying the position of stressed syllables within the individual lines. But in skaldic terms this is a remarkably simple piece of work. Other examples can be more complex in form and wording, so difficult sometimes that modern readers find them impossible to interpret, or discover in them too many possible interpretations. Sentences can be intertwined; words that agree together be far distant. Here is an example, one for which there is an impeccable Viking Age text cut on a rune-stone at Karlevi on the Swedish island of Öland in the Baltic. The inscription begins with a prose section commemorating one Sibbi Foldarsson. Transliterated from its runic form the verse reads:

> **fulkin:likr:hins:fulkþu:flaistr:uisi:þat.maistar.taiþir:tulka**
> **þruþar:traukr:i:þaimsi.huki:munat:raiþ:uiþur:raþa:ruk:starkr**
> **i:tanmarku:aintils:iarmun:kruntar:urkrantari:lanti**.

Set in verse form and with its runic spelling normalised to agree with the 'standard' form of Old Norse, this reads:

> Fólginn liggr hinns fylgðu
> (flestr vissi þat) mestar
> dæðir, dólga Þrúðar
> draugr í þeimsi haugi.
> Munat reið-Viðurr ráða
> rógstarkr í Danmörku
> Endils iörmungrundar
> ørgrandari landi.

The rules of the *dróttkvætt* form apply (though the reader will have to note that in Norse terms *–stark–* is a full rhyme with *–mörk–*; and all initial vowels alliterate together so *Endil–* and *iörmun–* begin with the same sound). But the sentence structure of the first half is complex indeed. Dividing these four lines into individual clauses by the use of different styles of print, we arrive at:

> Fólginn liggr, *hinns fylgðu*
> (**flestr vissi þat**) *mestar*
> *dæðir*, dólga Þrúðar
> draugr í þeimsi haugi.

This when translated is: 'Concealed in this mound lies the warrior *whom the greatest virtues accompanied:* **most men knew that**.' The three clauses interweave.

Even this does not give the full complexity of the half-verse. The words I have translated 'warrior' are *draugr dólga Þrúðar*, literally 'the one who carried out the work (*draugr*) of the goddess (*Þrúðr*, a goddess, daughter of Thor) of battles (*dólg*)', who would either be a fighting-man or the leader of an armada. This type of circumlocution is common in skaldic verse and is called a kenning. The second half of this verse has two of these kennings: *reið-Viðurr* means 'chariot-god' (*Viðurr* being a name of the great god Odin); *Endils iörmungrund*, 'the giant land of Endil (a sea-king)' is the sea. The

'Odin of the chariot of the sea' is the ship's skipper. Thus the half-verse means: 'No skipper more honourable (*ørgrandari*), strong in battle (*rógstarkr*), will rule land in Denmark.' In one sense the text is a simple one and its historical importance might be judged to lie in the fact that, on an island off the Swedish coast, there is commemorated a Viking seaman who held land in Denmark and whose epitaph is carved in runes of Danish form. Equally important from the point of view of social history is the elaborate form of the epitaph, which would need professional understanding both to compose and to appreciate. The Vikings may have been ruffians, but they were cultured ruffians.

They would have to know the names of the gods, their various nicknames or soubriquets, their relationships to other gods and the adventures they had undertaken, as well as the names and attributes of early heroes and legendary kings, since a skald might refer obliquely to all these in the kennings of his poem. They must also command the vocabulary proper to skaldic verse, for this type of poetry tended to use specifically poetic words, words that we now find hard to translate precisely. For instance, since skaldic verses often refer to battle, murder and sudden death, there were numbers of words for fighting-man, king or warfare. This faces the modern reader with a problem for we have relatively few words to cover these ranges of meaning. How many modern synonyms can we find for 'king', for instance? 'Monarch', 'sovereign', 'royal', perhaps 'prince', 'ruler'. Old Norse had dozens: *buðlungr, hilmir, iöfurr, dróttinn, allvaldr, þengill, fylkir, siklingr, gramr, folkrekr, döglingr, harri, skiöldungr, mildingr* and many others. Yet these are not strictly synonyms since they illustrate different aspects of the king's person, as their derivations suggest. Some define the king as a battle-leader: *hilmir* is related to the word meaning 'helmet', *fylkir* to a verb meaning 'to marshal men into line of battle'; *iöfurr* means literally 'wild boar' and refers to, among other things, the king's valour and ferocity in warfare; *gramr* is primarily an adjective meaning 'stern, fierce, wrathful', referring to his power of command. Others show the king as ruler, leader of a retinue: *allvaldr* means 'all-powerful'; *folkrekr* has the first element meaning 'people' (though it can also mean 'army') and presumably indicates the king as elected by his people, leading and perhaps protecting them; *dróttinn* is 'head of a *drótt*, the king's retinue or court'. Others again refer to the king's descent from royal ancestors or his relationship to legendary kings. *Skiöldungr* means 'descendant of *Skiöldr* (a king of prehistory)'; *buðlungr* refers the king's ancestry to one *Buðli*, in Norse tradition the father of Atli (Attila the Hun); *siklingr* means 'descendant of *Sikki*'. Such rather artificial words are called *heiti*, related to the verb *heita*, 'to be called'. But a king could also be called by a kenning that is a single word. For instance, *menfergir* means literally 'enemy of the neck-ring'. A neck-ring or collar was made of silver. A prince, if he was wise, was its enemy because he hacked it in pieces and gave it out to his men in reward for, and indeed to ensure, their loyalty. *Menfergir* thus means 'generous prince' and is parallel to the *heiti mildingr* which is derived from the adjective *mildr*, 'free-handed'.

Obviously it is impracticable in a translation to render this aspect of the richness of skaldic verse. Indeed, it is likely that Vikings themselves found difficulty in some of this complex use of vocabulary and imagery. To help his contemporary students to understand and poets to compose similar verse the thirteenth-century skald, prose-writer and politician Snorri Sturluson compiled (*c.*1220) his *Prose Edda*, an account of the nature of poetic language and the complexities of skaldic metrics. To explain the elaborate kennings containing references to the exploits of gods and legendary heroes he had to expound the mythology and legendary history of the Viking Age as he understood it; and scholars have seen this material through Snorri's eyes ever since. How accurate Snorri was in depicting the lore of earlier centuries is another and often disputed matter.

Perhaps the complexity of form weakens the force of skaldic verse as source material for Viking history. The poets were so concerned with details of verse structure and vocabulary that often they had little space or energy for historical fact, and the poems tend to be formulaic in wording and limited in subject matter. Yet here and there are poems that transcend these limitations, such works as the 'Plain-speaking verses' and the 'Verses on his eastern journey' by the eleventh-century poet Sigvat Thordarson. Indeed, for centuries skaldic verses have been adduced to illustrate Viking history. The classic statement of their use is in an introduction (extant in three versions) by Snorri Sturluson to his history of the early Norwegian kings, a work known as *Heimskringla*, 'The circle of the world'. Discussing what information the scholar can gain about the Viking Age Snorri listed the evidence of learned writers, genealogies and 'ancient verses or historical narrative poems that men recited for entertainment. And though we do not know the truth about it, yet we have this to support them, that learned men of old times believed such things to be true.' Which may or may not convince us of their validity as primary sources. But he adds:

> At the court of King Harald [Finehair, *c*.900] there were poets, and today we still know their poems, and the poems of [the skalds of] all the kings who ruled Norway after him. And we regard as most reliable what is said in the poems that were recited before the great men themselves or their sons. We accept as true everything that is said in them about their travels and battles. It is the practice of court poets to praise most fulsomely the man they are reciting to, but no-one would dare to tell in a man's presence anything about his exploits that everyone who listened – even the man himself – knew to be falsehood and invention. That would be mockery not praise.

We who live in a more sceptical world, where public flattery has become accepted rhetoric, need not put too much trust in this argument. Certainly it is unlikely that any public verse would contain a clear factual error (though one might well remember George IV's public insistence that he led the German charge at Salamanca, or according to some versions of the tale displayed his heroism at Waterloo, and the Duke of Wellington's drily ambiguous reply when called upon to substantiate the claim, 'I have often heard Your Majesty say so'). Yet it is unlikely that any professional poet, reciting for reward before a prince, would mention shameful acts of his or describe any of his defeats in anything but glorious terms.

Snorri is only one in a sequence of history writers who used skaldic verse as evidence. Indeed, this is how the greater part of the known corpus of skaldic verse has survived, as quotations within prose works. Such a historian will describe an incident and then add: 'as NN says', and quote the verse that provides his material. Thus a longer poem is likely to be extant only as a series of verses or verse groups scattered through a prose work, and we do not know if we have the whole of the poem, or sometimes indeed if we know the original verse order. Moreover, we do not know how accurately the prose writer received his verse from oral tradition or whether he passed it on or interpreted it correctly. When we find the same verses used by two or three historians, we do not find their prose accounts identical in detail though they may be generally alike (which suggests there was an accepted tradition of interpretation of the verses). Here is an example of a bit of unpalatable news being given to a king by his skald. The king is Hakon Athelstan's foster-son, called the Good, who ruled Norway in the mid tenth century, having expelled his elder brother Eirik Bloodaxe.

Snorri's *Heimskringla* tells the tale thus:

> When King Hakon Athelstan's foster-son had been king of Norway for twenty-six years after his brother Eirik [Bloodaxe] left the land, this is what happened. King Hakon was based in Hordaland, quartered at Fitje on Stord. There he had his retinue and a host of free farmers on call. The king was sitting at his midday meal when the guard outside saw a number of ships sailing northwards, not far from the island. They talked among themselves, saying the king should be told they believed there was an armada approaching. But nobody found it easy to tell the king of an enemy approach because he had firmly ruled against anyone doing that; yet it seemed to them not feasible for the king to be kept ignorant of it. Then one of them went into the hall and asked Eyvind Finnsson to come out with him at once – he said it was a matter of great need. So Eyvind went straight out and came to where he could see the ships. At once he could see it was a great force approaching.
>
> He went directly back into the hall, walked up to the king's table and said, 'A short time to travel, a long time to spend over a meal.' The king looked at him and said, 'What's going on?' Eyvind recited:

> > Avengers of bold Bloodaxe
> > Demand a meeting of mail-coats
> > And scabbard-points. No chance
> > Of a sit-down for us.
> > A problem for me, king,
> > To tell my lord of this attack.
> > It's your honour I look to.
> > Quick, let's take up tried weapons.

> The king said, 'You're such a fine fellow, Eyvind, you wouldn't have told me of an attack if it were not true.' The king had the tables cleared. Then he went out and looked at the ships, recognising they were men-of-war. He asked his men what action they ought to take, whether they should fight with what forces they had or take to their ships and sail off northwards.

'It's clear to me,' the king said, 'that we would have to fight against much greater odds than we have done yet. But I have often thought there was inequality in our forces when we did battle against the sons of Gunnhild [widow of Eirik Bloodaxe].'

To this there was no immediate response. Then Eyvind said:

> God of spear-rain, not right
> Is it for men of courage
> To take ocean-steeds northwards.
> We risk disaster.
> Now Harald brings his mighty
> Fleet north on the crashing road
> Of the sea-king Rakni.
> Let us grab our battle-shields.

The king answered, 'That's a bold speech. Just what I feel. Yet I would like to hear the opinions of more of you about this.' And when the men understood how the king wanted things to be, many of them replied saying they would rather die valiantly than run from the Danes without a trial of strength. They said they had often gained victory when they had fought against odds. The king thanked them for what they said and ordered them to arm themselves, and so they did.

The writer of the history called *Nóregs konunga tal* (The list of Norway's kings, commonly known as *Fagrskinna*) from roughly the same date uses the same verses but with a rather different, and shorter, prose explanation:

Now it happened that the sons of Gunnhild sailed north from Denmark. They used the outer route, not approaching the land - though their expedition was spotted. They in turn had information about where King Hakon was quartered. Their ships were well manned and fully armed, and they had with them a great Viking called Eyvind 'swagger'. As they journeyed King Hakon was in quarters at Fitje on Stord. Neither he nor any of his men had news of what was going on till the ships came in view sailing northwards, not far from the island. King Hakon was then sitting at table. The rumour reached his retainers that ships were to be seen approaching. Some who had the keenest sight went outside and each said to the other that these must be enemy vessels. Everyone said somebody else ought to tell the king. There was nobody to do this but Eyvind Finnsson, whose nickname was 'plunderer of skalds'. He went in before the king and this is what he said: 'It's a short travelling time, sir, and a long mealtime.' The king replied, 'Well, poet, what's happening in the big world?' Eyvind said:

[The first verse is quoted in the same form]

Then the king replied, 'You are a good fellow, Eyvind, and a sensible man. You wouldn't report an attack if it were not true.' Then everyone said it was true, that there were sailing ships approaching, not far from the island. Thereupon the tables were cleared and the king went out to see the armada. When he had seen it he called on his advisers and asked what should be done. 'There are a lot of ships sailing here from the south and we have only a small force, even though it is a good one. Yet I don't want to lead my best friends into peril. Certainly I would be prepared to run if sensible men didn't think that would be great disgrace or folly.' Then Eyvind replied:

[The second verse is quoted in very similar form]

At that they all said, one after the other, that they would rather fall in battle together than run before the Danes. Then the king said, 'You speak like the finest of all fighting-men. Everyone pick up his sword. It won't matter how many Danes there are against each Norwegian.'

The phrase with which Eyvind reports the coming of the enemy is virtually the same in each version: *lítil er líðandis stund, en löng matmáls stund* in *Heimskringla*, and *lítill er líðandi stund, herra, en langt matmál* in *Nóregs konunga tal*. There is similarity too in the reply Hakon gives to Eyvind's first stanza. Presumably these derive from an oral prose tradition that was attached to the verse. Otherwise the wording in the two accounts varies greatly; speeches are invented for the main character and motivation is added. *Heimskringla* tells more of the nature of the forces Hakon could call upon, *Nóregs konunga tal* perhaps more of the purposeful nature of the attacking forces, and the friendly relationship that existed between King Hakon and his retainers and the charisma that made Hakon such a good leader. But such things are apparently inventions of thirteenth-century historians and can only be used with caution as source material for Viking history. Yet there is a further common point that may be significant. In both stories it is the court skald who presents the unpalatable news to the king, in *Heimskringla* the others deliberately choose him to do this task, in *Nóregs konunga tal* the motivation is not so precisely stated. The skald stood a little outside the main body of a king's court servants and indeed was often a foreign national, an Icelander. This gave him a degree of independence which could be put to good use, as on this occasion (and on the occasion of the presentation of the 'Plain-speaking verses' to Magnus the Good). We have here some indication of Viking court etiquette.

Skaldic poems are of two types: the longer poems, composed for public occasions, made up of a group of verses, perhaps in versions of *dróttkvætt* metre, perhaps of simpler form; and individual verses, *lausar vísur*, 'free verses', each of which is a poet's reaction to a contemporary event.

The longer poem has often a clear formal structure with introduction and epilogue, and must have taken some time to prepare. It might have a refrain, a *stef*, and then would be called a *drápa*; or it might not, in which case it would be a *flokkr*. If you were a travelling skald presenting your poem to a Viking leader, it would be advisable to know whether he was entitled to a *drápa* or if the less laudatory *flokkr* would serve. A famous example of a *drápa* (though its authenticity as a Viking Age poem has been questioned) is one that the great Icelandic poet Egil Skalla-Grimsson recited before Eirik Bloodaxe, then king of York, to assuage his anger and save the skald from execution at his hands: Egil's 'Head ransom'.

An introduction explains the poet's intent:

> West over sea I came
> With me I carried
> The sea of Odin's breast.
> Such is my profession.
> At breaking of the ice-floes
> I dragged my oak-ship to sea.
> I loaded my vessel's hold
> With its cargo of praise.

Egil claims – what was not the case – that his intent in travelling abroad was to bring Eirik a poem of praise: the 'sea of Odin's breast' is the mystic mead that Odin stole (and swallowed) and which endows a man with the gift of poetry.

There are two more verses in this strain, then the theme changes to one of battle. Egil praises Eirik for his valour in warfare, though the warfare is described very generally. No specific fights are named, and all we get are advancing warriors and missiles flying; lots of row, with clashing of swords, bashing of shields, and blood pouring out like rivers; and the beasts of battle, raven and wolf, licking their lips in the expectation of plenty to eat. After two verses of this comes the refrain, half the length of a verse:

> At arrows' weaving
> Men sank to the ground.
> In this action Eirik
> Won a glorious name.

Two more verses and again the refrain, its first two lines different from last time, its last couplet a repetition. Two more stanzas then a new refrain. Two more and the second refrain again, with once more only the last two lines a repetition. Hitherto all the verses have glorified Eirik as war-lord. There follow two praising his generosity (a poet was, after all, a professional). Then a final three verses echoing the three opening ones. The whole a polished product of twenty stanzas altogether, containing practically no facts for the historian. But fortunately not all major skaldic poems are so empty – in Egil's case he was, says his saga, declaiming a poem he had hastily made up only the night before to save his life. The Norse poetic corpus has many poems more carefully researched, that may list a leader's battles, travels and other exploits, his respect for the law, his protection of the people, his wardenship of the sanctuaries and so on, often giving an idealised picture of what a Viking king should be.

In contrast the 'free verses' are individual responses to particular situations (as the two by Eyvind Finnsson just cited). Their contents will vary with circumstance, and their range is likely to be wider than that of the public poetry. Here are a few examples:

i)  From the Saga of Olaf Tryggvason as told in the fourteenth-century compilation *Flateyiarbók* (there are several variants, notably the one in *Heimskringla*). Hallfred Ottarsson had shown himself a difficult person to deal with, and King Olaf had given him the nickname *vandræðaskáld*, 'awkward skald'. Hallfred tried to free himself from the king's ill opinion. The king asked him to go on a mission:

> '...and we shall be friends again if you succeed. By the way, have you still got that sword I gave you?'
>
> 'I certainly have, sir,' he replied, 'and it hasn't been put into a scabbard yet. But for all that it hasn't done anyone any harm.'
>
> The king said, 'Well, it's right that an awkward skald should own an awkward bit of property. Do you think you can compose a verse that has the word "sword" in every line?'
>
> Hallfred answered, 'I'll try if you want. I'll do anything to escape your anger.' Then he recited:

> > 'This is a sword of swords
> > That made me sword-rich.
> > For this swift Niord-of-swords
> > My verse becomes sword-full.
> > Not short of swords shall it be.
> > I shall be worth three swords
> > Should I get an inlaid
> > Sheath for this sword.'

> The king thanked him for the verse and said he had a great gift in his poetry, and then gave him a scabbard for the sword, richly decorated.

ii)  Sigvat Thordarson had been on a trading voyage to England where he met Cnut the Great. On his return to Norway King Olaf Haraldsson (later to be St Olaf) greeted him coldly. *Heimskringla* tells the tale:

> King Olaf had heard all about Sigvat's travels and that he had met King Cnut. King Olaf said to Sigvat, 'I don't know if you expect to remain my chamberlain. Haven't you become King Cnut's man?'

> Sigvat declaimed:

> > 'Cnut, giver of fine rings,
> > Asked me if I were willing
> > To be serviceable to him
> > As to the great-hearted Olaf.
> > "One lord at a time,"
> > I answered him in truth.
> > To every man is given
> > A goodly example.'

Then King Olaf said that Sigvat should take up the seat he had always had.
Sigvat quickly won the same favour as he had enjoyed before.

(Though this looks like a 'free verse' it may in fact be a stanza quoted from a longer
poem.)

iii) In *Flateyiarbók* is this tale of King Harald Sigurdarson of Norway, nicknamed
*harðráði*, 'savage in counsel, tough, tyrannical'. Harald was himself a poet of sorts.

One summer King Harald's fleet was sailing along the coast when one day
they saw a man sitting by himself in a boat fishing. The king was in good
humour and said they must meet this fisherman. And as the man worked
his boat past the longship the king said, 'Can you by any chance make
verses, my man?' 'No, sir,' said the boatman. 'Oh yes,' said the king, 'just
make a verse for me.' He replied, 'Then you will have to make a verse in
return.' 'Just so,' said the king. The fisherman spoke this verse:

> 'I pulled up a haddock.
> It took long: it wasn't pleased.
> I bashed its head in.
> That was just now.
> Quite different, I remember,
> I had a sword, gold-wired.
> As a lad I splashed spears in blood.
> That was long ago.'

'A good verse, man,' said the king. 'Have you been among men of
authority or in battles?'

'Sir,' he answered, 'maybe I have been among men quite as powerful
as you are, though now everything seems lowly compared with you. Well,
sir, now make your return verse and pay your debt.'

'Just so,' said the king and declaimed this verse:

> 'My bloody bold retainers
> Chopped down sturdy Danes,
> Chased the fleeing enemy
> Onwards – that was just now.
> Another time, earlier,
> Far from my homeland
> I reddened swords in Serkland.
> That was long ago.'

Then the king said to Thiodolf, the skald who was with him, 'Now it's
your turn to produce a verse, Thiodolf.' Thiodolf declaimed this verse:

> 'Our gracious king was reddened
> In the spear-river: a tough encounter.
> The Danes had angered the gods.
> That was just now.

The prince set his standard
Down in flat Serkland.
Its staff stood at the king's bidding.
That was long ago.'

The story continues with the king criticising his skald's stanza on technical grounds. Then they have a second round of verses, and finally it is revealed that the fisherman is not a fisherman at all but *hinn vaskiligsti maðr*, 'a very valiant man' in disguise.

iv)  In the thirteenth-century Icelandic saga called *Egils saga* is the following episode:

> Then Egil went aboard. They hoisted sail and put out to sea. Then the following wind grew stronger, making the weather keen yet favourable. The ship sped ahead. Then Egil declaimed:
>
> > 'Before the stem of the prow-beast
> > The hostile monster of the mast
> > With his strength hews out a file
> > On ocean's even path.
> > With it the chill wolf of the willow
> > With its gusts files away,
> > Showing no mercy to Gestil's swan,
> > Over the stem, before the prow.'

The poem is full of kennings: 'the hostile monster of the mast', 'the chill wolf of the willow' are both metaphors for the stormy wind which is liable to dismast the vessel. 'The prow-beast', 'Gestil's [a sea-king] swan' refer to the ship. The whole verse is an image, appropriate to a blacksmith's son like Egil: the wind cuts the smooth surface of the sea into sharp teeth like a file, and this then files away at the ship's timbers.

v)  *Flateyiarbók* has the following incident taking place at the court of King Olaf Haraldsson:

> When Sigvat and Ottar [two of Olaf's skalds] were not in such favour with the king as they had been, it happened one day that the king sent nuts down to them from his table. Then Sigvat declaimed this verse:
>
> > 'The great king of the people
> > Sent down nuts to me.
> > So the king remembers his servants.
> > Yet I'm slow to hold back my praise.
> > Often what is said is done,
> > And the valiant prince bade us two,
> > Ottar and me, divide them
> > As brothers their father's heritage.'

This is what the king had said – that they should divide the nuts fairly between them as though they were brothers sharing what their father left.

Then Ottar declaimed a second verse:

> 'To me down here this ring-sharer,
> The king up there sent nuts.
> A time there was when my state,
> I well recall, was higher.
> But small may lead to great,
> I hope for more from him.
> Do not humiliate us otherwise,
> Ruler of ice-clad heaths.'

The king chuckled at the verses they had recited.

From these tales the reader might deduce a number of things; that men of rank and others took an interest in the techniques of skaldic verse and enjoyed discussing it; that an appreciation of this type of poetry was to be found in other social ranks, even in the working man; that there was a democratic tone to Viking society that allowed a fisherman to speak to a king in familiar terms; that Viking kings were jealous of the loyalty of their officers, who did well to keep that in mind; that skaldic verse could deal as well with low as with elevated themes and could use images from working life (Egil sprang from a family of blacksmiths and so would be familiar with the technology of file-hewing and the use of tools); that poems of praise could be presented, even if sardonically, in gratitude for a meagre gift as for a great one. Certainly the reader *might* deduce all these things but he would be wise to be cautious about it; for the conditions that Snorri set out for accepting skaldic verses as reliable historical sources do not necessarily apply to such minor episodes and to 'free verses'. These are not public poems declaimed before great men and so need not have Snorri's required accuracy. We do not know, in some of the cases given above, that 'learned men of old times' did believe the verses to be true. Indeed, of the *lausar vísur* attributed to the poet Egil in his saga a number are now generally agreed to be spurious, perhaps invented to illustrate episodes in the story rather than being the sources from which those episodes were derived. Though the one above has no great tale to illustrate, and it could be a remembered verse of an admired skald.

Medieval Scandinavia, and in particular Iceland, had a great tradition of historical writing in prose, one that culminated in the great cycles of *konunga sögur*, the sagas of kings, mainly of Norway but showing some interest also in those of Sweden and Denmark, and in the *Íslendinga sögur*, the sagas of the men and women who settled Iceland and of their descendants over several generations. These sagas, however, are mainly thirteenth-century compilations and in some cases even inventions; they must be thought of as historical novels rather than histories; and their authenticity must be continually questioned, which is a pity because some of the best-told and best-known adventure stories of the Viking Age are found in these writings. The Viking historian must feed on more austere fare.

Ari Thorgilsson (*c.*1067–1148) was an Icelandic cleric and scholar, much respected throughout the Middle Ages. Certainly attributed to him is *Íslendingabók*, 'The Ice-landers' book', a short account of early Iceland from its settlement at the end of the ninth century to the early twelfth. We have only a revised version of this text: Ari's preface tells us the first draft was rewritten after submission to the two Icelandic bishops and the older scholar Sæmund. Even this second version survives only in seventeenth-century transcripts of a now lost twelfth-century manuscript; fortunately their authenticity is generally accepted.

In comparison with later histories and with contemporary histories from other parts of Europe Ari's book is a slight one, yet it gives important information on the settlement of Iceland and the development of its political and legal system. Ari wrote at the very end of the Viking Age, even just after it, for *Íslendingabók* dates from the 1120s. But he had access to historical tradition that went back a couple of centuries. In the first chapter he gives the date of the first settlement of Iceland, 870, which he equates also with the dates of Harald Finehair's reign and of the killing by Vikings of King (St) Edmund of East Anglia; he gives his authority for this dating, which is:

> according to the opinion and calculation of my foster-father Teit, the most informed man I ever knew, son of Bishop Isleif; and of Thorkel Gellisson, my uncle, whose memory stretched far back; and of Thorid, daughter of Snorri the *goði*, who was very well-informed and reliable.

From time to time in his book he quotes the source of his story, which may or may not go back to an eye-witness account. It is this recorded acknowledgement of his sources that gives Ari's history its sense of trustworthiness. To take an example: on the establishment towards the end of the settlement period of a legislative and judicial assembly for the whole of Iceland Ari wrote:

> The Althingi [General Assembly] was set up where it now is [at Thing-vellir] on the advice of Ulfliot and all the settlers. Before that there was an assembly at Kialarnes which Thorstein son of Ingolf, one of the original settlers, father of the lawspeaker Thorkell mani, held there with the leading men who decided to join it. But a man incurred outlawry because he had killed a slave or a freedman. He held land in Blaskogar. His name was Thorir Crimp-beard and his grandson was called Thorvald Crimp-beard who later went to the Eastern fiords and there burned his brother Gunnar to death in his house. So Hall Orœkiuson said. And the man who was killed was called Kol. After him was named the gully that has been known ever after as Kolsgia, where the body was found. That land then became public property and the people put it at the disposal of the Althingi. That is why there is freedom for everyone to collect wood from the thickets for use at the Althingi and on the heaths there is pasture for their horses. Ulfhedin told me that.

Ari's reputation as a reliable historian has always been high. As early as Snorri Sturlu-son's *Heimskringla* preface there is commendation of his skill and explanation of the sources of his knowledge. Snorri wrote:

> [Ari] was very learned and so old that he was born the winter after the death of King Harald Sigurdarson [that is, in 1066/67]. As he himself

says he wrote the lives of the kings of Norway according to the account of Odd, son of Kol, son of Hall of Sida, and Odd learned from Thorgeir afradskoll, a man who was learned and so old that he was already living at Nidarnes when Earl Hakon the Mighty was killed [995] ... Priest Ari came to Hall Thorarinsson in Haukadal when he was seven years old and stayed there for fourteen years. Hall was a very learned man with a good memory. He remembered being christened by priest Thangbrand when he was three – that was the year before Christianity became law in Iceland. Ari was twelve when Bishop Isleif died. Hall travelled from land to land and was in partnership with King Olaf the Saint and benefited greatly from that. So he was well-informed about his reign. And Bishop Isleif died nearly eighty years after the fall of King Olaf Tryggvason [1000]. Hall died nine years after Bishop Isleif. He was then ninety-four years old. He had settled in Haukadal at the age of thirty and lived there sixty-four years. So Ari wrote. Teit, son of Bishop Isleif, was Hall's foster-son in Haukadal and lived there afterwards. He taught Priest Ari and told him many things worth knowing.

The range of concerns here, family, local, religious and political history, chronology, the relationships between Norway and Iceland, all fed into the second historical work that Ari's name is associated with, *Landnámabók*, 'The book of the settlements'. This work is in part attributed to one Kolskegg Asbiarnarson, in part to Ari. It tells of the discovery and early landings on Iceland, and then records the individual settlers, their families and dependants, their places of origin and the territories taken by each. Presumably this sort of information came from such ancient and learned men and women as Snorri discusses in his *Heimskringla* preface, the material passed down in families and localities. For example:

There was a man called Yngvar, father of Bera whom Skalla-Grim married. Grim gave him land between Leirulœk and Straumfiord and he lived at Alptanes. His second daughter was Thordis who was married to Thorgeir lambi of Lambastadir, father of Thord whom the slaves of Ketil gufa burned to death in his house. Thord's son was Lambi the strong.

There was a man called Steinolf who took both Hraundals as far as the River Griota by permission of Skalla-Grim. He was the father of Thorleif from whom the Hraundalers are descended.

The original *Landnámabók* does not survive. Extant versions date from the late thirteenth century and after. The relationship between these and the original text is complex (as I discuss in more detail below, pp. 59–60. Yet this collection of texts is obviously important to family historians and genealogists, to those concerned with historical geography and settlement patterns. It is also of more general interest, for it contains some valuable accounts of the problems Vikings faced in settling a land often poor in quality and hostile in weather: the sort of fact that is not recorded for other regions of the Viking world. And it recounts some of the brutality common enough among people living far from central authority and control. As:

There was a man called Thorbiorn bitra. He was a robber, a bad character. He went to Iceland with his dependants. He took the fiord which is now called Bitra and lived there. A bit later Gudlaug, brother of Gils skei-darnef, was wrecked out by the headland there, at the place now called Gudlaugshofdi. Gudlaug, his wife and daughter managed to get ashore, but the rest were drowned. Up came Thorbiorn bitra and murdered the two grown-ups and took away the girl and looked after her. And when Gils skeidarnef got to know of this he went over and took revenge for his brother. He killed Thorbiorn bitra and more of his men too. After Gudlaug is named Gudlaugsvik.

Or again:

Thorarin krok took Kroksfiord from Kroksfiardarnes to Hafrafell. He quarrelled with Steinolf the Low about Steinolfsdal and rowed in chase of him, ten ['twenty' in another version] of them altogether. And Steinolf was just leaving his *saeter* with six men. They fought on the sandbank by Fagradalsaros. Then men came up from the house to help Steinolf. There Thorarin and four of his men fell, and seven of Steinolf's men. Their grave-mounds still stand there.

And again:

There was a man called Onund the Wise who took land upstream from Merkigil, all the land on the eastern side of the eastern dale. And when Eirik intended to go and take the whole western side of the dale, Onund consulted the oracle to make sure he knew when Eirik was going to make the journey to claim the dale. So Onund got there first and shot a flaming arrow across the river; by this he took ownership of the land to the west. And he lived there between the rivers.

And again:

Hrafn 'harbour-key' was a great sea-robber. He went to Iceland and took land between the two rivers Holmsa and Eyiara, and lived in Dynskogar. He foresaw a volcanic eruption, so he moved his farm to Lagey. His son was Aslak aurgodi from whom the Lageyings are descended.

Many of the individual entries in the existing texts of *Landnámabók* have close connections with tales from the *Íslendinga sögur*. To take an example. The account of the killing of Thord Thorgeirsson/Lambason by slaves, given above, has a parallel in *Egils saga*, The saga of Egil Skalla-Grimsson.

By the time Ketil gufa reached Iceland the land was already widely taken up ... He came by way of Ireland and had with him a number of Irish slaves ... Thord Lambason was then living at Lambastadir. He was married and had a son called Lambi. By this time he was fully grown, as big and strong as anyone of the same age.

The next summer when it was time for men to ride to the Althingi, Lambi rode there as well. And Ketil gufa had gone to the west of Iceland, to Breidafiord, to see if he could find somewhere to settle there. That's when his slaves ran off. They came by night to Thord's at Lambastadir, set fire to the house and burned Thord and all his household inside it. They broke open his store-house and carried away goods and materials. Then they drove horses in from the fields and saddled them with packs, and then went out to the coast at Alptanes.

At daybreak next morning Lambi came home. He had seen the flames during the night. There was a group of men with him. He rode off at once to trace the slaves, and men joined him from the farms nearby. When the slaves saw they were pursued they ran off leaving their plunder behind. Some rushed off out to Myrar; others along the sea-shore until they came to the fiord. Lambi and his men attacked them and there killed the one called Kori (the place has been called Kora-headland since then), and Skorri and Thormod and Svart plunged into the water and swam out. Then Lambi and his fellows looked out boats and rowed in pursuit, and they came upon Skorri on Skorra Isle and killed him there. Then they rowed out to sea to Thormod's Skerry and there they killed Thormod (the skerry is named after him.). They picked up more of the slaves, and the early place-names are given after them.

Clearly there is some relationship between the *Landnámabók* and *Egils saga* accounts, and it is commonly thought that here the late version of *Landnámabók* has taken material from the somewhat earlier – yet still thirteenth-century – *Egils saga*. This demonstrates two points: that it is wise to be cautious about treating *Landnámabók*, as it now survives, as a primary source; and that the *Íslendinga sögur* may contain a good deal of useful historical material, if we could only determine how much is history, how much historical novel. The *Íslendinga sögur* both have some of the most evocative tales of the Viking Age and record fact; the difficulty is evaluating the two. It is unlikely that any two scholars will agree fully on how far such sagas can be taken as history, so the easy way out is to reject them altogether. Yet by such rejection the historian probably deprives himself of significant material.

Here, for instance, is an fascinating passage from *Eyrbyggiasaga*, an account of the settlement and early history of part of Snæfellsnes, the peninsular on the west coast of Iceland. The first settler was Thorolf Mostrarskegg, devotee of Thor and major landowner in Norway, who left that land to escape the wrath of the great king Harald Finehair towards the end of the ninth century:

> He established a great farm at Hofsvag which he called Hofstadir. There he had a temple put up. It was a big building. There was a door in the side-wall near one of the ends . . . Inside, the building was protected by the laws of sanctuary. At its inner end was a room resembling what now is the choir in a church, and there stood a stone in the middle of the floor like an altar. Upon it lay a pennanular ring weighing twenty ounces. On the ring

all oaths must be sworn. The temple priest had to wear it on his arm at all formal meetings. On the altar too should stand the sacrificial bowl, and in it a twig as though it were an aspergillum. And with that should be sprinkled from the bowl the blood called *hlaut*. That was blood from slaughtered beasts that were dedicated to the gods. About the standing stone and in the side-room were set up figures of the gods. To this temple all men should pay toll and have the duty of accompanying the priest on all formal journeys (as men must now do for their legal lords). And the priest must keep up the temple building at his own expense and ensure it did not fall into decay. And he must hold sacrificial feasts in it.

Thorolf gave the name of Thorsnes to the region between Vigrafiord and Hofsvag. On that headland stands a mountain. Thorolf had such superstitious belief in this mountain that nobody must look at it un-washed, and no living creature should suffer death on the mountain, neither beasts nor men, until it left of its own accord. He called this mountain Holy Mount, and believed that, when he died, he would go inside it, he and all his kin on the headland.

At first glance this looks an important and detailed account of an Icelandic temple and of pagan practice and belief, but scholars are sceptical of it. Its phraseology occurs in other sources, suggesting it is something of a conventional description. Archaeologists point out that they have no evidence for major buildings designed solely for religious use in pagan Iceland: instead they suggest that the *hof*, 'temple', was commonly the main building of an important farm, used for both secular and religious activity. Textual scholars have noted the comparisons made between pagan and Christian buildings, implying that here a Christian writer was trying to define the pagan temple (which he knew nothing of) as though it were a church. Yet despite these objections there are some aspects of the *Eyrbyggiasaga* account that look factual. Other sources make clear that a *baugeiðr*, 'ring-oath', was one of peculiar sanctity: the *Anglo-Saxon Chronicle* for the year 876 (an impeccable authority here) writes of the Vikings swearing an oath 'on the holy ring, which they had never before done for any other people'. And folklorists have adduced later beliefs that the dead continued some sort of life in a hill, mound or barrow close to the ancestral farm. It seems, then, that in this *Eyrbyggiasaga* account there is a mixture of fact and fiction that calls for careful scrutiny.

In view of their uncertain authority *Íslendinga sögur* are not commonly cited nowadays as historical sources save by those who have failed to keep up with the scholarly times. Hence they are not much in evidence in this book, though I use them for introductory and comparative material.

The same applies to the 'kings' sagas', the *konunga sögur*, which again give an entertaining picture of Viking life and certainly contain material of historical and social interest if only it could be properly evaluated. Here is an illustration of the type of problem they offer us, an incident in the life of the young Hakon the Good, later to be king of Norway. The most famous of the collections of kings' sagas is that known as *Heimskringla*, whose author is commonly said to be the Icelander Snorri Sturluson.

This is what *Heimskringla* tells us of how Hakon came to be brought up in the court of the English king Athelstan, and so became a Christian at a time when most Norwegians were pagans.

There was a king in England called Athelstan: he had just taken the throne. He was known as the Victorious and the Faithful. He sent messengers to King Harald [Finehair] of Norway with this errand. The envoy came into the king's presence and presented him with a sword, with gilt sword-haft and guards, and its scabbard all splendid with gold and silver and set with gems.

The envoy held the hilt out to the king and said, 'Here is a sword that King Athelstan asked you to take as a gift.' The king took hold of the hilt and the envoy said at once, 'You accepted it as our king expected you to. Now you must be his subject since you have accepted his sword.'

At this King Harald realised he was being held up to scorn since he had no intention of being any man's subject. Yet he kept in mind his usual way of behaving; whenever rage and anger seized hold of him he allowed his mind time to settle down and let his wrath subside so that he could look at things calmly. This is what he did now. He consulted his friends and they all reached the same conclusion; in the first place to allow the ambassadors to journey back unharmed.

Next summer King Harald sent a ship west to England, and put it under the captaincy of Hauk habrok. He was a very valiant man, close to the king. Harald gave his son Hakon [who was also son of the king's mistress Thora, who had the nickname 'the king's servant-girl'] into Hauk's charge. He went west to England to reach King Athelstan, and came upon him in London. A reception was being held, and a splendid banquet.

When they reached the king's hall Hauk told his men how they were to order their entrance. He gave instructions that the first in should be last out, that they should stand together in a row before the table, each of them with a sword on his left hip and his cloak so arranged that the sword was hidden. Like this they all marched into the hall, thirty men together.

Hauk walked up to the king and made his greeting. The king bade him welcome. Then Hauk picked the lad Hakon up and put him on the king's knee. The king looked at the lad and asked Hauk what he meant by this.

Hauk answered, 'King Harald bade you foster up his servant-girl's child.' The king lost his temper, grabbed at his sword that was set near him and drew it as though to kill the lad.

'You have taken him on your knee,' said Hauk. 'You can slaughter him if you want, but you won't be able to destroy all King Harald's sons like that.'

Out marched Hauk again, and all his men with him. They went off to their ship, put to sea, sailed back to Norway and came to King Harald. He was very pleased with what had happened because it is common knowledge that a man who fosters another's child is lower in rank than him.

In this pair of dealings it was manifest that each of the kings wanted to go one higher than the other, but of course it had no effect on their relative ranks, each remaining over-king until his dying day. King Athelstan had Hakon baptised and taught the true faith, sound morals and all patterns of courtly behaviour. King Athelstan was very fond of him, more indeed than of his own family, and what's more every man who knew him loved him. Ever after he was called *Aðalsteinsfóstri*, 'Athelstan's foster-son'.

So much for *Heimskringla*. Roughly contemporary with it is the history known as *Nóregs konunga tal* which tells the same tale in slightly different form.

At this time a young king called Athelstan the Good ruled England. He was one of the most noble men in the northern lands. He sent messengers to King Harald in Norway with this errand. The envoy came into the king's presence and presented to him a sword, with gilt haft and guards, and its scabbard all splendid with gold and silver and set with gems.

The envoy held the hilt out to the king and said, 'My lord king, here is a sword that Athelstan, king of England, sends you as a gift.' The king took hold of the hilt and the envoy said at once, 'You accepted it as our king expected you to. Now you must be his man and his "sword-taker".' King Harald then realised the sword had been sent in mockery. He took deep thought and consulted his counsellors as to whether the envoy should be killed or the king injured in some way or other. He had no intention of being Athelstan's man, or indeed the man of anybody else in the world. On the advice of his men King Harald concluded that it was not kingly behaviour to kill the envoys of another king if they carried their lord's message unadorned. Rather guile should be met with guile, saying with saying. So he let the English king's men depart in peace.

Next summer King Harald sent a ship west to England, and put in charge of it his best friend Hauk habrok. King Harald put under his care a lad whom Thora Mostrstong, his servant-girl, had given birth to. She came from a family in Mostr in South Hordaland. This lad was called Hakon, and the mother claimed he was King Harald's son. So Hauk came west to England and met up with King Athelstan in London. When the tables were cleared Hauk marched up to the king and made his greeting. The king bade him welcome.

Then Hauk said, 'Lord, King Harald of Norway has sent you his kind regards. Further he has sent you a white bird, well trained, and asks you to train it even better in the future.' He pulled the lad out of the lap of his cloak and put him on the king's knee. The king gave him a look, but Hauk stood firmly before the king and did not flinch. Under his cloak, on his left hip, he had a sharp sword, and indeed his men, thirty of them in all, were similarly equipped.

Then Athelstan said, 'Whose child is this?'

'A servant-girl's in Norway,' answered Hauk. 'King Harald said you should foster up her child.'

King Athelstan said, 'This lad's eyes are not those of a servant.'

Hauk answered, 'The mother is a servant-girl. She says King Harald is the father. Now you have taken the lad on your knee you must treat him just as if he were your own son.'

The king replied, 'Why should I foster up Harald's child, even if he were legitimate? Much less his servant-girl's child.' With one hand he reached for the sword that lay nearby, with the other the child. Then Hauk said, 'You have taken King Harald's child on your knee as your foster-son. You can slaughter him now if you want, but for all that you won't be able to destroy all King Harald's sons like that. And from now on everyone will say, as they always have done, that a man who fosters another's child is less noble than him.'

Thereupon Hauk turned away and threw aside the left edge of his mantle and had a drawn sword in his right hand. The last of his men to go in was the first to come out. And so they went off to their ships. The winds were favourable for putting out to sea, so they took advantage of them and sailed to Norway. And when they came to the king's he gave Hauk his best thanks for his mission. And King Athelstan had Hakon brought up at his court, and ever since he has been known as *Aðalsteinsfóstri*.

In this pair of dealings it was clear that each of the kings wanted to be recognised as higher than the other, but of course it had no effect on their relative ranks, each remaining king of his land until his dying day.

The two stories are obviously closely related; not only in their incidents but even in the wording of individual sentences. There are differences of detail and emphasis, but the two must derive ultimately from a single source. But was that source history or anecdote? To put it another way, to what extent can such tales supply historical source material? Athelstan came to the throne in 924, and Harald's long reign traditionally ended *c*.930, though that date is much disputed. At any rate the incidents, if they happened, took place in the second quarter of the tenth century. *Heimskringla* and *Nóregs konunga tal* date from the early thirteenth century, some three hundred years after the events they portray. Is there any way we can check their truth?

Three aspects are to be considered. Were there diplomatic contacts between English and Norwegian kings that might be expressed by Harald's son being brought up at Athelstan's court? Are the social values accurately represented in the tale: someone of lower rank than the parents fostering a child, the need for a king to assert his greatness by vying with those of other countries? Are there obvious fictitious elements here?

To the last we can say, yes. The claim (only in the *Nóregs konunga tal* version) that a child born to parents of rank can be readily identified by its clear and piercing eyes (as in the poem *Rígsþula* below, p. 153) is a known feature of Norse narrative. The other two questions require scrutiny. Certainly the practice of fostering up children was common in western Scandinavia. It was one of the bonds that could link a man to his social superior and add to his own standing and security. Foster-parent and -child had an intimate and profitable relationship. A runic memorial inscription at Kirk Michael, Isle of Man, hard to translate because its grammar is so unconventional, seems to show a foster-son commemorating his foster-mother. It adds the pregnant aphorism: 'it is better to leave a good foster-son than a bad son', which many would agree with. Whether Athelstan of England would recognise this relationship is a different matter. Whether tenth-century kings behaved to one another in the rather childish way the story describes is perhaps unlikely. Yet most societies have some element of one-upmanship, and Vikings often responded to challenge arrogantly.

That diplomatic contacts were initiated between Athelstan and Harald is clear, for William of Malmesbury, writing in the twelfth century, describes ambassadors coming to Athelstan at York, sent by 'a certain Haroldus, king of the Norsemen' with the gift of a splendid ship. That there was a tenth-century English Christian mission to Norway is also suggested by William, who commemorates one Sigefridus who was 'bishop in Norway' at that time. That Athelstan made a practice of bringing up at his court the sons of neighbouring princely houses (presumably to extend his influence abroad) is recorded in contemporary Frankish texts. That Hakon's Christianity got him in trouble with his fellow-Norwegians when he took over the throne is a long-standing tradition in Scandinavian narrative. That Hakon had the nickname *Aðalsteinsfóstri* no later than the early eleventh century is shown by its use, unexplained, to refer to him in Sigvat Thordarson's 'Plain-speaking verses' (below, p. 162). It is pretty evident from all this that Athelstan brought up Hakon at his court as a Christian, and to that extent the stories in *Heimskringla* and *Nóregs konunga tal* record the truth. But this truth must be quarried from a complex pair of tales that may be largely fiction. And this is typical of the problems involved in evaluating the 'kings' sagas'.

Perhaps the most serious gap in our prose sources is in the field of law, which is so informative on conditions of life in comparable civilisations like the Anglo-Saxon. We know that law was important to the Vikings, that they were, despite their reputation among their contemporaries abroad, a legal-minded race. Ari's *Íslendingabók* shows something of the significance of legal process in early Iceland. Yet vernacular legal codes from the Viking Age do not survive since so much depended on oral transmission of precedent and rule. We know, for Ari tells us, that Icelandic law was written down 'in the first summer when Bergthor [Hrafnsson] was lawspeaker', which is calculated as the year 1117/18; but the earliest legal manuscripts surviving from Iceland are a good deal later than that. Of early Norwegian law we hear in *Heimskringla*, in its Saga of Hakon the Good:

> [Hakon] was a very knowledgeable man and paid great attention to legislation. He established the Gulathing law with the advice of Thorleif the Wise, and the Frostathing law with the advice of Earl Sigurd and the wisest of the rest of the men of Trøndelag. But the Heiðsævislaw had already been established by Halfdan the Black.

Whether Hakon in the tenth century established such law codes or whether he was only instrumental in amending them is a matter for thought. It is most likely that provincial assemblies like these had existed for centuries, but there was need to adapt them to the requirements of a new, more ambitious, monarchy. Unfortunately there are no legal texts surviving from Viking Age Norway, for the earliest is the law of the Gulathing (held somewhere in Gulen in western Norway) in a mid-thirteenth-century version. This already shows the adaptation needed for a Christian society, and its opening sections contain provisions 'for keeping the Christian religion', some of which are ascribed to the late Viking Age king Olaf kyrri (the Quiet), others to the later Magnus Erlingsson (1162–84). So individual provisions begin: 'Both Olaf and Magnus said this', or 'Olaf said this but Magnus deleted it', or 'Only Olaf declared this'. Thus even the earliest surviving Norwegian laws are already influenced by high medieval concerns. This does not mean they do not also contain material of considerable age, provisions that may reflect Viking Age patterns of judgment (and I suggest a couple of examples below). Only that it is hard, often impossible, to identify such material. The introduction to the Frostathing law (extant text from the 1260s when Hakon Hakonarson ruled Norway) is explicit in its appeal to Viking Age practice. Regretting the growth of violent crime, it says:

> It will be known to many a man how much harm and how many injuries most men's kin in the land have suffered through homicides and killing of the best men, something that has been more common here than in most other lands ... It is shameful that in those more law-abiding countries people should claim that there is more crime here than in any other land ... So it seems appropriate at the beginning to insist that the law of King Olaf the Saint should be observed just as he ordained it, though hitherto that has not been the case because of men's greed. Whoever kills a man without cause shall forfeit property and legal protection. Wheresoever he be found let him be declared an outlaw for whom no compensation can be accepted, either by king or kin.

The earliest Swedish and Danish law-codes to survive are from an even later date than the Norwegian.

The vernacular sources I have noted for use hitherto are (save in the case of some of the rune-stones) all from the West Norse area, from Iceland and Norway. There are no comparable texts from Denmark and Sweden, and to illuminate these Viking regions we must have recourse to writings composed outside Scandinavia. Naturally, such material must be chosen with care, because it is unlikely that Christian Europe would give a fair verdict on pagan peoples it was familiar with only as invaders, plunderers, tiresome incomers wanting land to settle on. It comes from a wide geographical region, from the British Isles in the west to the Arabic-speaking communities of the east. I give here two examples:

One major source is the *Gesta Hammaburgensis ecclesiae pontificum* (Activities of the prelates of the church at Hamburg) by the eleventh-century cleric Adam of Bremen. The cathedral of Hamburg-Bremen held claim, disputed by the English church, to control the Christian church in Scandinavia, and Adam's work is in part historical, recounting among other topics the missions to the north mounted by the

German church, in part geographical and ethnographical, recording the state of the northern countries and the practices of their peoples. Some of his material comes from earlier written sources, some from popular misconceptions about the nature of Scandinavia, some from eyewitness accounts. For instance, he made acquaintance with the Danish king Svein Estridsson/Ulfsson and quoted him as an authority:

> To anyone who has crossed the islands of Denmark another world opens up in Sweden or Norway which are the two most extensive kingdoms of the north and are practically unknown to our world to the present day. About them I was informed by the most learned king of the Danes; that Norway could scarcely be crossed in a month while Sweden was not easy to get over in two. 'For,' he said, 'I had tested that myself some time ago when I fought for twelve years under King [Anund] Jacob in those territories, both of which are surrounded by very high mountains – Norway rather more since it encloses Sweden with its alps.'

From a completely different world comes a Greek work by the learned Byzantine Emperor Constantine Porphyrogenitos, usually known by its Latin name of *De administrando imperio*, 'On administering a realm'. This was a private work written *c*.944 for the edification of the emperor's heir Romanus who seems to have benefited little from it. Amidst its material is a chapter on the people called *Rhos*, who made the perilous journey down the river Dnieper to Constantinople (below, pp. 94–6). These were Viking traders who took over a network of settlements in western Russia which they used as trading posts; the Norse name for this region was *Garðaríki*, 'the kingdom of the towns' or simply *Garðar*, 'the towns'. Constantine's text is of immense importance because there are few detailed reports on this aspect of Viking life and the Emperor wrote with authority and knowledge. Indeed, it is suggested that this bit of *De administrando imperio* derives from the official archives of the Byzantine foreign ministry.

These two examples, so different in nature, origin and background, suggest something of the complexity of the evidence from outside Scandinavia. It is unlikely that any single scholar will control the full range of material – the languages needed (to those used already we must add early Slavonic and Arabic), the knowledge of manuscript tradition, historical analysis and the detailed study of word meanings. Inevitably therefore this type of material will be the most weakly represented and inadequately examined, and I quote it only tentatively in this book. Inevitably too there are valuable materials relevant to the social history of the Vikings which cannot find a place in this book since they derive from sister disciplines such as archaeology, numismatics, historical geography, place-names and so on. Here I am content to draw attention to their existence and to stress their importance.


A word on translation. A translation can never be a substitute for the original, it can be only an interpretation of it. It is impossible to recover the tone the writer used or the pattern of thought he held to, and we naturally tend to replace these with our own. To take two simple examples from my translations above. When Eyvind Finnsson apprised Hakon Athelstan's foster-son of an attack by an enemy fleet, the king was sitting *yfir dagverðarborði*; he was at a trestle table eating *dagverð*, the main meal of the day taken in the forenoon (p. 18). How to translate *dagverð*? 'Lunch' would sound prissy, 'breakfast' inadequate in our degenerate days, 'dinner' would mislead. An accurate translation is 'brunch', but that has the wrong register, suggesting a leisured society that gets up late and combines two meals. I evaded the problem by using 'midday meal', but it is a compromise. When Onund the Wise outwitted his neighbour, I said he did so after 'consulting the oracle' (p. 28). He certainly got supernatural advice, but 'oracle' again has not the correct register. Onund cast *blótspánn*, 'sacrificial sticks' presumably marked with mystic symbols to direct the man who could interpret them. But what would these be in modern English?

In many ways the values of the Viking Age differed from those of our times, and we must resist the temptation to conflate the two. A word in one language cannot adequately represent one in another; it can only approach it. A translator will try to pick the nearest approximation but it will be only that. Hence there will be ranges of meaning unrepresented, even unsuspected. In early texts – particularly verse but not only verse – there will be obscurities; and the translator may have to choose between several possible interpretations of the evidence. It is not practicable, in a work like this, to annotate translations so as to indicate all these obscurities/interpretations. In the case of verse there is always the conflict between representing the form and giving the meaning. On the whole I have preferred the latter but in approaching Old Norse poetry, particularly that of the skalds, some formal aspects (unusual words, complex images, contorted sentences) must be included. Nevertheless I am aware that many of my renderings of verse sound flat-footed, and I can only plead in extenuation that some of the originals sound equally so. In the case of prose I have translated into as fluent modern English as the original and my limited talents allow.

The translations given here are only a small sample of the material available for the Viking Age. Readers may wish to follow them up. On the runic material there are good general books available for Sweden and Denmark: Sven B. F. Jansson's *Runes in Sweden*, translated Peter Foote (Stockholm, 1987) and Erik Moltke, *Runes and their origin, Denmark and elsewhere*, translated Peter Foote (Copenhagen, 1985). For those prepared to venture into French there is a more wide-ranging work, Lucien Musset, *Introduction à la runologie*, Bibliothèque de philologie germanique 20 (Paris, 1965). Some may wish to read my own introductory book *Runes* (London, 1987) in the British Museum Press's 'Reading the past' series, which has chapters on the Viking runes and on Scandinavian runes in the British Isles.

On the (mainly Icelandic) written sources there is a good general introduction in Jónas Kristjánsson, *Eddas and sagas: Iceland's medieval literature*, translated Peter Foote (Reykjavík, 1988). More formal is the excellent collection edited by Carol J. Clover and John Lindow, *Old-Norse-Icelandic literature: a critical guide*, Islandica 45 (Cornell, Ithaca, 1985) with valuable bibliographies.

There is no very adequate translation of the whole of the *Poetic Edda*. Those by Henry Adams Bellows (*The Poetic Edda* [New York: the American-Scandinavian Foundation, 1923]) and Lee M. Hollander (*The Poetic Edda* [Austin, Texas, 1928]) are, for my taste, vitiated by the archaic mode into which the verse is translated. W. H. Auden and Paul B. Taylor's *Norse poems* (London, 1981) gives the Eddic poems in idiosyncratic order (and sometimes idiosyncratic form), and sacrifices accuracy of translation to what I suppose to be Auden's poetic enthusiasm. A few of the heroic poems are edited and translated in Ursula Dronke, *The Poetic Edda:* vol. 1, *Heroic Poems* (Oxford, 1969), vol. 2 promised shortly: Mrs Dronke's translation sometimes makes the poems sound better than they in fact are.

There are a number of useful introductions, with texts, translations and commentaries, to skaldic verse. I name E. O. G. Turville-Petre, *Skaldic poetry* (Oxford, 1976); Roberta Frank, *Old Norse court poetry: the dróttkvætt stanza*, Islandica 42 (Cornell, Ithaca, 1978); and most recently, R. G. Poole, *Viking poems on war and peace: a study in skaldic narrative* (Toronto, 1991) which examines a group of skaldic poems, with a critical discussion of the position of the verses within prose texts. There is also Lee M. Hollander's *The skalds: a selection of their poems* (Princeton: the American-Scandinavian Foundation, 1945) wherein Professor Hollander renders select skaldic verses in a contorted English almost as hard to follow as the original Norse. Finally, Christine Fell translates a major skaldic poem with important historical implications, *Víkingavísur* in Ursula Dronke *et al.* eds., *Speculum Norroenum: Norse studies in memory of Gabriel Turville-Petre* (Odense, 1981), pp. 106–22.

For those who want to follow up the mythology behind both Eddic and skaldic poetry Snorri Sturluson's *Prose Edda* is easily available in Anthony Faulkes's full and accurate translation *Snorri Sturluson: Edda* (Everyman's Library, London, 1987).

Of the historical prose texts in Old Norse a text and translation of *Íslendingabók* appears in Halldór Hermannsson, *The book of the Icelanders (Íslendingabók)*, Islandica 20 (Cornell, Ithaca, 1930). It is also one of the texts translated in Gwyn Jones, *The Norse Atlantic saga: being the Norse voyages of discovery and settlement to Iceland, Greenland, and North America* (Oxford, 1964, revised edition, 1986). That work also contains a good selection from *Landnámabók*, and material from a number of the *Íslendinga sögur* dealing with Viking adventuring to Greenland and the New World. One of the versions of *Landnámabók* is presented in Hermann Pálsson and Paul Edwards, *The book of settlements: Landnámabók* (Winnipeg, 1972). For what they are worth as historical sources, there are translations of a number of the *Íslendinga* and *konunga sögur* in the Penguin Classics series, notably for our purposes *Egil's saga*, translated by Hermann Pálsson and Paul Edwards (1976) and *King Harald's saga: Harald Hardradi of Norway*, translated by Magnus Magnusson and Hermann Pálsson (1966) with their important skaldic verses. Christine Fell also translated *Egils saga* for Everyman's Library (London, 1975) with imaginative versions of the poems by John Lucas but a salutory set of literal translations in the notes. Other saga translations that readers might wish to consult - cautiously– include *Eyrbyggja saga*, translated by Hermann Pálsson and Paul Edwards (Toronto 1973; Harmondsworth, 1989); *Njál's saga*, translated by Carl F. Bayerschmidt and Lee M. Hollander (London, 1956), also by Magnus Magnusson and Hermann Pálsson (Harmondsworth, 1960); *Grettir's saga*, translated by Denton Fox and Hermann Pálsson (Toronto, 1974). A rather archaic translation of the whole of *Heimskringla* by Samuel Laing was reissued with new introductions in Everyman's Library, 3 vols., (London, 1961–4) and there is a rather more up-to-date version by Lee M. Hollander (Austin, Texas: the American-Scandinavian Foundation, 1964). A useful reference book is D. K. Fry, *Norse sagas translated into English: a bibliography* (New York: AMS Press. 1980) together with a supplement by P. Acker in *Scandinavian Studies* 65 (1993), pp. 66–102.

The texts of two of the medieval law-codes, to be used with great caution, are in Laurence M. Larson, *The earliest Norwegian laws: being the Gulathing law and the Frostathing law* (New York, 1935). There is a useful discussion of the laws of medieval Scandinavia and their importance as evidence, or non-evidence, of Viking/Norse society in Ruth Mazo Karras, *Slavery and society in medieval Scandinavia* (New Haven, 1988), pp. 167–83.

The past, we are told, is a foreign country: they do things differently there. This is true to a degree for the Viking Age. In the physical apparatus of their living, in their moral attitudes, social codes, views of the natural and the supernatural, the systems of law and maintenance of order, in the qualities they admired and despised, and in many other things they responded in their own way, which is very different from ours. At the same time, they faced eternal problems, problems that we too recognise: how to survive against competition, how to get enough food and shelter, how to struggle against sickness, old age, injury, oppression, even fight against boredom, how to adjust to injustice. There is much in this book that we will find familiar, even if in unfamiliar guise. A formulation as modern as Sod's Law, the inevitable cussedness of life, was not unknown to the Vikings. Here is their version:

> Much too early I've often arrived.
> Sometimes much too late.
> Either the beer was finished or not yet brewed.
> It's hard to hit the right moment.
>
> Here and there I'd be invited out
> When I had no need of a meal.
> Or two hams would hang in a good friend's house,
> And I'd already polished off one.

# CHAPTER 2

# The Viking homelands and their peoples

The Scandinavia of the Viking Age was very different from that of today. We think of Scandinavian societies as peaceful, sophisticated, well-ordered, industrious and rich, and their countries as either forbidding but picturesquely beautiful, like Norway and northern Sweden, or fertile, flourishing and agricultural, as Denmark. Viking Age records often show Scandinavia as danger-ridden, disorganised, barren and poor. Travel can still be toilsome in parts of the north, but Viking wayfarers had a much harder time of it; roads were poor and dangerous, river and fiord crossings troublesome, hostel accommodation almost non-existent. Even today in parts of mountainous Norway distances are measured in time rather than space. This was commonplace even in lowland or coastal parts of Viking Scandinavia. When, in the mid twelfth century, an Icelandic cleric Nikolas, later to be abbot of the monastery at Thvera, made his pilgrimage to Rome, he defined the first part of his journey thus:

> † It is said that to sail right round Iceland takes seven days with a fresh following breeze, which has to change as is needed since you cannot always make use of the same wind. The journey from Iceland to Norway takes the same time. From Norway to Denmark you first make for Ålborg. Travellers to Rome count it a two-days' journey from Ålborg to Viborg, then a week to Haddeby, from which it is a short distance to Schleswig. Then a day's journey to the Eider, where is the boundary common to Denmark, Holstein, Saxony and Wendland. †

To give some idea of the travel difficulties involved: the distance from Ålborg to Viborg, as the crow flies, is some 75 km.

## A German cleric reports on the northern lands

Adam, a German perhaps from Bamberg or its neighbourhood, moved to Bremen in 1066–7 and died in the 1080s. He became a canon of the cathedral church of Bremen, and wrote his *Gesta Hammaburgensis ecclesiae pontificum* (above, p. 35) in thanks for his reception there, and to record 'the list of prelates of Bremen or Hamburg' so that posterity should not neglect their achievements. Since the see had taken responsibility for converting the north and controlling its churches, a good deal of Adam's work deals with Scandinavia in Viking times. Indeed, the fourth book of his *Gesta* is a *Descriptio insularum aquilonis*, 'Account of the islands of the north'. At its beginning he describes geographical conditions in eleventh-century Denmark, apparently on the basis of local general knowledge. However, his detail is a little shaky. Oddesund is, if it is correctly identified below, a strait of the Limfjord, the inlet that cuts off the northern tip of Jutland, rather than being the sea beyond it. Perhaps *Ottinsand* should be translated Skagerrak here. The geographical relationship of the various Danish islands is hardly precisely given. Following his Danish report are accounts of Sweden and Norway, again with errors of detail here and there. Adam included a good deal of fabulous stuff about the far north, material derived from earlier geographers rather than contemporary travellers. This I omit. There is, however, also much accurate information such as that provided by Svein Estridsson of Denmark whom Adam knew personally, while the geographical information is supplemented by valuable notes on the nature of Scandinavian society and practices.

Like many medieval writers Adam provided etymologies of place-names, usually 'learned' and erroneous. There are some in these extracts. The first element of *Oddesund/Ottinsand* is not the personal name *Otto* but the Old Norse word *oddi*, 'angle or tongue of land'. *Skåne* is not related, as Adam implied, to an Old High German adjective *scôni*, Old Saxon *skôni*, 'shining, beautiful'.

### (a) Denmark

The main part of Denmark (which is called Jutland) extends its full length north from the River Eider, three days' journey if you turn off through the island of Fyn. But if you travel the direct route from Schleswig to Ålborg you will have a five to seven days' journey. This is the high-road of Emperor Otto, and goes the whole way to the sea at Wendila [Vendel, now called Vendsyssel, the northern coastal district of Jutland], a sea which even today is named Ottinsand [Oddesund on the Limfjord] after that king's victory. At the Eider Jutland is quite broad, but then it gradually narrows rather like a tongue to the point that is called Wendila where Jutland comes to an end. From there it is a very short passage to Norway.

The land there is infertile. Apart from places near a river practically the whole of it looks waste-land: 'a salt land and not inhabited'. Moreover, if every region of Germany looks terrifying with its steep mountain glens, the desert of Jutland is more savage than any other. The land is avoided because of the poverty of its crops, the sea because of marauding bands of pirates. Hardly any cultivated land is to be found in any region, hardly anywhere fit for human habitation. But wherever you come upon inlets of the sea, there it has very large towns ...

Fyn is a fair-sized island beyond the one called Wendila, situated at the entrance to the Barbarian Gulf. It lies close to the region called Jutland; the passage to it from every part of Jutland is very short. There is the great town of Odense. Around are tiny islands, all rich in produce. And note that if you make your way through Jutland to Fyn you travel due north. On the other hand, anyone going through Fyn to Sjælland faces east. There are two passages to Sjælland, one from Fyn, the other from Århus, the two of equal length. By nature the sea is tempestuous, full of double peril, since even if you have a favourable wind you are not likely to escape the hands of pirates.

Sjælland is an island, large in area, lying in a bight of the Baltic Sea. This island, well famed both for the toughness of its men and the plenty of its crops, is two day's journey in length and about the same in breadth. Its biggest town is Roskilde, seat of the kings of Denmark. The island, equally distant from Fyn or Skåne, can be crossed in a single night. To the west it has Jutland, with the cities of Århus, Ålborg and Wendila. To the north, where indeed it is desert, are the straits of Norway. And to the south the aforesaid Fyn and the Slavic Gulf. To the east can be seen the hills of Skåne where the town of Lund is.

There is lots of gold there piled up through pirate raids. The pirates themselves, whom they call Wichingi and we call Ascomanni, pay tribute to the Danish king for leave to plunder the barbarians, who live in large numbers round this sea-coast. In effect it can just as well happen that the licence they apply to their enemies recoils on themselves. So little faith has each in the other that anyone, if he can capture another, will quickly sell him without compunction into a state of slavery either to a comrade or to a barbarian. And both in their laws and their practices the Danes hold to many other things that are contrary to virtue and justice. So there seems no point in my speaking of any of them save to note that they immediately sell any woman who has yielded to seduction. Men who have been apprehended for high treason or some other crime would rather be beheaded than flogged. There is no other sort of punishment there but the axe or slavery, and when a man has been condemned it is his glory to put on a cheerful face. For tears and complaint and other signs of remorse which we generally regard as wholesome, the Danes so loathe that no-one is allowed to weep either for his sins or for the dear departed.

From Sjælland to Skåne there are many routes, the shortest being to Hälsingborg, which is in fact within range of sight. Skåne is the prettiest province of Denmark as its name indicates, strong in its men, rich in crops and wealthy in commodities – and now full of churches. Skåne has twice as many as Sjælland – three hundred churches; while Sjælland is said to have half that number and Fyn a third. Skåne is the most distant part of Denmark, almost an island, for it is surrounded on all sides by the sea, except for a stretch of land adjoining it to the east which divides Sweden from Denmark. There are dense forests and towering mountains which the paths from Skåne to Götaland are obliged to cross, so you may wonder whether it is easier to avoid the perils of land by taking the alternative of the sea, or whether to prefer the first to the second.

## (b) Sweden

Sweden is a very fertile country, the land abundant in crops and honey. Further, it excels all others for cattle breeding, is very favoured in its rivers and woods; and the whole region is everywhere full of imported merchandise. So you can say the Swedes are poor in nothing rich save the pride that we love – or adore rather. For all the materials of empty pomp (that is to say gold, silver, regal steeds, the pelts of beaver or marten), things that drive us mad with desire, they think nothing of.

Only in their relations with women do they know no bounds. Any man may have at the one time two, three or even more, depending upon the extent of his powers; the rich and the nobles innumerable. For even the sons of such unions they accept as legitimate. Yet it is a capital offence for a man to know another's wife or to take a virgin by force, to despoil another of his goods or do him an injury.

Though all Northerners are noted for their hospitality, our Swedes are supreme. To them worse than any infamy is to deny hospitality to travellers, so there is rivalry or competition as to which of them shall have the honour of entertaining a guest. To him they extend all the humane courtesies for as many days as he wants to remain there, and they take him to their friends in their various homes. Good things like this are part of their customs . . .

There are many peoples in Sweden outstanding in strength and warfare. Moreover, as excellent fighting-men they are equally good on horseback or shipboard. Indeed that is why they seem to keep the rest of the northern peoples under their thumbs. They have kings of ancient family. *Their* power, however, is dependent on the will of the people – what everyone has approved by common agreement the king must confirm; unless his decision turns out more sensible, when the people sometimes accept it though reluctantly. So they enjoy equality at home. When they go to war they display complete obedience to the king, or to whoever is put forward by the king as being more competent than his fellows. If ever in battle they find themselves in a perilous situation they call for help to one of the host of gods they worship. After victory they then remain faithful to that one, and set him above the rest. Yet now, by common consent, they claim that the God of the Christians is stronger than any others; that other gods often fail but that He always stands by them, 'a refuge in times of trouble.'

## (c) Norway

As Nortmannia is the ultimate region of the globe, so I properly put it in the last bit of this book. By people today this land is called Norway. We have already mentioned its position and size in connection with Sweden. Now we must deal with it specifically. Its length extends to the most distant shores of the north, and from that it gets its name. But it begins with mountainous crags by the sea that is commonly called the Baltic. Then its spine turns north and after following along its coastline the shores of the raging ocean it eventually reaches its end at the Riphean mountains, where the weary world too fades away. Because of the savagery of its mountains or its immoderate cold Norway is the most infertile of all lands, suited only to beasts. They harbour their cattle far off in the wilderness, like Arabs. And they manage to keep life going from their herds by using the beasts' milk for food and their wool for their clothes. As a result the land produces the most powerful fighting-men, who are not enfeebled by any luxury of produce and so are more likely to take the fight to other nations than to be molested by anybody. They hold no ill-will towards their nearest neighbours the Swedes, though they are sometimes tested by the equally poor Danes, who suffer for it. Thus they are forced by daily lack of commodities to travel the whole world, bringing back from their forays a plentiful supply of the riches of all countries, and so they sustain the penury of their own. Since their conversion to Christianity, however, they have been inspired by better teaching, and have now learnt to love peace and truth and to be content with their poverty ...

In many parts of Norway or Sweden the most noble men are also herdsmen of cattle, living as the patriarchs and by the labour of their hands. But all who pass their lives in Norway are Christian through and through, except for those who live far off across the arctic regions by the ocean. It is said that these people are even now so skilled in magic arts or spells that they claim to know what everyone over the whole world is up to. By their powerful chants they even draw ashore the mighty monsters of the sea, and by practice easily do all sorts of other things that can be read of in the scriptures about wizards ... For clothing they use the skins of wild beasts, and when they speak together it is said to be more like grinding the teeth than uttering words, so as to be hardly intelligible even to neighbouring peoples ... These same mountainous regions the Roman authors call the Riphean range, terrible with their eternal snows.

The Skritefingi [Lapps] cannot live without the freezing snows, for they can even outstrip wild animals as they rush across the deepest drifts. In these mountains there is such plenty of wild cattle that the greatest part of the region subsists on forest animals alone. There they trap aurochs, stags and elks as in Sweden; but bison are found in Slavonia and Russia. Only Norway has black foxes and hares, white martens and bears of the same colour which live under water just like the aurochs. Since there are many more things to be seen there quite different and unusual to our eyes, I leave them and other things to be spoken of in more detail by the inhabitants of this same land.

The metropolitan city of the Norwegians is Trondheim which is now graced with churches and crowded with a great press of people. In it lies the body of the most blessed Olaf, king and martyr. To the present day Our Lord works such great miracles of healing at his shrine that those who do not despair of being given help through the saint's virtues crowd there from distant lands. The journey is like this: boarding ship at Ålborg or Wendila in Denmark it is a day's sea-journey to *Víkin*, a city in Norway [in fact *Víkin*, 'the bay', is a regional name given to the area on the approach to the entrance to the Oslofiord]. From there you should veer to port round the coasts of Norway, and on the fifth day arrive at the city which is called Trondheim. It is possible to go another way too, by land from Skåne in Denmark to Trondheim, but this is slower in mountainous country and because it is full of danger travellers avoid it.

## A Norwegian merchant reports to King Alfred on his life-style and exploits

This is a unique piece, the record of a Norwegian merchant at King Alfred's court, and it gives a unique picture of the ordinary yet varied life of an important Viking, how he made a living and what countries he visited. It reads like a statement based on an interrogation – the Viking was assisting Alfred with his enquiries. What languages the two spoke, how well they understood one another, we do not know, and so we must be unsure about the interpretation of some passages here. The Viking is given the anglicised name Ohthere, which Scandinavian scholars usually turn back to Norse as Ottar. He addressed Alfred as 'his lord', presumably because, as a foreigner with no kin to support him in England, he came under royal protection. Alfred's regnal dates are 871 – 899, so this gives a dating range for Ohthere's visit to England. His account of Norwegian life is preserved rather by chance. Under Alfred's direction a group of scholars produced a series of translations into Old English of 'books that were most needful for all men to know'. One of these was a rendering of Paulus Orosius's *Historia adversum paganos*. An early part of this work is a geographical introduction to the countries of Europe, and into the translated version was inserted Ohthere's description of Scandinavia (and an English fellow-traveller's account of journeys across the Baltic not included here).

Ohthere's homeland was in the far north of Norway, and his farm may have resembled that recently excavated at Borg in Lofoten (reported by Gerd Stamsø Munch *et al.*, 'Borg in Lofoten. A chieftain's farm in arctic Norway', *Proceedings of the tenth Viking Congress: Larkollen, Norway, 1985*, ed. James E. Knirk, Universitetets Old-saksamlings Skrifter ny rekke 9 (Oslo, 1987), pp. 149–70.) His farming, however, occupied only part of his life, for the land was poor and the upland pastures not yet in use (contrast Adam of Bremen's account here). Much of his income came from exploiting the half-wild reindeer. To this was added the profit from whaling and walrus-hunting, and the tribute enforced from the neighbouring Lappish peoples. The last of these was in kind, and had to be converted into other goods, so Ohthere had to visit the great trading marts of northern Europe, Kaupang (which has undergone systematic excavation since 1956) and Hedeby (Haddeby near Schleswig, excavated over many decades). He presumably owned and sailed his own ship. So altogether he was farmer, herdsman, hunter, fisherman, local worthy, master mariner and trader, local defence commander; a versatile fellow.

There are numbers of difficulties in interpreting Alfred's record of Ohthere's conversation. Not all the place-names in it are securely identified, and the distinction Ohthere made between *Finnas* (translated here conventionally as 'Lapps'), *Cwenas* (= modern Norwegian *Kvener*, a Lappish people) and *Beormas* (modernised here as 'Beormians') is difficult to render. Nor do we know whether Ohthere (or the interpreter) used terms of measurement like 'ell' and 'mile' precisely. Even fairly ordinary words may pose problems. The text uses two words for 'to dwell': *buan* which implies permanent residence, and *wician* for temporary lodging, camping. I have tried to distinguish these by using longer phrases. But *buan* can also mean 'to cultivate' of land, so in its past participle, defining land, it could signify either 'inhabited' or 'cultivated'. In practice there would probably be little distinction between these two; nevertheless such imprecision of translation needs noting. For discussion of some of the general difficulties of translating this text see Christine Fell's essay in Niels Lund, ed., *Two voyagers at the court of King Alfred* (York, 1984) and the explanatory notes in Janet Bately's edition, *The Old English Orosius*, EETS SS 6 (Oxford, 1980), pp. 179–97.

Though Ohthere's account of late-ninth-century Norway is immensely important it must not be considered complete. The original version may have been edited to fit the particular geographical concern of its context in the Orosius translation. Perhaps in consequence of this Ohthere's tale gives no indication of the political turmoils of Norway at this crucial period of the development of its kingship – the late ninth century was the period when, traditionally, Harald Finehair was taking control over large stretches of the land and founding a major dynasty, meeting savage resistance from some of the old noble families and wealthy farmers. Of this there is no sign in Ohthere's tale, and I find it hard to believe that King Alfred, who was intensely interested in the theory of kingship, should not have asked what was the nature of royal rule in Norway.

> Ohthere told his lord, King Alfred, that the farm he lived on lay further north than that of any other Norwegian. He said he lived in the north of the country on the Atlantic coast. Yet, he said, the country stretched a very long way farther north but it is all uninhabited, save that here and there Lapps had their encampments, hunting in winter and in summer fishing along the sea-coast.
>
> Once, he said, he determined to explore how much farther north the land stretched or whether anyone lived to the north of the uninhabited land. So he sailed north along the coast. The whole way the waste land was to starboard and the open sea to port; this went on for three days. By then he was as far north as the whale-hunters reach at their farthest. Then he continued north as far as he could sail in the next three days. Then the land curved eastward (or the sea formed an inlet in the land – he didn't know which). All he knew was that he waited there for a west-north-west wind and then sailed east along the coast as far as he could reach in four days. At that point he had to wait for a wind from due north because the land turned south there (or the sea formed an inlet in the land – he didn't know which).

From there he sailed due south along the coast as far as he could reach in five days' sailing. There a great river opened up into the land. So they turned in along it because they did not dare sail beyond the river since they had no secure right of passage there and the land was continuously settled on its far bank. He had not come upon any cultivated land before since he left his own home; but the whole way there was uninhabited territory to starboard – except for nomadic fishermen, fowlers and hunters, and they were all Lapps – and to port was nothing but open sea. The Beormians had made good use of their land, though Ohthere and his crew did not venture ashore there; but the land of the Lapps was quite empty, except where hunters or fishermen or fowlers had their camps.

The Beormians told him many tales both of their own land and of the lands that encompassed them, but he didn't know how much truth there was in them because he did not see for himself. He got the impression that the Lapps and the Beormians spoke almost the same language.

He made this journey – apart from the desire to explore the country – mostly for the walrus-hunting since they have most excellent ivory in their tusks (some of these tusks he brought to the king), and their skins made excellent ships' cables. This whale (the walrus) is much smaller than other whales – it is not more than seven ells long. But in his own country there is the very best whaling; they are forty-eight ells long and the biggest fifty. He said that he and a group of six others killed sixty of these in two days.

He was a very rich man in the sort of things their wealth is counted in, that is to say, wild beasts. When he visited the king he still owned six hundred tame beasts not yet sold – the sort of beasts they call 'reindeer'. Six of them were decoy deer. These are very valuable to the Lapps because they use them to catch wild reindeer. He was among the most important men of that country, but for all that he possessed no more than twenty cattle and twenty sheep and twenty pigs, and what little he ploughed he ploughed with horses.

Their wealth comes mostly from the tax the Lapps pay them. This tax consists in the pelts of wild beasts, in birds' down and whale-bone and in ships' cables that are made of the skins of whale and seal. Each pays according to his rank. The highest has to pay the skins of fifteen martens, five reindeer and one bear, and ten bushels of down and a short coat of bear- or otter-skin and two cables – each must be sixty ells long, one of whale-hide and one of seal.

He said that Norway was very long and narrow. All the land fit for grazing or arable lies along the sea-coast and that is very rocky in places. To the east and higher up, wild fells lie alongside the worked land. In these fells live the Lapps. The worked land is broadest in the south, and the further north you get the narrower it becomes. In the south it may be sixty miles across or more; in the middle thirty or more; and in the north, he said, where it is narrowest, it may be three miles to the fell. And then the fell is in some parts as broad as can be crossed in two weeks, and in other parts as broad as can be crossed in six days. Alongside the southern part of this land, beyond the fells, is Sweden, extending up to the north of the land. And alongside the northern part of the land is the territory of the *Cwenas*. Sometimes the *Cwenas* attack the Norwegians across the fell, sometimes the Norwegians attack them. Scattered over the fells are very large fresh-water lakes, and the *Cwenas* carry their boats over land to the lakes, and from there attack the Norwegians. They have very small, very light boats.

Ohthere called the district he lived in Halogaland. He said that nobody lived north of him. But there was a certain market-town in the south of the land called *Sciringesheal* [Kaupang]. He said it took at least a month to get there under sail if you laid up at night and had a favourable wind every day. All the time you must sail along the coast. To starboard there is, first, Ireland; and then the islands that lie between Ireland and England; and then this country until you get to *Sciringesheal*. And to port Norway all the time.

South of this place *Sciringesheal* a great sea opens out into the land, broader than anyone could see across. Opposite on the other side is Jutland and then *Sillende*. This sea reaches many miles into the land. From *Sciringesheal* he said he sailed in five days to the trading town called *æt Hæthum* [Hedeby]. This is set between the lands of the Wends, the Saxons and the Angles, and it owes allegiance centrally to the Danes. When he sailed there from *Sciringesheal* he had Denmark to port and open sea to starboard for three days; then, two days before arriving at *æt Hæthum*, he had to starboard Jutland and *Sillende* and a lot of islands – these are the lands the Angles lived in before they came to England – and for two days there were to port the islands that are part of Denmark.

In this account Ohthere defines fairly precisely two voyages. On one he sailed the coastal route to the northern tip of Norway (Nordkapp, the North Cape), then east along the north coast of the country until he reached the White Sea. His farthest point was one of the rivers that flows into the White Sea. His second voyage was south along the Norwegian coast until he reached Kaupang, south-east of Larvik on the Skagerrak. From there he sailed across the entrance to the Oslo fiord, then followed the coasts of Norway and Sweden (at that time Denmark) until he reached the northern point of · Sjælland, and then he threaded somehow through the cluster of Danish islands until he reached the great mart of Hedeby on the Schlei close by the present-day town of Schleswig.

## A poet complains of an arduous journey

The poet in this case is Sigvat Thordarson, who was court poet to King Olaf Haraldsson, the Stout (later the Saint), of Norway. This is an example of a court skald being used for a diplomatic job. Olaf of Norway was on poor terms with his namesake Olaf, called *skottkonungr*, of Sweden. The Swedish Olaf had agreed to marry his daughter Ingigerd to the Norwegian king, and then had gone back on his pledge, betrothing her to the Slav king Iarizleif. This caused a coolness between the Olafs. An important political figure in this situation was Earl Rognvald of Västergötland, Sweden, presumably based at Skara. It was necessary for Olaf of Norway to know the earl's loyalties, hence this mission.

I tell the tale as Snorri Sturluson gives it in *Heimskringla*. There Snorri includes several verses of a poem of some length which, he tells us later, was called *Austrfararvísur*, 'Verses on the eastern journey'. These he scattered about his tale and expounded in prose in between. The stanzas are in *dróttkvætt* and some of them are in surprisingly simple wording. Others are fuller of the kennings common to this poetic type. Because of the piecemeal distribution of the individual verses it is not possible to be sure (a) what order they were originally intended in, (b) how many belong to this one poem, (c) how much of the whole poem has survived. In what follows I give only a selection of the verses that various scholars have linked to this poem, choosing those that fit the theme of travel. It is noteworthy that Sigvat's experience of Swedish (or at least Gautish) hospitality hardly tallies with Adam of Bremen's enthusiastic commendation (above, p. 43).

† There were very differing reports about Earl Rognvald. Some accounted him a true friend to King Olaf [it is not clear if the Swedish or Norwegian Olaf is meant]. Others were not so certain. They said he could bring pressure upon the king of Sweden, making sure he kept his promise and the terms of his agreement with King Olaf the Stout. The poet Sigvat spoke in friendly words of Earl Rognvald and often mentioned this to King Olaf. He offered to go on a visit to Earl Rognvald to see what he could learn about the Swedish king and find if he could bring about some sort of settlement. The king approved this because he thought it pleasant to talk often to his confidants about Ingigerd the [Swedish] king's daughter.

At the beginning of winter the skald Sigvat and two companions left Borg [Sarpsborg, Norway] and went east through the forests to Götaland. Before he parted with King Olaf Sigvat spoke this verse: †

> Rest here in safety, here again
> We shall meet in your hall.
> By then I'll have completed
> Everything I've promised.
> This I pray: may the tree
> Of the helmet's snow-storm
> Preserve both life and land.
> May your glory last. My verse ends.

[The 'driving snow of the helmet' is 'battle', whose 'tree' is a fighting king.]

† Then they went east to Eid and took a wretched ferryboat over the river and had difficulty in getting across safely. Sigvat declaimed: †

I was soaked. The swaying ferry
Was hauled across to Eid.
Too scared to turn back, like a fool
I risked my life on that boat.
The ship was a joke. The devil take it!
Never a worse have I seen.
In peril I lay in that old tub.
Yet things turned out better than expected!

† Then they went across Eidaskog forest. Sigvat recited this verse: †

Not for the first time – that's clear –
We met trouble. I was furious.
Twelve leagues and one we went
Walking the forest from Eid.
You can bet we plodded on foot
Speedily through the day.
Blisters blotched the feet
Of all the king's servants.

† Then they journeyed across Götaland. In the evening they reached a farm
called Hof [the noun *hof* means 'temple']. The door was shut firm and
they could not get in. The people of the household said it was sacred.
They turned away, and Sigvat declaimed: †

To Hof I struck the path.
The door was shut. Outside
I had to ask. I bent down,
Poked my nose in to see.
Not much I learned from that household.
They said, 'Today is holy.'
Heathen bullies threw me out.
To Hell with them, say I!

† They came to another farm. The lady of the house was standing outside.
She told them not to come in, saying they were celebrating the 'elf-
sacrifice'. Sigvat declaimed: †

'No farther can you enter,
You wretch!' said the woman.
'Here we are heathens
And I fear the wrath of Odin.'
She shoved me out like a wolf,
That arrogant termagant,
Said she was holding sacrifice
To elves there in her house.

[The term *álfablót*, literally 'elf-sacrifice', needs explanation. The word *álfr* is akin to
our 'elf' but it has quite different connotations, lacking the 'elfin' quality of the English.

In literature the *álfar* were closely linked to the great gods, the *Æsir*, and the two words form an alliterating pair that was common in verse texts. However, the *álfar* were subsidiary deities whose cult seems to have been a group rather than an individual one. They were connected to specific localities, and had some similarity to the *landvættir*, the 'land-spirits' recorded in other sources. They were perhaps something like 'guardian spirits' of the region and helped ensure its prosperity.]

† The next evening they came to three farmers. All of them were called Olvir and they all drove him away. Sigvat declaimed: †

Now three of the same name,
Turning their backs on me,
Have thrust me away.
These sword-trees show no courtesy.
What I fear over all
Is that every sea-going skipper
Who bears the name of Olvir
Will drive away all strangers.

[The image 'sword-tree' is in fact more complex in the original: *heinflets þollr*. *Hein* means 'hone, whetstone'. Its *flet*, 'bed' is the sword-blade on which it rests while the edge is sharpened. *Þollr* means 'fir-tree'. *Heinflets þollr* is one of those kennings that uses the image of 'tree' for 'man'. Here a 'tree of the sword', 'fighting-man'. The phrase I have translated 'sea-going skipper' is in fact *hlæðir hafskiðs*, literally 'loader of the snow-shoe of the ocean'.]

† So they went on further through the night and came upon a fourth farmer. He was said to be the best of the king's men there. Yet he too drove them away. Sigvat declaimed: †

I went to see the giver
Of ocean's glitter, one
Whom all men said would greet me.
I hoped to find a welcome.
That farm-hand scanned me sourly
- I don't shout men's faults -
But if this one is the best,
What can the worst be like?

[The 'ocean's glitter' is gold, for in Norse verbiage gold is associated with Ægir who personifies the ocean (below, p. 220). The 'giver of ocean's glitter' is thus a generous prince who rewards his servants liberally. The words I have translated 'farm-hand' are more subtle than that: *gætir grefs*, literally 'guardian of the hoe'. *Gætir* is usually used in complimentary kennings, as 'guardian of men, or the land' for 'king'. Here Sigvat uses a deliberately ironical and insulting kenning.]

On the foot-track east of Eidaskog
How I missed the house of Asta!
I asked a heathen man

> For some place to put up at.
> Great Saxi's son I never met.
> No decency did I find.
> Four times in a single evening
> I was shown the door!

[Asta was the mother of St Olaf and *Heimskringla* celebrates her for her hospitality. Saxi is otherwise unknown.]

† When they came to Earl Rognvald's he said they must have had a toilsome journey. Sigvat declaimed: †

> Ambassadors of the ruler
> Of Sognfiord, coming to princes
> With their retinue
> Have had a monstrous journey.
> Little we spared ourselves
> For men find toil in travel.
> Norway's strong defender
> Gave us this southern mission.

> The path through Eida forest
> Was a tough road to take
> East to the warrior's tamer.
> That prince's glory I praise.
> The sea-flame's trees
> Of that battle-leader
> Should not have thrust me away
> Before I found my gracious lord.

[Rognvald is called 'tamer of warriors' presumably because he holds strong discipline and stands no nonsense from his retinue. But the word for warrior here is *iöfurr*, literally 'wild boar', which can also have the connotation 'noble warrior, prince'. So Sigvat may here be flattering Rognvald by calling him 'tamer of princes', perhaps referring to his powerful position situated between the territories of the kings of Norway and Sweden. In the second half of this verse Sigvat indulges in a complicated kenning that needs explanation and must have puzzled his first hearers. I have simplified it above as 'the sea-flame's trees'. A literal translation is 'the trees of the precious fire of the bench of the ship's roller'. *Hlunnr*, the 'ship's roller', one of the logs used to roll a ship down to the water or to support the ship when it is hauled ashore', is commonly used in kennings for ships, and the 'ship's bench' is the sea. The 'sea's precious fire' is, as has been seen, gold. The poetic word *runnr* is a *heiti* for 'tree' and is often used in kennings for fighting-men (who, it is hoped, will stand in battle firm as trees). And a 'tree of gold' is a fighter well rewarded by his prince with gifts of gold arm-rings and other finely decorated gear. The hearer would not have been helped by the word order of this complex kenning in the poem, or the fact that it is split up into three sections by intervening words: *hlunns . . . hilmis runnum . . . dýrloga bekkiar*. The word for prince here, *hilmir*, is etymologically related to *hiálmr*, 'helmet', so I have translated it 'battle-leader', but perhaps 'protector' would be an equally appropriate rendering.]

† Earl Rognvald gave Sigvat a gold arm-ring. One of the women said that he
had achieved something with those dark eyes of his. Sigvat declaimed †

> Good woman, these dark eyes –
> Icelandic ones – have shown me
> The long and uphill road
> Towards that glittering gold.
> This foot of mine, my goddess,
> Has stepped so valiantly
> Over ancient pathways
> Unknown to *your* man.

[The translation 'my goddess' is something of a travesty. Sigvat calls the woman by a
goddess name, but only in poetic licence. She is given the title *miöð-Nanna*; the first
element is the word 'mead' presumably because she takes round the drink at a formal
feast, the second is the name of the god Baldr's wife.]

† When Sigvat returned to King Olaf and walked into his hall, he looked
round the walls and said: †

> Men of the king's guard
> Who feast the wound-swan
> Array the prince's hall with helmets,
> Mail-coats. Here they hang.
> No other young ruler
> Can boast richer wall-hangings.
> No fear of that.
> Glorious is this hall.

[The 'swan of wounds' is the eagle or raven which, as all ornithologists know, feeds on
the corpses of those killed in battle.]

† Then he spoke of his travels and declaimed these verses. †

> Swift man of battle, I beg
> This noble company hear
> These verses I made on my journey.
> I suffered teeming rain.
> I was sent to ski over the field
> Of the swan, east,
> Distant, to Sweden.
> Little sleep for me that autumn.

[Literally Sigvat said he was sent 'aboard the swan-field's ski'; the 'swan-field' is water,
its 'ski' a ship.]

† And when he spoke with the king he declaimed: †

> With thought and with honour
> I kept my word to you,
> When, King Olaf, I visited

The noble, mighty Rognvald.
Many a long talk I had
At the court of that fee'd man of yours.
To you, my weaponed prince,
No man more true than he.

[There follow a group of stanzas more concerned with the negotiations with Earl
Rognvald than with Sigvat's dreary journey. A number of other verses ascribed to Sigvat
are included by some editors among the *Austrfararvísur* though they appear elsewhere
in the *Heimskringla* Saga of St Olaf and are used there to tell of a different journey to
Earl Rognvald. Certainly their tone is different from that of the *Austrfararvísur* quoted
so far. Among them are:]

Glad I was often when out
On the fiords the harsh storm
Drove the wind-filled sail of the king
Of the Strinda-men across the water.
The sea-stallion made a fine gallop.
The keels made Lista's neck-ring shudder
As we sailed our pinnace, fiercely rushing
Out across the ocean.

[Strinda and Lista are coastal places in Norway. 'Lista's neck-ring' is the sea that more or
less surrounds it.]

We let the noble Skioldung's ships,
Canopied, lie at anchor
By the island off the glorious land
Through the opening summer.
But in autumn it was our lot
To ride our horses, kicking,
Through thickets of hawthorn.
I showed the women my skills.

The horse, unfed, covers the long paths
Through evening's dusk.
Its hooves slash the turf before the hall.
The light fades.
Now my steed carried me
Across waters, far from Denmark.
My nag's foot struck the river bank.
Now day meets night.

Quickly the stately ladies
Gaze out to view us
Riding through Rognvald's courts.
They see our cavalcade.
We spur on our horses
So the lady within her house
Hears from far away
The pounding of hooves.

## Roads, bridges, hostels

Travel overland was always difficult in the Middle Ages. One act of social charity a rich man could undertake was build a bridge over a watercourse or a causeway over a fen (the word *bró* is used for both and so is not easy to translate precisely); or make a ford in a river. Such a work would sometimes be marked by a rune-stone asserting the local distinction of the man's family and in Christian times stressing the religious import of the deed. Here are examples from late Viking Age Sweden.

1. Sälna, Uppland: in the nineteenth century the stone was moved from its original site by a stone bridge. It is a pillar over three metres high, with a long, partly lost, inscription, part in verse. Some of the loss is supplied from early drawings.

   > Oystæin and Iorund and Biorn, [brothers, set up] ... their father. God help his spirit and soul, and forgive him his offences and sins. |
   > > Ever will stand, while man lives on
   > > This strong-built broad bridge, to the good man's memory.
   > > Lads made it for their father.
   > > There can be no better way-monument.

2. Årby, Uppland: a stone boulder, with an inscription divided between the two sides. It once served to mark the road leading to a river crossing.

   > A. Nasi and his brothers raised this stone
   > B. in memory of their good father Iarl and made a bridge to God's glory.

3. Näs, Uppland: two inscriptions on a rock face by the side of the road leading to the farm.

   > A. Lifstæin had made, for the benefit of his own soul and the souls of his wife Ingirun and his sons Iarund and Nikolas and Ludin, these causeways.
   > B. He owned the farm at Torsholma and had the right to call on a ship's crew from Rolsta.

The last part of inscription B is difficult, partly because the important word is damaged. It is usually completed [s]**kibliþ**, *skiplið*, 'ship's crew', and presumably refers to a duty the farmers at Rolsta had to supply men for Lifstæin's ship.

4. Gryta, Uppland: a wayside stone with a snake-like band of runes, surrounding a pair of decorative crosses. A chunk has broken away from the left-hand side, with part of the text, which fortunately can be supplied from an earlier account.

   > Thialfi made [this bridge in memory of Bolla, his daught]er. Ali and Olæ[if had] ⟨the stone⟩ carved in memory of their father Thialfi. And Inga in her husband's memory. May God give ease to their souls.

5. Runby, Uppland: a stone with two related inscriptions set in decorative snakes.

A. Ingrid had the loading-bridge made and the stone [carved in memory of | her husband Ingimar] and her sons Dan and Banki.

B. They lived in Runby and owned the farm. Christ help their souls. This shall commemorate | the men as long as mankind lives.

The 'loading-bridge', *hlaðbró*, was presumably an embankment by the waterside to allow ships to be loaded and unloaded.

6. Täby, Uppland: one of the most famous of bridge/road monuments is that set up by the local landowner, Iarlabanki, to honour his own achievements. He built a causeway (which still stands) some 150 metres long and apparently marked at each end by two rune-stones, more or less identical in content. Two remain in place.

   Iarlabanki had this stone put up in his own honour during his lifetime. | And he made this bridge for his soul's sake. And alone he owned the whole of Täby. May God help his soul.

Iarlabanki did not want to be lost sight of, for he also put up at nearby Vallentuna a stone with two inscriptions, recording his greatness. It declares that 'he alone owned the whole of Täby' and 'he made this moot-place, and alone held this whole district'. The same man occurs also on a memorial at S. Sätra, Uppland together with his brother.

   Hæming and Iarlabanki, they had a road cleared and bridges made in memory of their father, and Æstrid in memory of | her sons Ingifast and Ingvar. +God hel | p their souls.

After his death he was commemorated by his son on a memorial stone at Fällbro, which also mentions bridge-building.

7. Kullerstad, Östergötland: the rune-stone, which has a prominent cross in its design, stands close to a bridge across a stream.

   Hakon made this bridge, and it shall be called Gunnar's bridge, and he | was Hakon's son.

8. Glömsjö, Småland: the runes are cut on a snake-like band surrounding a cross. The stone stands by the way-side near the bridge across the river.

   Thormar had this bridge built in memory of his son Saxi. May God give | his soul good help.

9. Södertälje, Södermanland: on a rock face by the roadside (Gamla Turingevägen) are carved a pair of adjoining inscriptions of related content, the first rather damaged. They are on a couple of snakes, the second enclosing a cross, the first not.

   A. Holmfast had the road cleared in memory of his mother Ing[iger]d . . .
   B. Holmfast had the road cleared and a bridge made in memory of his father Gam[al] who lived at Näsby. God help his soul. | Øystæin ⟨cut the runes⟩.

10. Karberga, Uppland; a very elaborately decorated boulder, partly damaged and partly supplied from an older drawing, though some details remain uncertain.

> Ingrid and Ingigærd had this stone erected and a ford made out in the sound in memory of their father Thorir. Thorir had a hostel built in memory of Ingithora his wife and in memory ...

What the two sisters made was an *aurr*, which means something like 'gravel bank, sand-bank'. Thorir set up a *sáluhús/sæluhús*, literally a 'soul-house' or possibly a 'comfort-house'; a shelter set up in desolate territory to give the traveller somewhere to lodge for the night. This again was an act of social charity, and the Christian word for it presumably implies it helped or gave comfort to the soul of the giver.

# CHAPTER 3

# Settlement and land-holding

Iceland is the only Viking land where we have detailed accounts of the process of settlement. There are, of course, saga tales of the Vikings setting up farms in Greenland and bases in North America, and there is plenty of archaeological evidence for the first of these. But for Iceland there are the primary sources – to be used with some caution – of *Íslendingabók* and *Landnámabók*, which demonstrate the problems a people of primitive technology have when faced with virgin territory.

When the Vikings settled down in northern England says the *Anglo-Saxon Chronicle* for 876: 'Healfdene divided up the land of the Northumbrians and they set about ploughing and cultivating it'. Viking fighting-men became instant farmers, but there was no problem here for the land had already been divided into holdings and tilled for many years. Settling a new land was a different business. How to control the size of a man's claim? *Landnámabók* records some pragmatic methods of control, but also gives a more general account. The various texts do not all agree at this point; here is the most detailed version.

† This opens the account of the settlement of the Southern Quarter which has the best quality land in the whole of Iceland. The most outstanding men lived there, both clerics and laymen.

The Eastern fiords were the first part of Iceland settled, but the land between Hornafiord and Reykianes was the last to be fully occupied. There the winds and the rough seas determined where men landed since there was a shortage of harbours and the coasts were forbidding. Some of the first to reach there settled land nearest the fells, for they spotted this fact about the conditions, that beasts were very ready to leave the seashore for the hills. The men who came here later thought the earlier settlers had taken too extensive estates. Then Harald Finehair made this regulation, that nobody should take over land broader than he and his crew could bear fire across in a single day. They had to make a fire when the sun was in the east. Then they should make other smoking fires so that each could be seen from the others. And the fires that were made when the sun was in the east must burn until nightfall. Then they should march forward until the sun was in the west and there make other fires. †

## Problems of settling a new land

Iceland was a virtually empty land when Vikings found it. Ari Thorgilsson's *Íslendinga-bók* tells us of the first settlements and also gives a working chronology: according to him the main body of settlers took land in the new country between 870 and 930.

> Iceland was first settled from Norway in the days of Harald Finehair, son of Halfdan the Black, at the time ... when Ivar, son of Ragnar Lodbrok, had St Edmund, king of the Angles, killed. And that was 870 years after the birth of Christ, as is written in his biography.
>
> There was a Norwegian called Ingolf, of whom it is said in truth that he first made his way from Norway to Iceland when Harald Finehair was sixteen years old; and a second time a few years later. He settled in the south of Iceland, in Reykjarvík. The place where he first landed is called Ingolfshofdi, to the east of Minthakseyr; and Ingolfsfell, to the west of River Olfosa where he later took over the land.
>
> At that time Iceland was overgrown with scrub between fell and foreshore. There were Christian men here then whom the Northmen call *papar*. But afterwards they went away because they didn't want to stay here side by side with heathens. And they left behind them Irish books, bells and croziers; from which one might deduce they were Irishmen.
>
> After that a great emigration took place to Iceland from Norway, to the extent that King Harald had to forbid it because he was afraid it would lead to the depopulation of his country. The final agreement was that every man who was not exempt from it and who wanted to travel here from Norway had to pay the king five *aurar* ... Moreover men who know have said that Iceland was fully settled in sixty years, so that there was no more settlement after that.

If Ari's information was correct Iceland had only a small population of Irish monks/hermits who had come to the land to live in solitude. There is some – though of course disputed – archaeological support for the statement in finds in Iceland of ecclesiastical objects including bell fragments which some have identified as early Irish.

A much more detailed account of the settlement of Iceland appears in *Land-námabók*, 'The book of the land-takings', or as we would put it, 'The book of the settlements'. The original *Landnámabók* was apparently a work of the early twelfth century; thus it related events that had taken place two hundred years before. The records it relied on could not have been written; they must have been oral accounts given by the sort of people, skilled in traditional lore, that Ari named in the opening section of his *Íslendingabók* (p. 26 above). Even if we had the original version of *Landnámabók*, we would have to be cautious about using it as a historical source, allowing for later additions and alterations to the original reports, or exaggerations and amplifications in their tales of the settlement.

Unfortunately the original *Landnámabók* does not survive. A century or so after it was written, a copy was made by one Styrmir Kárason, called the Wise, who died in 1245; but this text too does not survive. In its turn it was copied by one Sturla Þórðarson, perhaps *c.*1275–80, and his work (named *Sturlubók* and referred to below simply as S) does remain to us, though in a seventeenth-century transcript. Sturla did not simply copy; he added material from a variety of other sources. So *Sturlubók* alone cannot be used to recreate Styrmir's book, never mind the original work. In the early fourteenth century a further version was made, by one Haukr Erlendsson, but he tells us he conflated Styrmir's and Sturla's versions. Haukr's autograph copy survives in part and there is also a seventeenth-century transcript of nearly all of it (*Hauksbók* = H). About 1300 a copy of Styrmir's book was made; it is called *Melabók* from its place of origin. Only two leaves of a fifteenth-century copy of this remain. However, it was used – with other material – in compiling a version called *Þórðarbók*. I list these various recensions only to show how hard it is to reconstruct an original text of *Landnámabók*. (For a more detailed account see Jakob Benediktsson's article '*Landnámabók*: some remarks on its value as a historical source', *Saga-book of the Viking Society*, 17, 4 (1969), 275–92).

The extracts that follow (only a small part of what survives) have therefore to be treated with caution as historical sources but I hesitate to jettison them altogether. They give vivid pictures of some of the problems of settling a waste and often inhospitable region, the difficulties of finding habitable land in an unmapped country, and so how incomers fixed on places to farm and why they sometimes moved to new sites. There are important details of the way the people managed to subsist, their qualities of life, the reasons for the feuds and killings that took place in early Iceland, and there is some mention of the superstitions and beliefs that governed their actions.

*Landnámabók* opened with the earliest sightings and landings on Iceland, and then Ingolf's first settlement on Reykjanes in the south-west. Thereafter it proceeded round the coast of the island in a clockwise direction, listing the settlers of each area, their alliances and descendants and the lesser people dependent upon them. The surviving versions often tell incidents in the lives of the first settlers, though how much of this was in the earliest *Landnámabók* and how much added at later stages is difficult to detect. Two writers are named in connection with the original *Landnámabók*, Ari Thorgilsson and one Kolskegg Asbiarnarson, the Wise, the two being roughly contemporary. Kolskegg was responsible for the section covering most of east and south-east Iceland. How much of the rest is by Ari, how much attributed to him because he was a respected chronicler of Icelandic history is a matter of uncertainty. It seems certain that, at the beginning of the twelfth century, there was an effort to collect together the traditions of the settlement of the country, and the existing versions of *Landnámabók* represent that collection in greater or lesser degree.

1. From S:

> † There was a man called Floki Vilgerdarson. He was a great adventurer by
> sea. He set out for Gardarsholm [an early name for Iceland], sailing from a
> place called Flokavardi [in Norway]. That is where Hordaland and Roga-
> land meet. First he went to the Shetlands and lay up in Flokavag there.
> There his daughter Geirhild was drowned in the Loch of Girlsta.
>
> In Floki's ship was a free-farmer called Thorolf and a second called
> Heriolf. A Hebridean called Faxi was on board too. Floki had three ravens
> that he took to sea with him. When he freed the first it flew aft to the stern
> of the ship. The second flew into the air, then back to the ship. The third
> flew off past the prow in the direction where they later found land. Floki
> and his crew came west to Horn [in Iceland]. They sailed south along the
> coast. And when they sailed west round Reykianes, the fiord opened up in
> front of them so that they could see Snæfellsnes. 'This is a huge land we've
> come to', said Faxi, 'look what big waterways there are!' That place was
> later called Faxaos.
>
> Floki and his company sailed over Breidafiord to the west of Iceland,
> and reached land at the place that is now called Vatsfiord, by Bardastrond.
> The fiord was well stocked with fish, and because of the plentiful catch
> they did not bother about hay-making, so all their cattle died that winter.
> The spring was pretty chill. Then Floki climbed up to a high fell and saw,
> to the north beyond the fells, a fiord full of drift-ice. So they called the land
> Iceland, and that has been its name ever since.
>
> That summer Floki and his comrades planned a move and were ready
> for sea just before winter. They could not round Reykianes, and the ship's
> boat was torn away from them: Heriolf was on it. He came ashore at the
> place now called Heriolfshofn. Floki stayed that winter in Borgarfiord,
> and there he and Heriolf were re-united. Next summer they sailed back to
> Norway. When they were asked about the land, Floki spoke unflatteringly
> about it, but Heriolf told everything about the land, both good and bad.
> In his turn Thorolf said that butter dripped from every blade of grass in
> the land they had discovered. So he was known as Butter-Thorolf. †

The H version has further details: it explains the ravens as sacrificial birds (the raven was
Odin's bird.) †He prepared a great sacrifice, and dedicated three ravens who were to
direct his journey, because at that time ocean-going sailors from the northern countries
had no lode-stones. † But the resemblance between this story and that of Noah at the
end of the Flood is unlikely to be coincidence, and at least in this form must be highly
suspect. Of the place where Floki over-wintered H adds: †You can still see the site of
their hut, in along the fiord from Brianslœk, and the boat-shed and cooking pit too. †
Which looks like a bit of local knowledge added to confirm the story. The tale of the
immigrants' neglect of their cattle (the writer has not told us they brought farm-stock
with them) is paralleled by a similar tale about the first settlers in North America,
recounted in *The Greenlanders' saga* and *Eirik the Red's saga*. It seems to be a common
theme of this sort of tale.

2. From S, H:

> † There was a man of Hebridean birth called Kalman. He went to Iceland and came to Hvalfiord, settling at the River Kalmansa. His two sons drowned there in Hvalfiord. Thereafter he took land west of the River Hvita, between there and the River Fliot, the whole strip of land called Kalmanstunga as far east up to the glacier as vegetation grows. He lived at Kalmanstunga. He drowned in the Hvita when he had gone south on to the lava-plain to meet his mistress, and his burial mound is to the south, on Hvitarbakki.
>
> His son was Sturla godi who lived in Sturlustadir, below the fells at Tungufell up from Skaldskelmisdal, and later lived at Kalmanstunga. His son was Biarni who had a dispute with the younger Hrolf and his sons about the land at Little Tunga. Then Biarni vowed to convert to Christianity. Thereafter the River Hvita broke a new channel through to where it flows now. Then Biarni took possession of Little Tunga and the land down round Grind and Solmundarhofdi.
>
> Kalman's brother was called Kylan. He lived below Kollshamar. His son was Kari who came to blows with Karli Konalsson from Karlastadir, a freed slave of Hrolf of Geitland. The cause of the quarrel was an ox, and it ended with Karli getting it. Then Kari egged on one of his slaves to kill Karli. The slave acted as though he were crazy and rushed off south across the lava-field. Karli was sitting at the threshold of his house. The slave struck him his death-blow. Thereafter Kari killed the slave. Thiodolf, Karli's son, killed Kylan Karason at Kylansholmar. Then Thiodolf burned Kari to death inside his house at the place now called Brenna [burning].
>
> Biarni Sturluson received baptism and lived at Biarnastadir in Little Tunga and had a church built there. †

The implication is that by turning Christian Biarni encouraged the River Hvita to change its course and so bring Little Tunga into his territory. There is in fact evidence of a former course of this river, so there is some sort of factual basis to the story. The bloody feud between Kari and Karli, carried on by the next generation, is typical of the subject matter of some of the *Íslendinga sögur* (Sagas of Icelanders) written in the thirteenth century but claiming to tell of events from the settlement period. The farm-name Brenna is known from other sources and may support – or it could be the origin of – this incident in the story.

3. From S:

> † One of Harald Finehair's fighting-men was called Vali the Strong. He killed a man in one of the sanctuaries and was outlawed for it. He went to the Hebrides and settled there, but his three sons went to Iceland. Their mother was Hlif 'horse-gelder.' One son was called Atli, the second Alfarin, the third Audun stoti. All three went to Iceland. Atli Valason and Asmund his son took the land between the rivers Fura and Lysa. Asmund

lived at Thorutoptir in Langaholt. He was married to Langaholts-Thora. When Asmund grew old he lived at Oxl, but Thora stayed on after him and had her great hall built across the main road. She had a table always laid, while she sat on a chair outside and invited any hungry traveller in to dine. Asmund was buried at Asmundarleidi, laid in a ship with his slave by his side. A passer-by heard this verse declaimed from inside the mound:

Alone in this berth of stones I lie
In the sea-king's raven's hold.
No press of men on the decking.
On the waves' steed I live.
Better for the battle-skilled fighter
Is space than this low companion.
The sea-beast is my command.
Long will that stand in man's memory.

Thereupon the mound was searched and the slave removed from the ship. †

Here is a clear case of unhistorical addition to a simple tale. The story of the woman who builds her hall across the road so that she can give (and get) entertainment is something of a commonplace, occurring elsewhere in *Landnámabók*, but it stresses the tradition of hospitality among the northern nations and the way by which news travelled. The dead man speaking from his burial mound is also something of a commonplace. The idea of the dead continuing some sort of shadowy life in the grave or funeral cairn is often rehearsed in Icelandic literature, and may have some basis in folk-belief. This dead man speaks a verse in good *dróttkvætt* metre, and with easily understood kennings: 'sea-king's raven', 'waves' steed', 'sea-beast' for 'ship', 'berth (or harbour) of stones' for 'mound enclosing a burial ship'.

## 4. From H:

† Sigmund, son of the Ketil 'thistle' who had settled Thistilsfiord, married Hildigunn. He took land between Hellishraun and Beruvikrhraun, and lived at Laugarbrekka and was buried there. He had three sons. One was Einar, who stayed there at Laugarbrekka. The father and son sold Lonland to [another] Einar who lived there afterwards. He was called Lon-Einar.

A whale was beached on his foreshore and he cut away part of the meat. The wind drove it to sea again, and it drifted on to Einar Sigmundarson's land. Lon-Einar claimed that Hildigunn had made this happen by witchcraft. When the whale had been driven from Lon-Einar's land he went in search of it, and came up just as Einar Sigmundarson and his labourers were cutting up the beast. He cut one of them down at once with a single blow. Einar of Laugarbrekka told his namesake to clear off 'because it will do you no good to attack us.' Lon-Einar went off for he had fewer men. Einar Sigmundarson transported the whale home.

And at a time when he was away from home, Lon-Einar came to

Laugarbrekka with seven men and summoned Hildigunn at law on a charge of witchcraft. She was the daughter of Beinir Masson, son of Naddodd of the Faeroes. Einar came back just as Lon-Einar had left. Hildigunn told him what had happened and gave him a jacket, newly made. Einar picked up his shield and sword, took his working horse and rode after them. He rode his horse into the ground at Thufubiorg, and then ran as fast as he could. As he came by Drangar he saw a monstrous creature sitting up on the top there, kicking his heels so that they swept the surf, and slapping them together so that they made spin-drift. He spoke this verse:

[There follows an eight-line *dróttkvætt* stanza but modern scholars have not been able to make much of it.]

Einar took no heed of this. They came together at the place called Mannafallsbrekkur and there they fought. No steel could penetrate Einar's jacket. Four of Lon-Einar's men fell and two ran away. For a long time the two Einars attacked each other before Lon-Einar's belt came in two, and as he grabbed at it his namesake struck him his death-blow. And Hreidar, Einar Sigmundarson's slave, had seen him hurrying along and ran towards him. Then he saw Lon-Einar's slaves fleeing. He ran after them and killed both of them at Thrælavik. For that Einar gave him his freedom, and as much land as he could fence round in three days. The place where he lived is now called Hreidarsgerdi. Einar lived on in Laugarbrekka and is buried not far from Sigmund's mound. His mound is green, winter and summer alike. †

Again there is a tale developed from a tradition, in part to explain a place-name – Thrælavik, 'Slave-bay'. Narrative elements are added to what is probably a historical record of a quarrel over the right to driftage on the beach that was part of a land-holding. A whale driven ashore would be a welcome addition to the red meat supply of a household, and its fat and bone could also be put to good use.

5. From S, H:

† There was a king of a band of fighting-men called Oleif the Fair. He was the son of King Ingiald Helgason . . . Oleif the Fair went on many a Viking raid in the west, took over Dublin in Ireland and the region dependent on it and became king there. He married Aud the Deeply-wealthy, daughter of Ketil flatnef. Their son was called Thorstein the Red. Oleif fell in battle in Ireland. Thereupon Aud and Thorstein went to the Hebrides. There Thorstein married Thurid, daughter of Eyvind the Norwegian and sister of Helgi the Skinny. They had a large family. Their son was called Olaf feilan, and their daughters Groa and Alof, Osk and Thorhild, Thorgerd and Vigdis.

Thorstein became king of a band of fighting-men. He joined up with Earl Sigurd the Mighty [of the Orkneys], son of Eystein glumra. They took over Caithness and Sutherland, Ross and Moray, and more than half Scotland. There Thorstein became king until the Scots failed him and he fell in battle there.

Aud was in Caithness when she heard of Thorstein's death. She had a ship built secretly in the forest, and when it was complete she set out for the Orkneys. There she married off Thorstein the Red's daughter Groa; she became mother to Grelod whom Thorfinn 'skull-splitter' married. After that Aud made for Iceland. On the ship with her she had twenty freemen ...

Aud came first to the Faroes and there married off Alof, daughter of Thorstein the Red ... Then she made for Iceland. She reached Vikrarskeid and was cast ashore there. So she went on to Kialarnes to her brother's, Helgi biola. He invited her to stay with half her crew. She thought that a mean offer, and said he would always be a man of little mind. So she went west to Breidafiord, to her brother Biorn's. He went to welcome her with all his household, saying he knew his sister's temper. He invited her to stay there with all her men. That she accepted.

Next spring Aud and her company went looking for land in along Breidafiord. They took their midday meal on the north side of Breidafiord at the place now called Dogurdarnes [Dinnerness]. Then they turned in along an inlet scattered with islands. They landed at a headland where Aud lost her comb; this she called Kambsnes [Combness]. Aud took all the dale-land at the inner end of the fiord between the Rivers Dogurdara and Skraumuhlaupsa. She lived at the place called Audartoptir in Hvamm by Aurridaaros. Her place of devotion was at Krossholar [Crosshillocks]. There she had crosses put up because she was baptised and a true believer. Later on the family had a superstitious belief about the hills there. A sanctuary was made there when sacrificing came into use. They believed that when they died they would go into the hills. And Thord gellir was taken to them before he came to man's estate as is told in his saga.

Aud gave land to her crew and to her freed slaves. †

[There follows a list of Aud's dependants and where they were settled.]

† Aud was a woman of great dignity. When old age wearied her she invited her relatives and kinsmen in and made a splendid feast ready. When it had gone on for three days she picked out gifts for her friends and wished them well. She said the feast must go on for another three days and that was to celebrate her passing. The following night she died. She was buried on the foreshore between high and low water-marks as she had stipulated, because as a baptised Christian she did not want to lie in unhallowed ground. After that her family's faith declined. †

Aud, sometimes called *diúpauðuga*, 'deeply-rich', sometimes *diúpúðuga*, 'deep-minded', is a well-known example of the great Viking lady, a widow in control of her own fortune and destiny. She appears elsewhere in Norse literature, notably in the

CHRONICLES OF THE VIKINGS

thirteenth-century saga *Laxdæla saga* where the account, in particular of her death and burial, is considerably different from the one above. There is no reason to doubt she was a historical figure, but a number of tales seem to have accumulated about her, and here the historicity is less certain. Some of her exploits were probably invented to account for place-names like Dogurdarnes and Kambsnes. Of the superstitious faith in hills or mountains linked to the fate of a family there are other records in Icelandic literature (p. 30 above) and it is likely some such belief existed – which may link to a type of ancestor-worship. The claim that many Icelandic families had roots in the Western Isles of Scotland and that there was a strong Celtic strain in the Icelandic settlers is attested in a number of ways, by archaeology, place-names and physical anthropology.

6. From S, H:

> † Thurid 'sound-filler' and her son Volu-Stein left Halogaland for Iceland and settled in Bolungarvik, living in Vatsnes. The reason she was called 'sound-filler' was that at a time of famine in Halogaland she cast spells that filled every sound with fish. She also set up the fishing-station at Kviarmid in Isafiardardiup and for it took a hornless ewe from every free-farmer in Isafiord. †

7. From S, H:

> † There was a man called Hrosskell who took all Svartardal and Yrarfellslond with the approval of Eirik [the major local landowner detailed later]. He took the land as far down as Gilhagi and lived at Yrarfell. He had a slave called Rodrek. He sent him up along Mælifellsdal exploring the country on the fells to the south. He came to the gully that runs south from Mælifell and is now called Rodreksgil. There he set up a staff, its bark newly stripped away, the sort they called a land-marker. Thereafter he turned back.
>
> There was a splendid man called Eirik. He left Norway for Iceland. He was the son of Hroald Geirmundarson ... Eirik took the land from the River Gila, all along Goddalir and down to the River Nordra. He lived at Hof in Goddalir ...
>
> There was a man called Vekel 'shape-changer' who took the land down from the River Gila to the River Mælifellsa, and lived at Mælifell. He heard of Rodrek's journey. A bit later he went south on to the fells to explore the country. He came to the cairns that are now called Vekelshaugar. He took a shot between the cairns and turned back from there. When Eirik in Goddalir heard that he sent out his slave called Rongud south on to the fells. He too went to explore. He came south to Blondukvislir and then up along the river that falls to the west of Hvinveriadal, and west onto the lava-plain between Reykiavellir and Kiol. There he came upon human tracks and noted that they led south from there. He built a cairn there which is now called Rongud's cairn. From there he turned back, and

Eirik gave him his freedom for his journey. From that time on there began travel over the fell between the southern and northern quarters [of Iceland]. †

The word translated 'took a shot' is the simple verb *skióta*, 'to shoot', but the writer does not tell what was shot. The answer is a *tundrör*, literally a 'tinder-arrow', a burning arrow that recorded symbolically the claim to a piece of land.

8. From S, H:

> † There was a man called Kraku-Hreidar; his father Ofeig lafskegg, son of Yxna-Thorir. The father and son got their ship ready for Iceland. When they came in sight of land, Hreidar came up to the mast and said he would not throw overboard the supporting beams of his high-seat. He said it would be commonplace to determine his future that way. He would rather appeal to Thor and ask him to direct him to somewhere he could settle. He would fight for the land if it was already taken up. When he came to Skagafiord he ran his ship straight at the shore at Borgarsand and wrecked it. Havard 'heron' came up and invited him to stay with him, so he stayed there that winter at Hegrines.
>
> In spring Havard asked him what his plans were, and he said he planned to fight Sæmund for his land. Havard discouraged him, saying it would lead to disaster. He told him to go to Eirik in Guddalir and ask his advice, 'because he is the shrewdest man in this district.' So Hreidar did. When he met Eirik, he discouraged him from fighting; he said it was inept for men to come to blows when there was such a shortage of people in the land. He would prefer to give him all the strip of land downstream from Skalamyr. That was where Thor had directed him, he said, and that is where his prow had pointed when he sailed ashore at Borgarsand. That was enough land for him and his sons. Hreidar accepted this offer and lived at Steinstadir; he chose to die into Mælifell. †

The *öndvegissulur*, the pillars (*sulur*) that supported the seat of honour in a house (*öndvegi*), represented the authority of the head of the household and in some way the continuity of the family and its prosperity. According to written sources, it was a common practice for Norwegians leaving their ancestral home to emigrate to Iceland to take with them these pillars and to throw them overboard on nearing land. They trusted the pillars to lead them to a suitable place to settle in. Sailing one's ship *til brots*, that is, sailing it straight at the shore to beach it with the strong risk of wrecking it, was a well-known manœuvre to a ship's captain in desperate danger. Here, however, Hreidar presumably does it as a gesture, to indicate his faith in Thor's guidance. Yet, if I have translated the last sentence correctly, he believes in some sort of after-life not connected with the gods but with the local 'sacred' mountain.

9. From S, H:

> † Hialti, son of Thord skalp, came to Iceland and took Hialtadal with the

agreement of Kolbein, and lived at Hof. His sons were Thorvald and Thord, both splendid men. When they inherited from their father they gave the most magnificent memorial feast there had ever been in Iceland. They invited all the leading men of Iceland. There were twelve hundred guests, and all the most honoured people took away gifts with them. At this feast Odd Breidfirding recited the ode he had made on Hialti. Earlier Glum Geirason had summoned Odd to answer a charge at the Thorska- fiord court. Hialti's sons brought their ship south to Steingrimsfiord and went south over the heath where now it is called Hialtdœlalaut. And when they reached the court, they were so splendidly dressed that people thought the great gods had arrived. This verse describes it:

> Each stock of the sword-blade
> Skilled in slaughter,
> Thought only that the almighty
> Gods were coming.
> When fierce Hialti's sons
> Brought to the court
> At Thorskafiord
> Their helmets of terror.

From Hialti's sons is descended a large and noble family. †

The etiquette of Icelandic life comes into view here, with a formal inheritance-feast celebrating the distinction of the dead man, and the recitation of an ode in his memory and honour. Odd repays with his poem the support he received from Hialti's sons at his court appearance. His poem is more complex than the translation here implies. The kenning in the first line 'stock of the sword-blade' (literally, 'of iron') for 'fighting-man' is simple enough. The image in the last line is not so easy. The Icelandic phrase *bera ægishiálm yfir*, 'to bear a helmet of terror over' means 'to overawe'. For 'helmet', however, Odd has used a complex kenning, 'metal beak of the forehead of the forest fish'. A 'forest fish' is a snake. The 'metal beak (the word here used of the metal-clad beak of a fighting-ship) of the forehead' is a helmet. A snake's helmet is the helmet of terror, because this was specifically connected, in Norse imagery, with the fear a great serpent spread through the neighbourhood. Such complexity had to be taken in by the audience of an orally presented poem.

10. From S:

> † There was a man called Thormod the Tough. He killed Gyrd, the grand- father of Skialg of Jæren [in Norway], and for that had to flee the land, so he went to Iceland. He took his ship into Siglufiord and sailed along it to Thormodseyr, and so he called it Siglufiord [Sailfiord, Mastfiord]. He took all Siglufiord between Ulfsdalir and Hvanndalir and lived at Siglunes. He quarrelled with Olaf bekk about Hvanndalir. This led to sixteen men's deaths before they reached the settlement that they should hold the land for alternate summers. †

11. From S, H:

> † Bard, son of Heyiangrs-Biorn, sailed his ship into Skialfandafliotsos, and
> took over all Bardardal upstream from the Rivers Kalfborgara and Eyiar-
> dalsa, and for a while lived at Lundarbrekka. Then he took note of the
> winds, observing that those driving from the land were milder than the
> ones from the sea. From this he thought that conditions south of the
> heath would be better. He sent his sons south towards the end of winter,
> and there they found horsetail and other vegetation. That spring Bard
> built a sled for every beast that was fit to move, and made each one draw its
> own fodder and part of the equipment. He went by the pass called
> Vanarskard, on the road later called Bardargata. Thereafter he took
> Fliotshverfi and lived at Gnupar; and then he was called Gnupa-Bard. †

The word I have translated here 'the end of winter' is *gói*, which is the name of a month
that covers the period from mid-February to mid-March. The word for the plant
horsetail, is *góibeytill*, '*gói*-prick', presumably because it flourishes early in the year and
the vulgar could compare its appearance to an erect penis. Dictionaries give an exact
identification of the plant, *equisetum hyemale*; certainly *equisetum* of some sort grew in
Iceland at the time of the Norse settlement though we cannot be sure what species it
was. In fact the plant is useless for grazing, being highly silicaceous and tough on the
teeth of any beast that eats it. It would hardly be a sign of rich feeding early in the
season, which is presumably what Bard was hoping for. Indeed, the region to the south
of Lundarbrekka is rough country by any standards and even today roads are open only
during the summer. Whether the compilers of *Landnámabók* knew of the infertility of
the area and treated this story ironically would be interesting to know.

12. From H:

> † There was a man called Arngeir who took all Sletta between Havararlon
> and Sveinungsvik. His children were Thorgils, Odd and Thurid who was
> married to Steinolf of Thiorsardal. As a young man Odd would sit by the
> fire like a sluggard, so he was nicknamed 'coal-biter'. A polar bear killed
> both Arngeir and Thorgils. Odd went looking for them, and there was the
> bear sucking their blood. Odd killed the bear, carried it home and ate the
> lot. So he claimed he had avenged his father in killing the bear, and his
> brother in eating it. In later life Odd was a harsh man in his dealings. He
> was something of a shape-changer too, for he left his home at Hraunhofn
> one evening and the next morning appeared in Thiorsardal to save his
> sister Thurid when the Thiorsdal people were going to stone her to death
> for witchcraft and sorcery. †

The 'coal-biter', the unpromising youth who later turns out well, is a common figure in
folk-tale. Odd's polar bear had presumably come over on an ice-floe, as is occasionally
recorded in Iceland in historical times. The word used to describe Odd, *hamrammr*,
normally means 'someone who could change his shape by magic'. Such people were
particularly powerful at night-times; hence Odd's midnight walk to the help of his

sister. Where in Thiorsardal Steinolf lived is unknown, but in any case Odd would have had to travel right across the centre of the island, from the north coast, where Hraunhofn is, to the dale of a river whose estuary is in the south. Stoning was the standard death for witches and wizards, and, if witchcraft went in the family, it looks as though Thurid deserved it.

### 13. From S, H:

† There was a man called Olvir the Fair, son of Osvald Oxnathorisson. He was a landed proprietor living at Almdalir [in Norway]. He fell into dispute with Earl Hakon Griotgardsson and went to Yriar [in North-Møre, Norway] and there he died. His son Thorstein the Fair went to Iceland, and took his ship into Vapnafiord after the land had all been taken. He bought land from Eyvind Vapni and lived for some years at Toptavoll out beyond Sireksstadir before he got the land at Hof. This is how; he asked for the return of money he had lent to Steinbiorn kort, and Steinbiorn had nothing to pay with except the land. Thorstein lived there for sixty years after and was a shrewd man, reliable in his advice. †

### 14. From S, H:

† Thorhadd the Old was priest of a temple at Mære in Trøndelag [Norway]. He was keen to go to Iceland, so he pulled down the temple and took with him some of its earth and the main timbers. And he came into Stod-varfiord, and declared the whole fiord Mære-holy. He let nothing be killed there save for farm-stock. He lived there throughout his life, and from him are descended the Stodfirdings. †

The temple was probably not a building specifically for religious use, but the main hall of a farm in which the seasonal feasts that celebrated the gods were held (see on this O. Olsen, *Hørg, hov ok kirke: historiske og arkaeologiske Vikingetidsstudier* (Copenhagen, 1966), with English summary pp.277–88). This held the fortune and continued prosperity of the family that lived in it, and so, in transporting part of it to the new country, the landowner was asserting the continuity of the family estate. Land that was deemed to be so holy that nothing could be killed upon it is recorded elsewhere in medieval Icelandic writings, notably in *Eyrbyggiasaga* (see p. 30 above).

### 15. From H:

† There was a man called Asbiorn, son of Heyiangrs-Biorn. He died on the sea-voyage to Iceland when he was planning to settle there, and his wife Thorgerd and their sons made the passage. Now it was decreed that a woman should take no more land than she could go round in a spring day between sunrise and sunset, leading a two-year-old cow not fully grown but in good heart. So Thorgerd led her beast below Toptafell, a short

distance from River Kvia in the south, and into Kidiaklett near Iokulsfell in the west. In this way she took land all over the Ingolfshofdi district between the Rivers Kvia and Jokulsa; she lived at Sandfell. †

Thorgerd ingeniously circumvented the legal process by taking her beast across country between two rivers, and cutting off a large tract of land bounded by the sea-shore.

## 16. From S:

† There was a man called Hrolf the Hewer. He lived at Moldtua in North-Møre [in Norway]. His sons were Vemund and Molda-Gnup. They loved fighting, and were blacksmiths. Vemund declaimed this verse when he was working in his smithy:

> Alone I carried news of eleven
> Men I killed. Blow harder, you!

Gnup went to Iceland because of some killings he and his brother had committed, and took land between Kudafliot and the River Eyiara, the whole of Alptaver. There was a great lake there, and wild swan to catch on it. Out of the land he had taken Gnup sold lots to many men. It became densely-populated there until molten lava ran down over it. Then they fled west to Hofdabrekka, and pitched tents at the place now called Tialdavoll [Tentfield]. But Vemund, son of Sigmund kleykir, refused to let them stay there. Then they went to Hrossagard and built cabins where they stayed over the winter. And soon there were disputes among them and killings.

The next spring Molda-Gnup and his companions went west into Grindavik and set up house there. They had little farm-stock. By this time Molda-Gnup's sons Biorn and Gnup, Thorstein hrungnir and Thord leggialdi were grown men. One night Biorn dreamed that a hill-giant came to him and offered him partnership, and, it seemed to him, he accepted. After that a billy-goat came to his she-goats and his stock bred so rapidly that he soon became very well-off. Then he was called Goat-Biorn. Then those with second sight could see that all the 'land-spirits' joined Goat-Biorn at legal meetings, and Thorstein and Thord in hunting and fishing. †

Another example of a family of roughnecks who got into trouble both in Norway and Iceland. Dreams are a common feature of Norse tale, and commonly direct or inform on the future. The *landvættir*, 'land-creatures, land-spirits', are seen as local semi-deities whose help is welcomed to bring success to a family.

## 17. From S, H:

† There was a man called Hrolf Redbeard. He took all Holmslond between the Rivers Fiska and Ranga and lived at Fors [Cataract]. His children were Thorstein Rednose (who lived there after him) and Thora . . . and Asa . . . and Helga . . .

Thorstein Rednose was a great man for sacrificing. He sacrificed to the cataract; all left-overs had to be taken and put into it. He could also see into the future. When his sheep were taken from the common fold he used to count up to two thousand of them, and then all the rest would jump out over the wall. This was the reason he had so many sheep. In autumn he could see which of them could not survive the winter, and them he had slaughtered. The last autumn he was alive he sat at the common fold and said, 'It's up to you to slaughter the sheep *you* pick out. Now I am going to die – or all the sheep are – or perhaps both.' And the night he died all the sheep were plunged into the cataract. †

This passage is put in to show something of the size of the flocks early Iceland supported (though whether the figure given is precise is a different matter – incidentally and on a pedantic point the text says that Thorstein had 'twenty hundred sheep' and an Icelandic hundred was 120). It also tells something of the economy of sheep-farming. The sheep were pastured in the open during summer and brought down to the common fold in autumn where the individual owners identified their own stock as they were brought out of the fold. Those that could jump out would presumably have strength to survive the winter. Thorstein could pick out up to two thousand that couldn't. There is also some indication of local superstitions here: the man who could read the future, the practice of sacrificing to natural features such as waterfalls. However, there are obscurities in the telling of this tale, and what happened to the sheep after Thorstein's death is not clearly expressed, though it is certain they perished in the waterfall.

18. From S, H:

† There was a man called Ozur the Fair, son of Thorleif from Sogn [in Norway]. Ozur killed a man in one of the sanctuaries in Uppland when he was on a wedding journey with Sigurd hrisi. Because of that he had to flee the country and went to Iceland, and first took all Holtalond between River Thiorsa and Hraunslœk. He was only seventeen when he did the killing. He married Hallveig Thorvidardottir. Their son was Thorgrim kampi ...

Ozur lived at Kampaholt. He had a freed slave called Bodvar, who lived in Bodvarstoptir, by the wood called Vidiskog. Ozur gave him a share of the wood, reserving the right to reclaim it if Bodvar died without issue. Orn from Vælugerdi (who has been mentioned before) summoned Bodvar on a charge of sheep-stealing; so Bodvar formally handed over to Atli Hasteinsson all his property, and that put an end to Orn's case. Ozur died when Thorgrim was young. Then Hrafn Thorvidarson took over the administration of Thorgrim's property.

After Bodvar's death Hrafn put in a claim for Vidiskog forbidding Atli to use it, but Atli considered it his own property. Atli and three of his men went to fetch wood ... A shepherd told Hrafn of this, and he rode after Atli with seven men. They came together in Orrostudal and there they fought. Two of Hrafn's household men fell. He was wounded. One of Atli's men fell, and Atli was mortally wounded and rode home. Onund bild parted the two sides and took Atli in. At this date Thord dofni, Atli's son, was nine years old. And when Thord was fifteen, Hrafn rode down to a ship at Einarshofn. He was wearing a dark-blue cloak. He rode back during the night. Thord lay in wait for him by himself at Haugavad, a short way from Tradarholt, and despatched him there with a spear. Hrafn's mound stands east of the road there, and the mounds of Hastein, Atli and Olvir to the west. These killings were balanced against each other.

Thord's reputation grew as a result of this. Then he married Thorunn, daughter of Asgeir 'Norseman-shaker', who had killed a whole ship's crew of Norwegians in Grimsaros in revenge for a robbery he had suffered in Norway. When Thord was twenty-two he bought a ship in Knarrarsund intending to go to Norway to collect his inheritance. He hid a lot of his property. For that reason Thorunn would not go with him, but took over the lands. Thord's son Thorgils was then two. Thord's ship foundered. A year later Thorgrim 'scar-foot' ... took over Thorunn's affairs. He married her, and their son was Hæring. †

Quarrels over the right to cut wood in a forest are quite common in medieval Icelandic tales and presumably represent what often happened. This entry shows one such, among a group of people used to violence. Yet there was a genuine attempt to put an end to further feud by balancing one lot of killings against another. To hand over a legal case to a more influential neighbour (with some such payment as Bodvar makes) was also apparently common practice; the two parties shook hands – the verb is *handsala*, cf. the modern English dialect word 'handsel' – to seal the agreement. In Norse tales a protagonist in an incident is frequently shown wearing dark-blue clothing (as opposed to undyed homespun); it is a literary device to signal to the audience that something significant will happen to him.

19. From S, H:

> † There was a man called Olaf 'twin-brows'. He came from Lofoten [in Norway] to Iceland. He took all Skeid between the Rivers Thiorsa and Hvita up to Sandlœk ... Olaf married Ashild and their son was Helgi trausti ...
>
> After Olaf died Thorgrim 'scar-foot' set his heart on Ashild, but Helgi made difficulties about it. He lay in wait for Thorgrim at the road junction below Ashildarmyr. Helgi told him to stop coming to the house. Thorgrim said he wasn't a child. They fought and Thorgrim fell. Ashild asked where Helgi had been. He declaimed this verse:
>
>> I have been where Scar-foot
>> Fell to feed the ravens.
>> Loud sang swords' mighty tongues.
>> Forward pressed the fighter.

> I sent Thormod's heir,
> Tough and bold, to Odin,
> The sacrifice to the Gallows-god,
> The carrion to the raven.

Ashild told him he had struck his own death-blow. Helgi got himself a passage abroad at Einarshofn. Hæring, Thorgrim's son, was then sixteen. He and two others rode to Hofdi to see Teit Gizurarson. Fifteen altogether rode in Teit's band to stop Helgi taking up the passage. The two groups met on the lava-plain at Merkrhraun, up the hill from Mork, by Helgahval. Helgi had two companions from Eyrar. Helgi and another man in his group and one of Teit's men fell. These killings were balanced against each other. †

Here is an example of the support a man gained from an extended family. Teit was the son of Ketilbiorn the Old, one of the first generation of settlers in Iceland. Ketilbiorn had taken a large stretch of land in southern Iceland and was also very rich in portable property. Teit occupied a major farm and so was an influential man in the south, the sort of man people would appeal to for assistance. But in addition he was Hæring's great-uncle and so a suitable ally in an act of vengeance. Helgi's verse has the usual skaldic complexities, such kennings as 'the swords' mighty tongues' for 'sword-blades' which 'sang' as they cut through the air. But it also makes use of punning. Instead of Thormod Helgi said Asmod, *Ásmoðr*. *Ás-* means 'god' and Thor was a god, so Asmod = Thormod.

20. From S:

> † Steinunn the Old, Ingolf's kinswoman, went to Iceland and stayed with Ingolf the first year. He offered to give her all Rosmhvalanes beyond Hvassahraun. And for it she gave a flecked hooded coat, claiming this made it a purchase. She thought it more likely to secure her against repossession. †

Transfer of land was not recorded in written deeds, so some action like this, vouched for by witnesses, could secure a landholder against a claim.

## Land-holding and inheritance

It is now accepted that rune-stones sometimes served as records of land-holding and inheritance. It would be natural enough in a semi-literate society to have some means, other than human memory, of advising the change of ownership that comes with death and the succession of heirs. Since rune-stones were often placed on prominent and frequented sites, they would be an obvious way of recording, for common knowledge, deaths of owners or heirs apparent (particularly if they occurred away from home) with the implication and sometimes the statement that the rightful heir had legally taken over rights and dues. Here are a few from Viking Age Scandinavia.

1. Gunderup, North Jutland, Denmark: two related inscriptions running vertically along a tall pillar stone.

    A. Toki put up these stones and made these monuments | in memory of Abi his stepfather, a well-born royal officer, and |

    B. of his mother Tofa. They both lie in this mound. | Abi left Toki his property as his heir.

This stone originally lay near a mound and by the roadside, so it must have been prominent. The precise meaning of the phrase translated here 'well-born royal officer' is uncertain. The noun is *þegn*, which originally meant simply 'servant', but in Viking times is certainly a word implying some important rank or duty, perhaps in the king's service. It may also have a more general meaning; as one scholar has put it, 'like the English "gentleman" in the variety of [its] connotations'.

2. Nora, Uppland, Sweden: on a rock face just south of the farm at Nora.

    Biorn Finnvid's son had this rock-slab carved in memory of his brother Olæif. He was betrayed ⟨to his death⟩ on Finnveden. God help his soul. This farm is the hereditary property and family estate of Finnvid's sons at Älgesta.

Älgesta is some 30 km from Nora, so this records a claim to ownership of an outlying piece of land, part of a family's inherited property. Olæif had perished some way from home, for Finnveden is in Småland, so it was presumably wise to have the fact of his death formally recorded.

3. Malsta, Hälsingland, Sweden: this standing stone has a group of related inscriptions in the peculiar and difficult version of the script called Hälsingland-runes or staveless runes. It is not all comprehensible, and there are some errors of carving.

    A. Frømund set up this stone (? these stones) in memory of Fægylfi Bræsi's son. And Bræsi was Lini's son, and Lini was Unn's son, and Unn was Ofæig's son, and Ofæig Thorir's son.

    B. Groa was Fægylfi's mother

    C. and ... and then Gudrun.

    D. Frømund Fægylfi's son carved these runes. We fetched this stone north at Balsten. Gylfi took over this land and then ⟨land⟩ north in Via in three townships and then Lönnånger and then Färdsjö.

The man commemorated was called Gylfi. Because he acquired extensive lands, as the stone records, he was nicknamed *Fægylfi*, 'Money-Gylfi'. Frømund was here declaring his legal right, by virtue of descent, to inherit the vast estates his father had possessed.

4. Hillersjö, Uppland, Sweden: this is the longest, and perhaps the most important, of the Uppland runic inscriptions, cut on the face of a natural slab embedded in the ground just by the farm at Hillersjö. Part of the text is missing (and was when it was first recorded, in the seventeenth century). A small part is incomprehensible to us. But the greater part can be followed, and it defines the detail of a complex series of

inheritances, showing how women could take over property and how it could pass from child to parent. The first word of the text is addressed to the passer-by, **raþu**, literally 'interpret!' or perhaps simply 'read!', confirming that this inscription is a public declaration of inheritance.

> Take note! Gæirmund married Gæirlaug as a maiden. Then they had a son before he [Gæirmund] was drowned. Thereafter the son died. Then she married [Gu]drik. He ... this. Then they had children but only one daughter lived. She was called [In]ga. She was married to Ragnfast of Snottsta. Then he died and their son afterwards. And the mother [Inga] took the inheritance after her son. Then she married Æirik. Then she died, so Gæirlaug took the inheritance after her daughter Inga. | Thorbiorn the skald cut the runes.

In this declaration Gæirlaug recorded the terms of her inheritance of the property of her first husband Gæirmund (through her son), Ragnfast (through her daughter who had come into it on the death of her own son), and perhaps Æirik (again through her daughter). If, as is likely, Gudrik had owned Hillersjö, Inga would have inherited it at his death, and it too would have passed to Gæirlaug. On the chain of inheritance Sven B. F. Jansson makes the interesting comment, 'The Viking Age rules of inheritance that were applied in this case agree with the statutes of the Uppland Law, codified in 1296'. Inga had already asserted her right to Snottsta on four rune-stones in that neighbourhood. One of them expounded Ragnfast's claim to the estate: 'Inga had these runes cut to commemorate her husband Ragnfast. He was the sole owner of this farm in succession to his father Sigfast'. Another, known only from a drawing, recorded her son's death: 'Inga raised staff and stones in memory of her husband Ragnfast. She inherited from her child'. Yet another listed Ragnfast's two sisters, who would have had no claim to the property since it had passed to his son, but would presumably have been a responsibility of Inga's after her inheritance.

5. Hansta, Hägerstalund, Uppland, Sweden: there are two related stones, on separate sites near the farmstead.

    A. Gærdar and Iorund have these stones put up in memory of their nephews Ærnmund and Ingimund.
    B. These markers are made in memory of Inga's sons. She inherited from them, and her own heirs were brothers, | Gærdar and his brother. | They died among the Greeks.

There is some ambiguity here. From the inscriptions it is not clear who died in the East, but it is usually assumed to have been Ærnmund and Ingimund. The story line then is: Inga married an unnamed man, probably the owner of Hansta. By him she had two sons. The husband died and the sons inherited the farm. They then went to the East and did not return. The mother Inga was their heir, and on her death the farm and other property went to her brothers, who recorded their inheritance publicly at places in the neighbourhood.

CHAPTER 4

# Vikings outside Scandinavia

Perhaps the word 'Viking' should properly be applied only to those medieval Scandinavians who journeyed overseas. Of these we hear a lot from the peoples they came into contact, often conflict, with, and it is not surprising that the Christian inhabitants of western Europe generally gave them a bad press. This is certainly the common British view of the Vikings, derived from such sources as the *Anglo-Saxon Chronicle*, whose account of the disastrous years 1010–11 shows the English, not quite 'lions led by donkeys', trying to cope with a determined, ruthless and mobile foe.

1010. After Easter this year the Viking army we spoke of before came to East Anglia. They landed at Ipswich and marched straight to where they had heard Ulfcytel was with his local forces. That was on Ascension Day. And the East Anglians ran off at once but the men of Cambridgeshire stood firm. And Athelstan the king's son-in-law was killed, and Oswig and his son, and Wulfric Leofwine's son, and Eadwig Æfic's brother, and many other good men of rank, and a mass of the people. Thurcytel Mare's Head it was who started the flight. The Danes held the battlefield. Then they got horses and afterwards took control of East Anglia, and plundered and burned the countryside for four months – they even went as far as the wild fens and killed men and beasts and set fires throughout the fens, and burned down Thetford and Cambridge and then turned south to the Thames.

Then their cavalry rode towards the ships and then suddenly turned west into Oxfordshire, from there to Buckinghamshire and then along the Ouse until they reached Bedford and so on to Tempsford, burning everything as they went along. Then they turned back towards their ships with their plunder. And as they were going to their ships, the English army should have come back into the field to prevent them turning inland again. And that's when the English army went home. And when the Vikings were in the east, the English army was kept to the west. And when the Vikings were in the south, our army was in the north. Then all the council was summoned to the king to determine how to defend the realm. But whatever was decided on did not last even a month. In the end there was no leading man who was prepared to call up his forces. Everyone ran off as best he could. And at last no shire was willing to help another.

Then before St Andrew's day the Vikings came to Northampton and straightway burned that market town down and grabbed as much as they wanted in the neighbourhood, and then crossed the Thames to Wessex, and so by Cannings marsh. And they destroyed everything by fire. And when they had overrun as far as they pleased, they got back to their ships by mid-winter.

1011. In this year the king and his council sent to the Viking army asking for truce. And they promised payment of tribute and provisions on condition that they gave up their plundering. By this time the Vikings had overrun i) East Anglia, and ii) Essex, and iii) Middlesex, and iv) Oxford-shire, and v) Cambridgeshire and vi) Hertfordshire, and vii) Buckingham-shire, and viii) Bedfordshire, and ix) half Huntingdonshire, and x) a good deal of Northamptonshire; and south of the Thames all Kent and Sussex and the region round Hastings, and Surrey, and Berkshire, and Hamp-shire, and a good deal of Wiltshire.

All these disasters came upon us through indecisive policy. Tribute was not offered them in time, and only when they had done their worst were they offered truce and terms of peace. Yet for all this truce and peace and tribute gangs of them went everywhere, plundering and robbing and killing our wretched folk.

And in this year, between the Nativity of the Holy Mary and Michael-mas they beseiged Canterbury, and by treachery were able to get inside because Ælmær (whose life Archbishop Ælfeah had once saved) gave Canterbury over to them. And there they took captive Archbishop Ælfeah and the king's steward Ælfweard and Abbot Leofwine and Bishop Godwine. And Abbot Ælmær [a different man from the traitor Ælmær mentioned above] they let go. And in the town they took prisoner all the clergy, both men and women – it is impossible for anyone to tell how large a proportion of the people that was – and they stayed within the town for as long as they wished. And when the Vikings had worked their way through the town they went to their ships, taking the archbishop with them.

> Then he was in chains who once had been
> Head of the English and of Christendom.
> There you could see misery
> Where once you saw bliss

> In that distressed town whence we first received
> Christianity and bliss with God and the world.

Or, in more ecclesiastical vein, the lament of the churchman over the despoliation of Christ's sanctuaries, with the suggestion that it was God's judgment on servants who had done those things which they ought not to have done. Alcuin, the great Northumbrian scholar, writes from the Carolingian court to Bishop Higebald and the congregation of St Cuthbert at Lindisfarne, devastated by an unexpected and ferocious Viking attack in 793; and puts the slaughter and destruction in historical and biblical perspective as one of the great crimes against the true faith.

> When I was with you the closeness of your love would give me great joy. In contrast, now I am away from you the distress of your suffering fills me daily with deep grief, when heathens desecrated God's sanctuaries, and poured the blood of saints within the compass of the altar, destroyed the house of our hope, trampled the bodies of saints in God's temple like animal dung in the street. What can we say except weep with you in our hearts before the altar of Christ and say, 'Spare thy people O Lord and give not thine heritage to the Gentiles lest heathens should say, "Where is the God of the Christians?"'
>
> What security is there for the churches of Britain if St Cuthbert with so great a throng of saints will not defend his own? Either this is the beginning of greater grief or the sins of those who live there have brought it upon themselves. This indeed has not happened by chance; it is a sign that someone has well deserved it ...
>
> Do not be cut to the heart by this terrible plight. 'God chasteneth every son whom he receiveth.' You he chastened more severely since he loved you more deeply. Jerusalem, God's beloved city, with its temple of God perished in Chaldean flames. Rome, encircled by the crown of saints, apostles and martyrs without number, was destroyed by the savagery of pagans but quickly recovered through the loving understanding of God. The whole of Europe almost was made a desert by the swords and flames of Goths or Huns. But now, God being merciful, it glitters with churches like the heavens with stars; and the observances of the Christian religion thrive and grow.

The Vikings did not view their incursions in quite this light. They saw them in part as adventure, the sort of thing a young man of good family might indulge in in youth. In part too as the proper work for a professional soldier, where he could get good money as a hired killer. Part too as a way of picking up the capital to put into a business, a ship or a farm. Equally important, not all Vikings were soldiers, professional or amateur, though like all Dark Age peoples they were wise to know enough of fighting to defend themselves. But many were primarily entrepreneurs, business men bringing cargoes from afar and exchanging the goods that the North produced for the luxuries of the south. Others were farmers who, as we have seen, were on the lookout for good land to settle on. And most, probably, would combine these roles.

## Swedish adventurers abroad

Swedish rune-stones are in the main, but not always (see the Stäket and Väsby examples below), memorials to the dead. It is quite common for them to include a brief summary of the career of a man commemorated, or at any rate some comment on how or where he died. From such records we can build up a minimal picture of the things Swedish Vikings got up to in the late Viking Age, where they went and why. And sometimes what they did with the money they made. There are, of course, problems of reading and interpretation that make parts of inscriptions ambiguous or obscure; but enough survives to demonstrate the energy and enterprise of the Swedes in the eleventh century, both to east and west, how they invested their capital (for instance, in merchant ships or land) and built up their labour force. These Swedes certainly ventured far and wide; east across the Baltic, through southern Finland and the Baltic states, down the Russian rivers to Byzantium; on forays westwards to the British Isles and the Continental mainland. In a more consciously imperialist age the large number of deaths on expeditions abroad might be defined as 'the price of empire'. As with modern epitaphs, these often conclude with a few lines of verse.

1. From Södermanland.
(a) Mervalla: a damaged inscription that can be supplied from early drawings.

> Sigrid had [this] stone put up [for] her husband Svæin.
> > He often sailed to Semgallia
> > In laden | ship round Domesnes.

The last two lines are simple verse. I translate *dyrum knærri* as 'laden ship'; the adjective means 'dear, precious' and presumably refers to the value of the cargo of a merchant vessel. This Svæin had a regular trading route into Russia, for Semgallia is roughly modern Latvia, and Domesnes was the northern tip of Courland, rounding into the Gulf of Riga.

(b) Åda: cut on a cliff face by the roadside.

> Hermod had this cut for his brother Bergvid. H | [e was] drowned | in Latvia.

The name I have translated 'Latvia' is in Old Swedish *Lifland*, Livonia.

(c) Tjuvstigen: two stones standing by a woodland road, though probably not on their original site.

> A. Styrlaug and Holm raised up stones,
> > Close by the road, for their brothers.
> > They ended their lives on the eastern route
> > Thorkel | and | Styrbiorn | good lads.

The epitaph is in four lines of alliterating verse.

B. Ingigerd had a second stone raised
   For her sons: she [? made a visible memorial to them]
   God help their souls. | Thorir carved ⟨the runes⟩.

This time the epitaph is only partly in verse. The meaning of the second part of line 2 is very uncertain.

(d) Fagerlöt: cut on a rock face overlooking a footpath.

Holmfrid, [and ?Hedinfrid] had this stone cut in memory of | their father Æskil.
   He waged war in eastern lands |
   Until that warlike leader was fated to fall.

Again, the inscription ends in alliterative verse, this time a couplet.

(e) Turinge: the text partly on the face, partly along the edge of a flat slab in the local church.

Kætil and Biorn raised this stone for their father Thorstæin, Anund for his brother, the 'huskarls' in memory of their equal, Kætiløy for her man. |
   Those brothers were among the best of men,
   Both at home | and in action abroad.
   They looked after their retainers well. |
   In battle he fell in Gardar in the east,
   Leader of his force, best of 'landmen'.

This epitaph, again with a verse supplement, is hard to translate, partly because it is difficult to make out how many are being commemorated altogether (more than one brother is celebrated but only one fell in battle), partly because the text uses several technical words of varying meaning. The word *húskarlar* which I give as 'huskarls' and later translate as 'retainers' is ambiguous. It means literally 'men of the household' and could be a fairly humble designation, a servant who was a freeman; here I assume it means men of a noble household, leading men of a courtly or at least wealthy circle. Similarly I take *landmaðr*, 'landman', to be something higher than a simple free farmer, though that has been disputed. The great man commemorated, whoever he was, fell *í Görðum*, which means literally 'in the walled towns' but is here used specifically to mean the region of western Russia dominated by the great Viking trading cities.

(f) Esta: on a natural boulder, a badly worn inscription which can be restored:

Ingifast had this stone cut in memory of his father Sigvid.
   He fell in Holmgard,
   A ship's captain with his crew.

Holmgard, *Hólmgarðr*, is Novgorod in western Russia. Though that town is a good way inland Sigvid was still regarded here as a seaman who perished in some sort of skirmish, with all his men. The word for 'ship' is *skæið*, usually used of a largish warship.

(g) Grinda.

> Gudrun raised this stone for Hedin who was Svæin's nephew.
> He was | among the Greeks; gold he shared. |
> Christ, help his soul. Christ he always loved.

References to Greece and the Greeks in these inscriptions are to the eastern Roman empire based on Byzantium/Constantinople, *Mikligarðr* 'the Great City' as it is known in Old Norse.

(h) Djulefors: a badly damaged inscription, some of which must be supplied from an early drawing.

> [Inga put up this stone for Olæif] her [heir].
> In the east his keel he ploughed.
> In the Lombards' | land he breathed his last.

(i) Kungshållet: an impressively tall stone standing by the roadside.

> Alrik Sigrid's son put up this stone for his father Spiut |
> Who had been in the western world
> Stormed cities and fought within them.
> He knew all the conduct of . . .

This is a fairly easy text until the last line, which has to be left incomplete because we do not recognise one of its most important words.

(j) Grinda.

> Griotgard, Æinridi, sons,
> Made ⟨this⟩ for their valiant father |
> Gudvær was west in England.
> He shared tribute.
> Cities in Sax | land.
> Like a man he stormed.

*Saxland* is a common name for Germany, Saxony, but in this context it is not impossible the epitaph refers to Anglo-Saxon land, England. The writer of this line needed a word that began with *s*- for his alliteration.

(k) Råby: most of this text is cut on the four arms of a cross incised in the surface of a stone block.

> Øybiorn put up this stone for | Skœrdir. He | met his death in England | in the army.

(l) Bjudby: a very elaborately carved stone, as is appropriate for one put up to the raiser's own glory.

> Thorstein had this stone put up in his own honour and in memory of his son Hæfnir.

He went to England as a young fighting-man
Then met a sorrowful death at home. |
God help their souls. | Bruni and Slodi [engraved] this stone.

(m) S. Betby: a fragmentary inscription.

]stone in memory of his son Iarund, who went westwards in the company
of Ulf Hakon's son.

Nothing is known of this Ulf, but he was possibly a local magnate, leader of a ship's
company venturing to the British Isles.

2. From Uppland.
(a) Ängby: the stone stands in the neighbourhood of unmarked standing stones and
burial mounds; that is, in its original setting in a grave-field.

Ragnfrid had this stone put up in memory of Biorn | her son by Kætil-
mund. God and God's mother help his soul. | He fell in Virland. | Asmund |
cut ⟨this⟩.

The name *Virland* is apparently linked to Viru, north-east Estonia.

(b) Söderby-Karl: a lost stone known only from drawings.

Biorn and Igulfrid put up this stone in memory of their son Otrygg.
He was killed in Finland.

(c) Veda: cut on a rock face near the farm at Veda.

Thorstæin made this in memory of his son Ærinmund. He bought this
farm and made his money in Gardar in the east.

(d) Vallentuna: only one stone remains, but the context of its inscription indicates there
must have been a pair of them; the text begins in mid-sentence.

]and Ingiberg in memory of her husband.
He drowned in Holm sea. |
His ship went down. |
Only three got away.

Holm sea, *Hólms haf*, should be the waterway near Novgorod (though the sea near
Bornholm has also been suggested as a possibility). The three lines of verse here, as well
as having alliteration, also rhyme.

(e) Sjusta: a great granite block in a woodland.

Runa had this memorial made after Spiallbudi and Svæin and Andvett and
Ragnar, her sons by Hælgi, and Sigrid after her husband Spiallbudi. He
met his death in Holmgard in Olaf's church. Øpir cut the runes.

If this interpretation is correct (and it must be admitted the reading of **i olafs kriki** as *i Ólafs kirki*, 'in Olaf's church', has been questioned), the Swedes in Novgorod had their own church dedicated to St Olaf of Norway. This implies a permanent Swedish presence in the town, perhaps because it was a place where Vikings congregated in their travels through western Russia.

(f) Låddersta.

> Alvi had this stone raised in memory of his son Arfast. He went east to Gardar.

(g) Skepptuna.

> Folkmar had this stone put up in memory of Folkbiorn his son. He also died among the Greeks. May God help his spirit and soul.

The word 'also' (**uk**) here suggests there was at least one more adventurer to Greece commemorated in this neighbourhood.

(h) Ed: there are two related inscriptions on a natural boulder.

> A. Ragnvald had these runes cut in memory of his mother Fastvi, Onem's daughter. She died in Ed. God help her soul.
> B. Ragnvald had these runes cut. He was in Greece as commander of a brigade.

Ragnvald used his mother's memorial stone to boast of his own distinction. He was *liðs forungi*, literally 'chief of a fighting force'. Presumably this celebrates his command of a brigade of the famous Varangian guard, the troop of mercenaries who protected the Byzantine emperor.

(i) Ulunda.

> Kar had this stone put up in memory of his father Mursi, and Kabbi for his ?father-in-law.
>
> > He journeyed boldly, made his money |
> > Abroad in the land of the Greeks for his heir.

Details of this text are obscure and it is not clear how much has been correctly interpreted here. But the phrase about making money among the Greeks for his heir is undisputed. Like other rune-stones this one is, as well as a memorial, a statement of inheritance.

(j) Fjuckby.

> Captain Liut erected this stone in memory of his sons. One was called Aki, who was lost overseas. ⟨?⟩ captained a merchant ship. | He reached | Greek harbours. At home he died. | [...]

A partly damaged stone, with important bits of the text missing – the name of the second, successful, son, for instance; but if this reading is correct, the omission was in the original text, not the result of damage.

(k) Lövsta: a lost rock recorded in early drawings.

> Fastvi had this stone put up in memory of Gærrar and Otrygg | his sons. The second met his death among the Greeks.

(l) Stäket: a now lost rock, known only from seventeenth-century drawings, which are not always accurate or at least which present forms hard to interpret.

> ?Ingirun Hard's daughter had these runes made on her own behalf. | She intends to travel eastwards, as far abroad as Jerusalem. ?Fot cut the runes.

A late inscription, perhaps towards the end of the eleventh century, that presumably records a pious Christian's intention to make a pilgrimage to the holy places.

(m) Broby: one of two memorial stones raised to the man by his wife and sons. The second is a bridge-stone.

> Æstrid had this stone put up in memory of her husband Øysten who visited Jerusalem and died ashore among the Greeks.

(n) Ubby.

> Kætilfast put up this stone in memory of his father Asgaut. He was in both the west and the east. May God help his soul.

(o) Husby-Lyhundra: an elaborate stone pillar with texts on three sides.

> A. Diarf and Orøkia and Vigi and Iogæir and Gærhialm, all the brothers, had put up
> B. this stone in memory of their brother Svæin. He met his death in Jutland. And he was
> C. to have gone to England. May God and God's mother help his spirit and soul better than his deeds deserved.

It looks as though Svæin was on his way to take part in a Viking raid on England when death caught up with him. Whether the cryptic last sentence has a deeper implication than simple Christian humility – that Svæin's Viking nature had led him to behave disgracefully, attacking Christian peoples, is a matter of opinion.

(p) Yttergärde: a pair of stones with related inscriptions. Unfortunately stone A is lost, known only from a seventeenth-century drawing.

> A. Karsi and [...]rn had this stone put up | in memory of their father Ulf. May God and God's mother help his [soul].
> B. And Ulf took three payments of *danegeld* in England. The first was what Tosti paid. Then [Th]orkætil [paid]. Then | Knut paid.

The second stone shows the Viking's attitude to the payment of *danegeld*. It is not a tribute exacted from beaten enemies; rather payment from a commander to one of his mercenaries. Two of the leaders are almost certainly identifiable: as the famous Thorkel the Tall, and Knut who later became king of England. Who Tosti was is less clear, but he has been linked to a famous Swedish Viking Skoglar-Tosti whom Snorri Sturluson mentions in *Heimskringla*.

(q) Väsby.

> Ali had this stone put up in his own honour. He took Knut's | *danegeld* in England. May God help his soul.

Ali's Christian conscience seems to have been untroubled by the fact that he plundered England with Knut; yet his personal memorial bears a prominent incised cross.

(r) Kålsta.

> Stærkar and Hiorvard had this | stone | put up for | their father Gæira who had his place in the *þingalið* in the west. May God help ⟨his⟩ soul.

Gæira was a fighting-man of distinction, belonging to the élite brigade of guards that Knut set up, the *þingalið*. The late twelfth-century Danish historian Sven Aggeson records this term as *Tinglith* in his treatise *Lex Castrensis sive Curie*, 'The law of the retainers or of the court' (on this see Erik Christiansen, *The works of Sven Aggesen: twelfth-century Danish historian*: Viking Society for Northern Research: text series 9 (London, 1992), pp. 14, 33), and it is there that the link is made with the great king Knut of Denmark and England. He was to select men *iuxta meritorum qualitatem et uirtutum experientiam*, 'according to the quality of their deserts and the test of their virtues'. Those outstanding in courage were to be linked more closely to the king. They must be of high birth; but to do proper honour to their king they had also to be able to afford the expensive uniform, and glitter *bipennibus mucronumque capulis deauratis*, 'with gilded axes and hilts of swords.' They were to number three thousand, and be chosen fighters. Gæira held a place (the verb in the original is *sat*, literally 'sat, stayed, dwelt') in this body of men.

3. From Småland.
(a) Transjö: a stone pillar with a line of text on each of its three sides. The epitaph ends with an couplet of alliterating verses.

> Gaut set this stone in memory of Ketil | his son.
> He was | most admirable of men
> Who lost his life in England.

The phrase rendered '(most) admirable' is (*mestr*) *úníðingr*, the opposite of *níðingr* which means something like 'traitor'. In later use *níðingr* came to mean 'an ungenerous, miserly man'. It is connected to the verb *níða*, 'slander, cast public scorn upon', so a *níðingr* is the sort of man who can properly be held up to public contempt; an *úníðingr* just the opposite.

(b) Nöbbelesholm: the stone appears to serve as a boundary stone as well as a memorial. It has a continuous text divided between two sides, indeed within a word.

A.  Gunnkel set this stone in memory of his father Gunnar, Hrodi's son.
    Helgi laid him in a stone coffin, his bro

B.  ther, in Bath, England.

## 4. From Östergötland.

(a) Högby: a stone with a text on three sides. Five sons are commemorated in a joint verse epitaph.

A.  Thorgærd put up this stone in memory of her uncle Assur who died
    out east in Greece.

B.  The good man Gulli begot five sons.
    Asmund, fearless warrior, fell at the River Fyris.
    Assur passed away among the Greeks in the east.
    Halfdan was killed on Bornholm.
    Kari [?was slain at Odd] |
    Dead too is Bui.
    Thorkel cut the ru | nes.

And so ended a whole family of sons. What happened to Kari we don't know for certain: the interpretation of this part of the text is disputed.

(b) Harstad.

Asgöta and Gudmund they put up this memorial after Oddløg | who lived
at Haddestad.
He was a good yeoman.
Dead among the Greek | s.

## 5. From Västergötland.

(a) Norra Åsarp: the stone probably stands on its original site, on a small mound near the farm at Frugården.

Gufi erected this stone in memory of his son Olaf, a very tough lad. He was killed in Estonia. | Havard cut the s[tone].

The phrase 'a very tough lad' is in the transcript *dræng harþa goðan;* where *drængr* is that difficult word that may be a technical one of status, 'free-born warrior', or may be something more general. The adverb *harþa* is an intensive, 'very', but possibly rather slang.

(b) Smula.

Gulli raised this stone in memory of his wife's brothers Æsbiorn and Iuli,
very tough lads. And they met their deaths on active service in the east.

The phrase I have rendered 'on active service' is *i liði*, 'in an army'.

(c) Dalum.

> Toki and his brothers raised this stone in memory of their brothers. One met his death | in the west and the other in the east.

(d) Vist.

> Geri set this stone in memory of his brother Guda, who lost his life in England.

## Rune-stones record a disastrous Viking expedition

A group of some thirty rune-stones scattered through central Sweden, mostly in the region round Lake Mälar, refer to the same event, a foray to the East made by a group of adventurous men of good family. The fleet was commanded by one Yngvar/Ingvar (who is later known in a romantic saga as *Yngvarr inn viðförla*, 'Yngvar the far-travelled'). On the evidence of the runic texts some members of this expedition reached the Middle East. Presumably some returned to tell the tale, but many perished and were commemorated at home. The stones date from the first half of the eleventh century. The elaborate decoration of many of these stones suggests wealth.

1. From Uppland.
(a) Svinnegarn: the inscription is cut on a pair of intertwined snakes surrounding an elaborate cross. From its text we can deduce the rune-stone formed part of a more extensive group of standing stones, though the others may not have been inscribed.

> Thialfi and Holmlaug had all these stones put up in memory of Banki their son, who had | a ship of his own and ste[ered] it eastwards in Yngvar's force. May God help Banki's soul. Æskil cut ⟨these runes⟩

(b) Steninge: the runes occupied two linking but not intertwined snakes which enclosed a cross patée. The interpretation of the last two words of this inscription is uncertain, and I present what is only a possible one. The stone once stood by the waterside at Steninge but has been missing for some centuries, and the inscription is known only from early drawings.

> Hærlæif and Thorgærd had this stone put up in memory of Sæbbi, | their father, who steered his ship east with Yngvar ?to Estonia.

(c) Ekilla: the runes are on two snakes that interlink, with interchange of text where the first link occurs; the stone has two decorative crosses. It stands by the former road, on a hillock with grave-mounds.

> Andvett and Kiti and Kar and Blesi and Diarf | they put up this stone in memory of Gunnlæif, their father. He fell in the east with Yngvar. | God help his soul.

There is a similar inscription on a stone at Varpsund, also Uppland, which is slightly more precise about Gunnlæif's fate: 'he was killed in the east with Yngvar'. It adds about him: 'he well knew how to steer his ship', which is to say, he was a good ship's captain. It also adds the rune-master's name: 'I Alrik cut the runes'.

(d) Råby: the inscription is on two coupled snakes surrounding a decorated cross. The stone stands in a large grave-field.

> Gæirvi and Gulla put up this stone in memory of their father Anund. | He met his death in the east with Yngvar. God help Anund's soul.

(e) Tierp: the inscription has largely vanished, and must be supplied from earlier drawings. It was on two opposed snakes surrounding a decorated cross.

> [Klint and Blæik put up this stone in memory of Gunnvid], their father. He | [travelled away with Yngvar. Lord God help the souls of all] Christians. [Thorir cut the runes.]

2. From Södermanland.
(a) Gripsholm: the inscription occupies the body of a snake curling round upon itself.

> Tola had this stone put up for his son Harald, Yngvar's brother.
> > Like men they journeyed for distant gold
> > And in the east they fed the eagle
> > In the south they died, in Serkland.

The epitaph begins in prose, but turns to heroic alliterative verse to describe the adventurers' exploits. The word translated 'like men' is the adverb *drængila*, 'behaving like a *drængr*', the latter a noun of shifting meaning but implying the concepts of bravery, loyalty and manliness. 'To feed the eagle' is a heroic way of saying 'to kill men in battle', since it was well-known, at any rate to poets, that eagles gathered about the battle-field in the hope of picking up easy meat. Serkland was a land where dark-skinned peoples lived – either Arab or Tartar, perhaps. Yngvar's expedition presumably went across the Baltic and down one of the great Russian river systems, perhaps to the Black Sea and then further east.

(b) Lundby: the inscription is set between roughly parallel framing-lines running vertically up and down the stone face. They surround a decorated cross. The stone was originally raised on a hillock which was also occupied by grave-mounds and stone-settings.

> Spiuti, Halfdan, they put this stone up in memory of Skardi | their brother
> > East he went | from here with Yngvar.
> > In Serk | land lies the son of Øvind.

Again the epitaph ends in a verse couplet.

(c) Tystberga: the inscription is cut on two snakes whose curving bodies follow the outline of the stone, one snake within the other. The rune-master failed to calculate his space accurately and had to finish his text within the inner snake. Incompetent layout like this is not uncommon on rune-stones.

> Mus-Gia and Mani had [this monument] put up [for their b]rother Hrodgæir and their father Holmstæin. |
>> Long had he been in the west.
>> They died | with Yngvar in the east.

The couplet is in fairly rough verse form. The reference to western travel, or indeed perhaps to residence, is another reminder that Swedish Vikings went on the western route (to the British Isles and Western Europe) as well as on the eastern, through Russia.

3. From Västmanland.
Berga: fragments of a rune-stone, with an inscription that can be supplied from older drawings and to some extent from context. The epitaph runs along the body of a snake which follows the outline of the stone face. It is not long enough to hold the whole text, which had to be continued elsewhere on the face. The stone is badly damaged and the text is restored from early readings.

> Gunn[ald had this stone put up] in memory of his stepson Orm, a [good] comrade, and he had gone east with Yng | var. God help [his soul].

The word I translate 'comrade' here is the difficult *drængr*.

4. From Östergötland.
Sylten: the inscription is cut on two bands, one within the other, following the curve of the stone's shape, and the final word is set on its own line. There is a decorated cross at the centre of the whole design.

> Thorfrid put up, in memory of her sons Asgaut and Gauti, | this stone.
> Gauti died in Yngvar's | squad.

## Danes and Norwegians abroad

Viking Age rune-stones are nowhere near as common in Denmark and Norway as they are in Sweden; for those countries there is not the same rich range of information. Yet surviving inscriptions make clear that Danes and Norwegians ventured both east and west. Here are a few examples. Medieval Denmark, of course, included the coastal areas of Sweden opposite, so some of these examples are from modern Sweden.

1. Hedeby/Haddeby, Jutland/North Germany.

> King Svein set | a stone in memory of Skardi | his retainer who had | travelled in the west and now | met his death at Hedeby.

On the social implications of this important inscription, see below, p. 167.

2. Kolind, North Jutland. A simple, but in its word order rather confused, inscription in four vertical lines of letters. The order has to be rationalised here to make sense.

> Tosti, Asvid's smith, put up this stone in memory of his brother Tufi who met his death in the east.

3. Uppåkra, Skåne. A granite boulder with texts on two sides.

> A. Nafni put up this stone | in memory of his brother Toki
> B. In the west he met | his death.

4. Valleberga, Skåne. Two related texts on a rough granite boulder, apparently part of a larger monument.

> A. Svein and Thorgot made these monuments | in memory of Mani | and Sveni.
> B. May God give good help to their souls, and they lie in London.

5. Galteland, Aust-Agder, Norway. An undecorated stone now broken into seven fragments, but whole into the nineteenth century. There were two texts. Early drawings allow us to reconstruct the first text fully.

> Arn[stein] raised thi[s] stone in memory of Bior his [s]on. [He met his] death in the army wh[en Knut attacked England.]

6. Alstad, Opland, Norway. An elaborately decorated rune-stone to which a second, slightly later, inscription was added. This second text, in three lines, reads:

> A. Engli put up this stone in memory of Thorald
> B. his son who met his death in Vitaholm
> C. between Vitaholm and Gardar.

Gardar is, as we have seen, the region of the Scandinavian/Russian towns. Where Vitaholm was can only be speculated. An informed guess puts it by the Baltic coast, near the mouth of the Vistula.

Two Viking rune-stones from southern England support the record of the Valleberga monument. One is from St Paul's churchyard, London. It is part of a composite grave monument and does not supply the name or exploits of the dead man; its two lines of runes give only the names of those who put up the memorial: 'Ginna and Toki had this stone laid down'. The runes are the so-called 'short-twig' ones, that is, less likely to be Danish than Swedish or Norwegian. From the wall of a medieval church tower in Winchester came a re-used stone, badly damaged but with enough surviving to show it was a Danish-type runic monument.

There are, of course, numbers of Viking rune-stones and fragments from northern England, Scotland, Ireland and the Isle of Man which need further study before their full implications can be assessed. On Manx stones see below, pp. 222-3.

## Ari Thorgilsson tells of Viking exploration in Greenland

This account of the tenth-century Norse settlements in Greenland comes from Ari's *Íslendingabók*. The hero/antihero is one Eirik the Red, a Norwegian whose quarrelsome disposition forced him to flee first from Norway to Iceland, and then from Iceland abroad – and so to Greenland. His concern, unlike Ohthere's, was not exploration as such but finding somewhere to live where the law could not touch him. Yet this account shows the same curiosity about the ways of life of other peoples that Ohthere's does. Eirik also seems to have had some of the qualities of a modern travel agent.

Though the Greenland settlements originated from Iceland, they developed independently of that country. There were two main Norse settlements both on the west coast, and their remains have been subjected to detailed excavation (K. J. Krogh, *Viking Greenland* [Copenhagen, 1967]: see also the periodical *Meddelelser om Grønland* for later reports, most recently, in its series *Man & Society* 18 [1993], C. L. Vebæk, *Narsaq – a Norse* landnáma *farm*). They continued until the fifteenth century, but eventually became unviable. The Norse explorations in Greenland and North America are described in the later (and so suspect) Vinland sagas, for which see M. Magnusson and H. Pálsson, *The Norse discovery of America* (Harmondsworth, 1965). The Vikings were not known for their tact. Their name for the aboriginal inhabitants of Greenland and North America was *skrælingar*, which seems from related words to mean 'feeble, stunted people'.

> The land called Greenland was discovered and settled from Iceland. There was a man from Breidafiord called Eirik the Red. He voyaged out there from Iceland and took land at the place that was later called Eiriksfiord. He gave the country a name, calling it Greenland, saying that people would be keen to go there if the country had a nice name.
>
> Both in the east [which probably here means south] and west of the country they found traces of human habitation, fragments of kayaks and stone implements; from which can be deduced the presence there of the race of people who colonised Vinland [the American coasts] and whom the Greenlanders call Skrælings. He began to farm the land fourteen or fifteen years before Christianity came here to Iceland [985 or 986] according to what a man who had himself accompanied Eirik the Red told Thorkel Gellisson in Greenland.

The journey from Iceland to Greenland was a perilous one. *Landnámabók* gives some chilling statistics. The H version reads: † Ari Thorgilsson says that that summer twenty-five ships set out for Greenland from Borgarfiord and Breidafiord. Fourteen reached their goal. Some were driven back and some were lost. † Presumably this derives from the first version of *Íslendingabók* – it is not in the surviving text.

## Svein Estridsson's report on Vinland

Adam of Bremen gives this account of the strange land of Vinland (in Old Norse *Vinland* is the name given to the Norse-colonised parts of North America) in book 4 of his *Gesta*. The 'he' mentioned in the first sentence is the Danish king Svein Estridsson, whom Adam knew personally. Svein died in 1076, and this is the earliest 'historical' account of the newly-found lands. There are also a couple of thirteenth-century 'Vinland' sagas which purport to tell of Norse adventurers into the New World (above, p. 92), but it is hard to distinguish their fact from their fiction. There is a single authentic Norse site in North America, defined in A. S. Ingstad, *The Norse discovery of America*, 1 ... *L'Anse aux Meadows, Newfoundland, 1961–68* (Oslo, 1985). Erik Wahlgren has written a fine sceptical account of the available evidence in *The Vikings and America*, Ancient Peoples and Places 102 (London, 1986).

> Furthermore he related an account of one more of the many islands discovered in that ocean. It is called Winland because vines spring up wild there, bearing excellent grapes. For that crops abound there unsown we have learned not from fable and fancy but from a factual report given by the Danes. Beyond that island, he said, there is no habitable land to be found in the ocean; everything beyond it is full of impenetrable ice and utter darkness.

## Viking river-traffic down the Dnieper

The ninth chapter of Constantine Porphyrogenitos's *De administrando imperio* (see above, p. 36) provides a seemingly authoritative account of the control Swedish expatriates exercised over a region of Western Russia in the tenth century. How far these people, known as the *Rhos*, thought of themselves as Scandinavians is a different matter; but they seem still to have used a Scandinavian tongue, though their names became progressively Slavonicised. In the heyday of the Soviet Union there was little talk there of this Scandinavian presence, and it was hard for Western and Eastern scholars to agree on its importance: on this see the discussion volume *Varangian problems*, Scando-Slavica, supplementum I (Copenhagen, 1970). More recently there has been some openness, one sign of which has been the increased speed of publication of runic inscriptions found on Russian territory, which if they do not testify to race at least show linguistic affinities: in English, for instance, Elena Melnikova, 'New finds of Scandinavian runic inscriptions from the USSR' in *Runer och runinskrifter*, Kungl. Vitterhets Historie och Antikvitets Akademien, Konferenser 15 (Stockholm, 1987), pp. 163–73, and E. A. Melnikova and E. N. Nosov, 'Amulets with runic inscriptions from Gorodische near Novgorod', *Nytt om runer* 4 (1989), p. 34.

The text of *De administrando imperio* is a complex one. There is an authoritative edition and translation by G. Moravcsik and R. J. H. Jenkins, vol. 1, revised text (Dumbarton Oaks, 1967), and vol. 2, commentary (London, 1962) which has detailed notes on chapter 9, with discussions of its vocabulary and place- and tribal-names to which I am much indebted; and there is a learned examination of the chapter in D. Obolensky's contribution, 'The Byzantine sources on the Scandinavians in Eastern Europe', to *Varangian problems*, pp. 149–69, particularly pp. 153–61. Moravcsik and Jenkins concluded that the author of the greater part of chapter 9 (section 1 below) derived his material from an informant who 'was in all probability a Northman who, living in the bilingual *milieu* of Kievan Russia, was familiar with the Slavonic tongue'. Obolensky thought it likely that the author himself was 'a Byzantine envoy who had been sent to Kiev on a diplomatic mission'. The shorter final part (section 2 below) is different in subject matter and to some extent language, and Obolensky regards it as 'a Greek translation of a Slav account . . . deposited in the archives of the foreign ministry in Constantinople'.

Section 1 has the unique account of the trade-route the *Rhos* used to get from *Garðar*, their outposts in what is now Western Russia and the Ukraine, to Constantinople/Byzantium. Gathering together from their various strongholds they moved down the Dnieper and past the perilous rapids that formed a danger to shipping for centuries until they were submerged in the great Dnepropetrovsk dam. Thence to the mouth of the Dnieper, where they rested on the island of Berezan', and then coasted round the Black Sea to their goal. The journey must have taken some six weeks, and preparations could not begin before the ice melted, in early April, while sailing conditions were most favourable in the Black Sea in June and July. The *Rhos* were required by treaty to leave Constantinople in the autumn (below, p. 100), so they had quite a tight time-table. How they got back to base again we are not told, and would be glad to know.

The word used for the type of boat the *Rhos* used is μονόξυλον, 'something made from a single trunk' or less likely in the passage 'made from wood alone'. From the context and its logistics they were simple hulls (or 'bottoms') made from hollowed out tree trunks. The *Rhos* fitted them out and added to them so that they could hold cargo, slaves and crew. They had to be manoeuvreable along a swift-flowing and often dangerous river and capable of being adapted for sailing over open sea when they reached its mouth. Inevitably scholars disagree a good deal over the technology of the shipping the *Rhos* commanded.

1. About the journeys of the Rhos in wooden hulls from Russia to Constantinople

The wooden boats coming down to Constantinople from outer Russia are some from Novgorod (in which Sviatoslav, son of Igor prince of Russia, had his seat), some from the walled town of Smolensk and from Lyubech and Chernigov and from Vyshgorod. All these come along the river Dnieper and converge on the fortress of Kiev (also called Sambatas). The Slavs who are bound to pay the Rhos tribute – those called Krivichians and Lenzanenes and the remaining Slav regions – hew the hulls in their wooded hills during the course of the winter, and when they have them ready, at the season when the frosts dissolve, they bring them to the lakes nearby. Since these discharge into the river Dnieper, these people come into the said river Dnieper, make their way to Kiev, drag their ships along for fitting out and sell them to the Rhos. The Rhos buy the plain hulls, and from their old ships, which they break up, they provide oars, rowlocks and whatever else is needed. So they fit them out. And moving off down the river Dnieper in the month of June they come to Vitichev, a town in alliance with the Rhos, and gather there for two or three days. When all the ships are assembled they set off and make their way down the aforesaid Dnieper. And first they come to the first rapid called Essoupi, which in Russian and Slavonic means 'Don't fall asleep'. This barrier is just as narrow as the width of the imperial polo-ground. In the middle of this rapid are rooted tall rocks, looking like islands. The water comes against them and, flooding up, dashes down to the depths below with a great and terrifying noise. So the Rhos do not dare to get through the midst of them but put ashore nearby and set the men on dry land leaving everything else in the ships. Then they strip off, feeling their way with their feet to avoid bumping against the rock. This is how they do it; some at the stem, some amidships, others again at the stern, they push along with poles. And by this caution they get through this first barrier, round the bend of the river bank. When they have got past this rapid they take the others from the dry land on board again and set off, and come down to the second rapid, called in Russian Oulvorsi and in Slavonic Ostrovouniprach, which means 'The islet of the barrier'. This one is like the first, tough and awkward to get through. Again they put the men ashore and take the ships past just as at the first one. They go through the third rapid in the same way; this is called Gelandri, which in Slavonic means 'Noise of the rapid'. And then the fourth rapid, the huge one, called in Russian Aeifor and in Slavonic Neasit because pelicans roost among the small rocks of the barrier. At this rapid all put ashore, stem foremost, and out get all those who are appointed to keep watch. Ashore they go, and unsleeping they keep sentry-go against the Pechenegs. The rest of them, picking up the things they have on board the ships, conduct the wretched slaves in chains six miles by dry land until they are past the barrier. In this way, some dragging their ships, others carrying them on their shoulders, they get them through to the far side of the rapid. So, launching the ships back on to the river and loading their cargo, they get in and again move off. When they come to the fifth rapid, called in Russian Varouforos and in Slavonic Voulniprach because it forms a great lake, they edge their ships again round the bank of the river, just as at the first and second rapids, and so they reach the sixth rapid, called in Russian Leanti and in Slavonic Veroutzi; that is, 'The boiling of the water'. This too they pass in the same way. From there they sail off to the seventh rapid, called in Russian Stroukoun and in Slavonic Naprezi, which is translated as 'Little rapid'. This they pass at the ford named Krarios [later called the ford of Kichkas], where the Chersonites cross from Russia and the Pechenegs to Cherson. The crossing is the width of the hippodrome, and its height from the bottom up to where the rocks project is the distance an arrow can be shot from a bow. It is at this point, therefore, that the Pechenegs come down and attack the Rhos.

After crossing this place they make the island called St Gregorios; on that island they conduct their sacrifices because of the huge oak that stands there. They sacrifice live birds. Also they stick arrows in a circle in the ground, and others of them provide bread and meat, bits of anything anyone has, as their practice demands. Also they cast lots about the birds – to sacrifice them, to eat them as well, or to let them live. From this island on the Rhos have no fear of the Pechenegs until they reach the river Selinas [Sulina]. So they set out from there and travel for four days until they reach the lake forming the mouth of the river, on which there is the island of St Aitherios. Reaching this island they take a rest there for two or three days. Then they fit out their ships with whatever they need [to make them seaworthy] – sails, masts and steering-oars – which they have brought on board. Since this lake is the mouth of the river (as has been said) and since it holds on down to the sea and the island of St Aitherios faces the sea, they come down from there to the river Dniester; and when they are secure there they have another rest. And when the weather is suitable they embark again and come to the river called Aspros, and after a rest there in the same way they move off again and come to the Selinas, to, as it is said to be, a branch of the river Danube. Until they are past the river Selinas the Pechenegs run alongside them. And if as often happens the sea casts one of the ships ashore, the whole lot land to make a common stand against the Pechenegs.

After the Selinas they are afraid of nobody; entering the region of Bulgaria they come to the mouth of the Danube. From the Danube they make for the Konopas and from the Konopas Constanza, from there to the river Varna [Provadiya], and from Varna they come to the river Dichina, all of them in Bulgarian territory. From the Dichina they get to the region of Mesembria, and at last their journey is at an end, full as it was of agony and fear, hardship and danger.

2. This is the harsh way of life of these same Rhos in winter. When November begins, their leaders with all the Rhos come out of Kiev and travel on πολυδια, that is to say 'circuits', to the Derevlyanians and Dregovichians and Krivichians and Severians and the rest of the Slavs who pay tribute to the Rhos. There they are provided for throughout the winter; then again, as from the month of April when the frozen river Dnieper frees itself, they come back to Kiev. Then they take up their ships as before and equip them and come down to Romania.

Of the nine notorious Dnieper rapids (the term used in this account is φραγμος, 'blockage, obstacle, barrier') seven are listed. They are given names in, the author claims, Russian and Slavonic, but there is general agreement that three of the names are Norse: Oulvorsi is interpreted as a form of *Hulmfors*, 'islet-cataract'; Gelandri as a present-participle *Gællandi*, 'howling, clanging', and Leanti the participle *Leiandi*, 'laughing', describing the distinctive sounds of the two rapids. Others too may be Norse. Varouforos is plausibly interpreted as a form of Old Norse *\*Bárufors*, 'wave-cataract'. Stroukoun, it has been suggested, is the dative-locative *(at) strukum*, 'narrows, swift currents'. It seems that what the writer calls 'Russian' is some form of Scandinavian.

The island of St Aitherios, at the mouth of the Dnieper, must be that now called Berezan'. On this island was found a runic memorial stone with the damaged inscription: '[B]ran[d] made this grave for his colleague Karl' (the first name is unclear). The word I have given as 'colleague' is *félagi*, which is probably to be taken in its primary sense of 'business partner'. Thus this is not only a memorial stone but a legal document, reporting to the world the death of Karl, and announcing that the trading business is henceforth to be carried on by the surviving partner, who is presumably responsible to Karl's heirs for his share of the profits.

The word πολυδια is a borrowing from early Slavonic *polyud'e*, a technical term which means, among other things, the journey a prince takes round his territories to collect tribute and administer justice. Something similar to this is the Old Norse term *fara at veizlum*, literally 'travel to receptions, feasts', or *taka veizlu*, 'receive entertainment'; used of the 'circuits' early Scandinavian kings made round their territories, accompanied by their retainers.

## Trade treaties with Byzantium

The first reference in a western source to a people called the *Rhos* with links to Sweden is in the second part of the *Annales Bertiniani* (Annals of Saint Bertin), written by the ninth-century bishop of Troyes, Prudentius. Under the year 839 he tells of envoys sent by the Byzantine Emperor Theophilus to the Holy Roman Emperor, Louis the Pious, then at Ingelheim:

> He sent with them also certain men who said that they - their race, that is – were called *Rhos*. Their king, *chacanus* by title, had directed them to him [Theophilus] in friendship, so they had claimed. In the above-mentioned letter Theophilus requested that by the favour of the emperor they might have help and opportunity to return home through his territories since the roads they had taken to get to Constantinople led through cruel and barbarous tribes of extreme savagery. He did not want them to return that way, fearing they might encounter danger. After carefully investigating the reason for their coming, the emperor [Louis] found them to be of the race of Swedes.

Such 'Scandinavians' are the subject of an early Slavonic work, variously called the *Russian primary chronicle*, or *Nestor's chronicle* (from the name of its supposed author), or *Povest'* from the first words of its title, *The narrative* (*of past times*). The work survives in two major versions, named from their earliest representative manuscripts: the Laurentian after its fourteenth-century copyist Lawrence, and the fifteenth-century Hypatian, after the monastery where it was discovered. Details are in the introduction to the American translation of the Laurentian text, *The Russian primary chronicle*, trans.

and ed. Samuel Hazzard Cross and Olgerd P. Sherbowitz-Wetzor (Medieval Academy of America publication no. 60, Cambridge, Mass., repr. 1973); also George Vernadsky *et al., A source book for Russian history from early times to 1917*: vol. 1 (New Haven, 1972), p. 19.

The *Chronicle* recounts the exploits of a people called *Rus'* (often translated as 'Russes') in the regions that now form parts of Russia, Byelorussia and the Ukraine. These include a number of expeditions from their base at Kiev to Byzantium. The tenth-century sections of the *Chronicle* record the terms of treaties between the Rus' and the Byzantine Greeks, dated 907, 912 and 945 (as well as one from 971, of less importance to the present purpose). They incorporate lists of names of Rus' envoys and merchants who negotiated the agreements. Most of them are interpreted as Scandinavian names lightly Slavonicised: forms of *Karl(i), Vermundr, Ingialdr, Hróarr, Óláfr, Sigbiörn* and others. There seem to be no Slav names among them, though there are a couple that have been identified as Estonian.

The extant forms of the *Chronicle* derive from a twelfth-century compilation. Of the treaty texts Cross and Sherbowitz-Wetzor comment (p. 26): 'the textual and archival history of the treaties of 907, 912, 945 and 971 is completely obscure, and it has never been satisfactorily determined whether the copies preserved in the *Povest'* represent Old-Russian texts of the treaties made when they were negotiated, or whether they are translations afterward prepared from Greek originals which subsequently came to light in Kiev itself.' They add a comment which suggests a hypersceptical approach to the material. 'It is not likely that the Russian princes of the tenth century, who were by no means superior to Scandinavian free-booters elsewhere on the Continent, attached any grave significance to these scraps of paper, and the fact that there is but one Greek allusion to them would indicate that to the Byzantine authorities they were more a gesture than a contract.' In fact, the treaties include provisions closely akin to those of Alfred and Aethelred (pp. 176–80 below); they define punishments for crimes committed by members of one race upon the other, record the terms of security for Rus' ships in Byzantine waters, and determine the treatment of slaves.

1. The 907 declaration comprises two paragraphs which list the rights and duties of Rus' envoys and merchants coming to Byzantium. The Russian requirements:

> † When Rus' come here ⟨as envoys⟩ they shall receive such supplies as they require. When they come as merchants they shall receive a monthly allowance for six months: including bread, wine, meat, fish and fruit. Baths shall be provided for them as often as they want them. When the Rus' go home again they shall receive from your emperor food, anchors, cables, sails, and everything they need for the journey. †

The requirements of the Byzantine authorities:

> † If Rus' come here without cargoes they shall receive no such allowances. Your prince shall personally order any of the Rus' who come here not to commit acts of violence in our towns and our territories. Such Rus' as come here must reside in the Saint Mamas quarter of the suburbs. Our authorities shall send officials to list their names. Then they shall get their

monthly allowances; first the men from Kiev, then those from Chernigov, Pereiaslavl' and the other towns. They shall enter the city by the one gate only, unarmed and in groups of fifty, escorted by an imperial officer. They may conduct such business as they need to without paying dues. †

2. The 912 treaty includes, among its many provisions, some to protect the interests of Rus' who served in the emperor's armed forces, as Harald *hardráði* was later to do (pp. 101–4, below).

> † Should the occasion arise that you must declare war, and some Rus' wish to honour your emperor with their service, as many as want to come to him of their own free will and remain under his command shall be allowed to do as they wish . . .
>
> Should any one of the Rus' who are in Greece in the service of the Christian emperor die without putting his affairs in order and he has no family there, his property shall be assigned to his heirs in Russia. If he make provision for the disposition of his goods, whoever he has made heir to his property by written testament shall receive what is assigned to him. †

3. Among other things, the 945 treaty ensures proper documentation and authorisation of Rus' ambassadors and merchants, a sensible, practical provision to enable the Byzantine authorities to tell friend from foe. The Greeks noted a tentative move towards a literate society:

> † The grand prince of the Rus' and his boyars may send to Greece, to the mighty Greek emperors, as many ships with envoys and merchants as they wish, as has been the practice hitherto. Envoys have customarily carried seals of gold, and merchants seals of silver. Now your prince has decreed that documentation shall be sent to our government. Henceforth envoys and merchants sent by the Rus' shall take with them a certificate to the effect that a certain number of ships has been dispatched. In this way we can be assured that they come in peace.
>
> If they come without documentation, they shall be surrendered to us and we shall hold them in detention until we have informed your prince. But if they refuse to surrender and offer resistance and are killed, your prince shall not exact compensation for their deaths. If they flee to Russia we shall inform your prince, and he shall take such action as is appropriate. †

The terms under which Rus' may trade in Byzantium are repeated and clarified:

> † If Rus' come here without cargoes, they shall receive no such monthly allowances. Your prince shall require his envoys and any other Rus' who come here not to commit violence in our towns and our territories. Such Rus' as come here must reside in the Saint Mamas quarter of the suburbs. Our officers shall list their names. Then they shall get their monthly allowances, envoys as is appropriate and merchants the customary

amount; first the men from Kiev, then those from Chernigov, Pereiaslavl' and the other towns. They shall enter the city by the one gate only, unarmed and in groups of fifty, escorted by an imperial officer. They may conduct such business as they need to, and then depart. A government official shall keep an eye on affairs, so that if any of the Rus' or Greeks commit a fraud, he may amend it.

Rus' who enter the city shall not have the right to buy more than fifty bezants' worth of silk. Anyone who buys such silks shall display them before an imperial officer who shall stamp and return them. †

[The word conventionally translated *bezant*, 'a gold coin originally struck in Byzantium', is *zolotn'ik*, which survives only as the name of an archaic unit of weight and is related to the word *zoloto*, 'gold'.]

† When Rus' travel back they shall receive from us supplies for the journey and such equipment as they need for their ships, as has been agreed above. Then they shall return to their land in peace. They shall not have the right to stay the winter in the Saint Mamas quarter. †

This last provision redefines the matter of an earlier clause on the relations of the Rus' to peoples in the Dnieper estuary:

† The Rus' have no right to over-winter at the mouth of the Dnieper, at Belobereg or Saint Eltherius. At the approach of autumn they must return home. †

There are a number of obscurities of detail in these texts (particularly to one with a minimal knowledge of early Slavonic languages), and I owe much to the translations of Cross & Sherbowitz-Wetzor and Vernadsky, as well as to others in a variety of modern European languages, for elucidation of such difficult parts as I have been unable to clarify.

## Harald Hardradi's exploits in the East

One of the most famous of Viking leaders, and for a time king of Norway, was Harald Sigurdarson. Various thirteenth-century kings' sagas recount his adventures as a young man when he was virtually in exile in the East, ultimately taking service in the Varangian guard of the Byzantine emperor. The stories are given authority by the many verses of poems written about him (as well as his own poems, for he was something of a skald himself), scattered through the prose lives of the hero. Here are a few samples from *Nóregs konunga tal*:

† When King Olaf the Saint had fallen at Stiklestad, his brother Harald left the country with Rognvald Brusason, and many others with them. Towards winter they came east to the court of King Iarizleif [of Russia] who received them graciously as Valgard á Velli tells in the poem he composed about Harald. †

Freehanded king, you cleaned down the sword's mouth
When you came from battle.
You gave the raven food enough – raw meat.
The wolf howled in the hills.
By the next year, battle-happy king,
You were east in the Russian towns.
I never knew a peace-destroyer
Bolder than you.

† King Iarizleif had always had Norwegians and Swedes with him. By this time earl Rognvald Ulfsson [who had held authority in Russia under Iarizleif] was dead and earl Eilif had taken his place. He too had a number of Norwegians with him as mercenaries. The terms of his position were that the earl should defend the kingdom against pagans. King Iarizleif made Harald the other captain of his army and hired all his men as mercenaries, as the skald Thiodolf says: †

Where Eilif had his seat
Two captains
Were at one.
Kept close formation.

† Harald stayed there a long time and fought often. Iarizleif was well-disposed to him. Then Harald became keen on travelling further to Byzantium. He set out with a great crowd of Norwegians, and travelled the whole way to Byzantium. Ruling Byzantium then was Zóe the Mighty who had governed the country with seven Emperors. At this time her joint ruler was Mikael kataláktus [the Greek form is καταλλακτης; this puts the events between 1034 and 1041]. Harald requested the emperor and empress to put him and all his men on contract as mercenaries. This they agreed to, ordering them all to man the warships †

. . .

† Then Harald took his force west to Africa . . . According to his saga it is said that he captured eighty towns there. Some were put under his control, others he demolished or burned. So Thiodolf says: †

You may say that eighty towns
Were seized in Serkland.
The young foe of the fire-red
Snake-ring risked his life.
Before the shield-bearing
Killer of warriors, terror of the men of Serkland,
Went to stir up the harsh sport
Of Hild on the plains of Sicily.

. . .

† Shortly afterwards he took his army from Byzantium to Jerusalem, and when he reached Jerusalem the whole country was given into his hands. This is what the skald Stuf says, who had heard the king himself speak of these deeds. †

> The sword-bold strong-willed victor
> Left the lands of the Greeks to subdue
> Jerusalem to his power.
> The land was an easy prey to the warrior king.
> With power enough he took possession
> Of land that fell unharmed
> Into the hands of a king tough in battle.

May the mighty king's soul live ever with Christ in the Heavens where it is well pleased.

[The final line as translated here is a conflation of the final lines of three of the verses in this poem; another bit of skaldic ingenuity.]

† He then went to the River Jordan and bathed there as was the pilgrim practice. He made gifts to the sepulchre of Our Lord and to the Holy Cross and to other sacred places in the Holy Land. Moreover he gave so much wealth in gold and silver that nobody could count its value. And he secured the road right up to the Jordan, putting to death robbers there and others who broke the peace, as Stuf says: †

> The decisions of Agder's prince
> Were held to with severity
> On both banks of the Jordan.
> It put a stop to men's treachery.
> For their certain ill-deeds,
> Their wicked plots,
> The prince put men in peril.

May the mighty king's soul live ever with Christ in the Heavens where it is well pleased.

† After this he returned to Byzantium, and at once a coolness developed between him and the Empress Zóe. The first charge was that he held on to gold that the Greek king owned, and would not pay up as the law required; that he had acquired more of it than the king had granted him. They also claimed that at the time he was in control of the king's forces, no gold had come from the warships. A second charge was Queen Zóe's accusation that he made love to her niece Maria – Harald had asked for her hand and been refused. But men who have been in Byzantium say that the Varangians remember the rumour that Queen Zóe herself wanted to have Harald. Queen Zóe and Emperor [Constantine] Monomachos had

Harald seized and put in chains in a dungeon, and two men with him, Ulf who later became his marshal, and Halldor Snorrason. King Olaf the Saint appeared to him in a vision on the street by the dungeon (later there was built there the chapel of St Olaf, and it is still standing), and they were then thrust into the dungeon. The following night a certain widow came along and opened up the dungeon – it is a tower, open at the top, now known as Harald's Dungeon. The woman had two servants with her. They let down a rope and pulled up Harald and the others who were with him. This woman St Olaf had healed, and he manifested himself to her, telling her to rescue his brother. Harald went straightway to Væringiaskipt – that is what they call the barracks they live in. When he got there he ordered them all to get up and take up their weapons. Then they went to the king's palace where he slept. They killed some Varangians who were keeping guard over the king, seized the king himself and put out both his eyes. As Thorarin says in his poem: †

> The prince took even more
> Glowing embers of the arm.
> The emperor of the Greeks became
> Stone-blind with savage injury.

Thiodolf too says this:

> Destroyer of the wolf's grief
> Bade stab out both eyes
> Of the throne-prince.
> Then strife arose.

[The two kennings in these verses are clear enough. A 'glowing ember of the arm' is a golden arm-ring. A fighting prince is 'destroyer of the wolf's grief' because his successful battles cheer the wolf with lots of corpses to eat. The word for 'wolf' in the poem is a *heiti*: *heiðingi*, 'heath-dweller', or even 'heathen'.]

Valgard speaks of the killing of the guards:

> King's son, you gave orders
> To hang the squad at once.
> You made sure there were fewer
> Varangians left.

† In many poems about Harald there is mention of this great action, and there is no point in saying anything other than that it was the emperor himself he blinded. One could have named some count or captain, but all the poems about Harald agree on this that it was indeed the emperor. †

In fact there was insurrection in Byzantium in 1042, and during it the emperor was blinded, but it was not Monomachos (who became emperor in that year), but his predecessor Michael Kalafates.

There is some confirmation of Harald's eastern exploits in an independent Byzantine record probably to be dated to the later eleventh century. The writer, traditionally one Kekaumenos, was presenting useful advice to an emperor; hence the title of the work, *Λóγος νουθετητικός*, 'A word of wisdom'. He quoted a series of examples to show how a foreigner in Byzantine (called here, as usually in Byzantine sources, 'Roman') service should not be honoured above a certain rank. One of his examples is:

> Araltes [Harald], son of the king of the Varangians, had a brother Ioulavos [Olaf]. After his father's death the latter took the father's royal power, placing his brother Araltes second to him in authority. But he, being still a lad, determined to visit the most blessed Emperor Michael the Paphlagonian, to pay his respects and to see for himself what Roman life was like. He brought with him a company of five hundred men of good family. He arrived there, and the emperor received him with proper courtesy and dispatched him with his force to Sicily; for a Roman army was engaged there in battle for the island. Harald reached the island and accomplished great deeds of valour. On the subjugation of Sicily he returned with his army to the emperor, and he conferred on him the rank of *manglavites*. Thereafter the emperor found Delianos stirring up trouble in Bulgaria, and Harald, taking his company, joined forces with the emperor and accomplished great deeds against the foe, worthy of his birth and noble character. When he had put down the Bulgarians the emperor returned. (I too was there fighting for the emperor to the best of my power). When we came to the town of Mesinos the emperor rewarded him for what he had done in the fight, giving him the title of *spatharokandidates*. After the passing of the Emperor Michael and of his nephew who had succeeded him, Harald wished in the time of the Emperor Monomachos to get royal permission to return to his own land, but it was not forthcoming. Indeed, the road out was obstructed. Yet he slipped away and took the throne in his own country in place of his brother Ioulavos. And he did not complain about the titles *manglavites* or *spatharokandidates* he had been honoured with; but instead, as king he showed good faith and brotherly love towards the Romans.

The terms *μαγγλαβίτης* and *σπαθαροκανδιδάτης*, *manglavites* and *spatharokandidates*, were in origin positions or ranks in the emperor's life-guard, but came to be used as honorific titles in the Byzantine court.

Harald's exploits must have been generally known in the west. In the twelfth century William of Malmesbury's *Gesta regum Anglorum* gave a passing reference to a romantic adventure Harald had in the eastern capital, which suggests the type of tale that was current about him as early as this.

> † Olaf was succeeded by Harald Harvagra [this wrongly for Hardrada], Olaf's brother, who had once, as a young man, been in military service with the Byzantine emperor. By the emperor's order he was thrown to a lion for seducing a woman of quality. He choked the great beast by the sheer power of his muscular arms. †

# CHAPTER 5

# The heroic life

A popular modern view of the Vikings sees them as heroes, their life as consciously heroic. They have an aristocratic society, with kings or nobles in charge of loyal bands of fighters, controlled by the rights and duties that lord and man owe each other. This, though a partial view, is not inaccurate, for many male Vikings also saw themselves as living a heroic life, or at worst dying a heroic death. Such a view of life was sustained by an Eddic poetic literature of adventure and entertainment, and represented in a skaldic poetry of formal eulogy of the courtly life. Both in their lives and their deaths great kings are glorified.

The heroic life is also celebrated in some of the runic memorial inscriptions, which report the great deeds of the dead in heroic terms. A pair of eleventh-century stones in Skåne (modern Sweden but medieval Denmark) show an inter-Viking skirmish regarded as a heroic conflict. From Sjörup comes a stone, sadly damaged in modern times but well recorded when it was in better state than now. It commemorates a fighting-man for his heroic defiance in defeat. The epitaph opens with a simple memorial formula:

Saksi set up this stone in memory of his comrade Asbiorn Toki's son.

Then it breaks into heroic verse:

He fled not at Uppsala
But kept on fighting while he could hold weapon.

Linked to the Sjörup stone is a composite memorial, three stones, at nearby Hällestad. All record a local magnate Toki Gormsson, and imply a close comradely relationship between a lord and his retainers. Hällestad 3, in plain prose, reads:

Toki's retainer, Asbiorn, put up this stone in memory of his brother Toki.

On which the great runologist Sven B. F. Jansson comments, 'it is interesting to see how the dead leader is called "brother" by his men.' The word translated 'retainer' is a technical one, *hempægi*, literally 'one who receives a home from someone else' and so 'dependant, member of a closed band of supporters'. Hällestad 2 remembers another retainer of Toki's and to the memorial inscription adds the verse line:

> Now the stone shall stand on its mound.

Hällestad 1 also commemorates Toki, echoing the wording of Sjörup:

> Askil set this stone in memory of Toki Gormsson, a most gracious lord to him.

> > He fled not at Uppsala.
> > 'Drengs' set up in their brother's memory
> > A stone on a mound, held firm by runes.
> > They were closest to Gorm's Toki.

I have left the word 'drengs', standard Old Norse *drengir*, untranslated because we are not sure of its meaning, or indeed if it had a single meaning on memorial stones from all lands and all dates. But here it is likely to mean 'fighting-men in the (perhaps temporary) service of a lord', members of an elite group, with the connotations of bravery, toughness and loyalty. For further examples of words in this semantic set and their help in defining 'the heroic life', see p. 167.

## A court poet sings in praise of his king

*Nóregs konunga tal*, 'The list of Norway's kings', is a thirteenth-century history of unknown authorship. It survived into the eighteenth century in two manuscripts which went up in the great fire of Copenhagen in 1728. Fortunately copies of both survived the blaze. One of the early manuscripts of this text was particularly handsome and was called *Fagrskinna*, 'the splendid codex', a name that is sometimes inaccurately applied to this historical text.

From it is this account of the first great king of Norway, Harald, whose soubriquet was *hárfagri*, 'Finehair/the Finehaired', and who by tradition controlled all Norway in the late ninth and early tenth centuries. The prose in this extract is thirteenth-century, but its writer illustrates his account with extracts from praise poems of Harald's skalds, his court poets. I quote examples from Thorbiorn hornklofi's poem *Haraldskvæði* (also known as *Hrafnsmál*, 'the raven's tale', because of its content. The raven is a bird of battle since it feeds on the corpses of the killed, as every ornithologist knows. It is also the bird of Odin, who is known as the 'Raven-god'. Thus it appears appropriately in any poem celebrating an important fighting-man. The raven's interlocutor is a *valkyria*, one of the supernatural pioneers of the women's movement who 'chose the slain' from the battlefield so that they could join Odin's great army on the final day of the world; again a suitable character for an ode on a fighting king.

Though the poem is linked to the name of the skald Thorbiorn, not all verses are said to be his and there may be more than one poet at work here. Nor is Thorbiorn's poem quoted in its entirety in this work, for further verses are known from other 'historical' sources, including Snorri Sturluson's *Heimskringla*. Thorbiorn's verse form is less complex than that of many later skaldic poems, which supports the claim of its early date. Thus the verses are likely to give a contemporary account of Harald's fame. He is seen in a number of aspects. He is a war-leader and controller of a formidable fighting army, and to be successful in this he must be a generous lord rewarding his followers adequately. So there is some description of the barbarous richness of a royal Viking court. And also, in the final verses, of the crude entertainment it offered.

† Harald, son of Halfdan the Black, took the office of king after his father's death. At that time he was a lad in years but mature in all accomplishments that a courteous king ought to command. His hair grew thick, with a magnificent sheen very like fine silk. He was the most handsome of men, very strong and big of build as can be seen by his grave-slab in Haugesund. He was a shrewd man, far-sighted and ambitious. Both destiny and planning gave him power to become overlord of the whole realm of Norway; which has been made glorious by his race hitherto and will be evermore.

Old men were associated with him in their wise counsels and their help in his plans. Young lads and men of courage were keen to join him because of his regal generosity and the magnificence of his retinue. This is what the poet Hornklofi says – he was a great friend of kings and had spent his time at their courts since he was a child: †

> Listen, ring-bearers, while I speak
> Of the glories in war of Harald, most wealthy,
> I will tell what I heard a young girl say,
> Fair, bright of hair, as she talked with a raven.
>
> That valkyrie was wise – men she despised –
> The clear-eyed woman knew the speech of birds.
> White of throat, bright of arm, she spoke to the raven.
> Hymir's skull-picker perched on the grassy rock face.

[There must be a story behind the image of the raven as *Hymis hausreyti*, 'Hymir's skull-picker', but it has not survived to us.]

> 'How is it with you, ravens? Where have you come from
> With bloody beak at the dawning of day?
> Flesh clings to your claws, your breath stinks of carrion,
> I think last night you nested where men lay dead.'
>
> The creature gray-feathered stirred, dried its bill,
> The eagle's sworn brother pondered its reply.
> 'We've been comrades of Harald, Halfdan's son,
> The young Yngling, since we broke from the egg.

[Harald's family traced itself back to the *Ynglingar*, a Swedish dynasty of kings; hence his title 'Yngling' here.]

'I thought you'd know that king – he lives in Kvinnar –
Prince of the Northmen, tall ships he governs,
With stained shields and red bucklers,
Tarred oars, salt-sprayed deck-covers.

'If that enterprising war-leader has his way,
He will drink Yule aboard ship, compete at Freyr's sport.
Even in youth he despised the warm fire,
Staying indoors, the cosy parlour, down-padded mittens.'

[Freyr's sport is 'battle', so the god Freyr must have had a formidable reputation as a fighter, even though he is commonly linked to the more peaceful aspects of life, fruitfulness and plenty.]

† In this account it is clear what was Harald's way of life at the time he was clearing his way to a kingdom. There is more in the same poem, for it tells of his free-handedness in this way: †

'How generous is he, that striker of terror,
Towards his great champions who defend his land?'

'Well-rewarded are they, those famed in battle,
Who sit gaming in Harald's hall.
They are graced with riches, with glorious treasures,
With Hunnish steel, slave-girls from the east.

'Eager they are when battle looms.
Fiercely they jump up, pull at their oars,
Cracking the rowlocks, tearing the thole-bands.
The wake creams behind them at their ruler's command.'

'Since you know all about it, of one thing I'll ask;
The standing of poets, the hosts of skalds –
You must know in detail – who live at Harald's court.'

'By their clothing, their gold armlets
You see they are the king's friends.
They bear red cloaks, stained shields,
Silver-clad swords, ringed mailcoats,
Gilded sword-belts, engraved helmets,
Rings on their arms, as Harald gave them.'

† This demonstrates the king's generosity. Among his following and his bodyguard he ennobled warriors who were so impetuous and unafraid that they held the front rank in battle. They had wolf-hides in place of mail-coats, as it says here: †

'I'll ask of the berserks, you tasters of blood,
Those intrepid heroes, how are they treated,
Those who wade out into battle?'

[The 'tasters of blood' are of course ravens, whose peculiarity is to feast on the corpses
of those killed in battle.]

'Wolf-skinned are they called. In battle
They bear bloody shields.
Red with blood are their spears when they come to fight.
They form a closed group.
The prince in his wisdom puts trust in such men
Who hack through enemy shields.'

† Here too it is said that King Harald had entertainers in his retinue. †

'Jugglers and jesters I've asked little about.
What sort of reception do Andad and his fellows
Get in Harald's halls?'

'Andad keeps a pet dog – it's crop-eared –
He plays tricks with it and makes the king laugh.
There are others too who can carry
Burning wood-chips around the fire;
Beneath their belts they tuck their fool's caps.
Such men deserve to be kicked out.'

† As a result of all this he became admired and secure in his inherited land,
and what's more he expanded his kingdom in many ways as can be seen
from the evidence: in part by fighting, in part by diplomacy and friendship
towards those who had been in control before, in part by providential
good luck, in part by subtle strategies and long-term planning or other
methods. †


## A great king dies in battle and goes to Odin's hall

Eirik, eldest of the many sons of Harald Finehair, gained the soubriquet *blóðøx*,
'bloodaxe' (or according to one source, *fratrum interfector*, 'brother-killer') because of
the savage feuds he conducted – and won – with some of his brothers in the dynastic
struggles that came with Harald's later years. After a short period of rule he was expelled
from Norway by his younger brother Hakon the Good, foster-son of Athelstan of
England. Eirik fled to England and for a time held power in the Viking kingdom of
York, but ultimately he was killed in rather mysterious circumstances and his memory
largely forgotten in England. However, *Norégs konunga tal* (see above, p. 106) tells a
heroic tale of his death in battle, and quotes part of the memorial ode composed for
him. This pictures him entering Odin's hall Valholl. Here he will join the great army of

warriors the god is collecting to defend him against Fenrir (the monstrous gray wolf of stanza 6 below). The other characters in the poem are Bragi, god of poetry, and Sigmund and Sinfiotli, two mighty heroes, uncle and nephew or father and son by an incestuous relationship, who take leading parts in the drama told in *Völsunga saga* (pp. 124–5, below). Eirik's triumphant approach makes such a din as to mislead even the clever Bragi into thinking it must be the dead Baldr returning to the world of the gods.

† When King Eirik gained the kingdom of Northumbria he took to heart how extensive had been his father's rule when he was king over the whole of Norway and many tributary countries too. He considered his own power was tiny and that was why he went a-Vikinging on the western route and plundered far and wide in the British Isles . . . One summer King Eirik was harrying throughout the west of Scotland, Ireland and Wales. And he did not pause until he came south to England. That he attacked as he had other regions because by this time King Athelstan was dead and King Edmund his son now ruled England.

Eirik had so great an army that it included five kings, for he was a tough and successful fighting-man. He had such confidence in his own prowess and in his army that he advanced far inland, plundering as he went. Against him came King Olaf, sub-king to Edmund. They fought, and Eirik was beaten down by superior local forces and fell there with all his host . . . After Eirik's death Gunnhild [his widow] had an ode written about him. It pictured Odin welcoming Eirik into Valholl. And it begins like this. †

'What dream was that', said Odin, 'when I thought before dawn
I was clearing Valholl for a slaughtered army?
I roused my great champions, bade the valkyries wake,
Strew the benches, wash out the beer-mugs,
Bring out the wine for a prince who was coming.
From the world I await such noble fighting-men
As will make my heart rejoice.'

'What's thundering there', said Bragi, 'like a host marching,
A huge multitude?
The panelled walls groan as though Baldr were coming
Again into Odin's halls.'

'One as wise as Bragi,' said Odin, 'must not talk such nonsense,
For well you know what it is.
That thundering portends that Eirik shall come
A prince into Odin's halls.

'Sigmund and Sinfiotli, get up at once
And go to meet that king.
Bid him come in, if Eirik it be,
For him I am eagerly waiting.'

'Why is it Eirik you wait for so keenly,' said Sigmund,
'Rather than other kings?'
'Because in many lands,' said Odin, 'he has reddened his sword,
And borne a bloody blade.'

'Why take victory from him if you thought him so bold?'
'What's to come cannot be known,' said Odin,
'The gray wolf glares at the homes of the gods.'

'Hail now Eirik,' said Sigmund, 'be welcome here,
Tried fighter, come into the hall.
There's one thing to ask you. In your company
What princes come from the clashing swords?'

'Kings there are five,' said Eirik, 'I'll give you their names.
The sixth – myself.'

† Here it says that five kings fell in battle with him, and also what a great
fighting-man he was. Further, Glum Geirason tells in *his* ode that before
King Harald died Eirik made attacks south on Halland and Skåne and
widely through Denmark, and he went through Courland and Estonia
and he attacked many other countries in the east. He also made inroads in
Sweden and Götaland. †

## Another Norwegian king is celebrated in a funeral ode

In his turn Hakon the Good, who had driven out his half-brother Eirik Bloodaxe, met
his end dying of wounds received in battle against Eirik's sons. Though he was a
Christian (above, pp. 31–3), his funeral ode was pagan in content and tone. Indeed, it
was copied from that made for Eirik for Hakon's skald, Eyvind, was a man of limited
originality and preyed on the ideas of other poets – hence his nickname *skáldaspillir*,
'plunderer of poets'. The poem is full of the kennings that delighted skalds and their
audiences; so it is hard to translate faithfully, while inevitably there is disagreement over
the meaning of some sequences.

This account of Hakon's death and commemoration is taken from Snorri Sturluson's *Hákonar saga góða* (in his *Heimskringla*), but that work scatters Eyvind's poem
here and there throughout the prose text. Here I put the text of the poem into a single
unit and supplement it from verses preserved in *Norégs konunga tal*. I begin the story in
the middle of Snorri's account of Hakon's last battle, which took place at Fitje on the
island of Stord off the west coast of Norway.

† After the death of the two brothers King Hakon mounted so savage an
attack that the whole enemy force fell back before him. Terror seized the
army led by Eirik's sons and then flight. King Hakon was fighting in the
front rank of his force and he followed closely on the fleeing men hacking
at them fiercely and vigorously. At that moment an arrow – the kind called
a *fleinn* – flew and struck King Hakon in the upper arm, in the muscle just

below the shoulder. And the way many men tell it, it was Gunnhild's servant, a man called Kisping, who pushed forward into the mêlée crying, 'Make way for the king-killer,' and shot the arrow at King Hakon. But some say that nobody knows who fired the shot; and that could well be, because there were arrows, spears and all sorts of missiles flying about as thick as driving snow.

Of the army of Eirik's sons many fell, some on the field of battle and some on the way to the ships and on the foreshore too. Some plunged into the sea. Many escaped to the ships, including all Eirik's sons, and rowed off at once with Hakon's men after them ...

King Hakon boarded his flagship and had his wound bandaged, but it bled so freely that it could not be staunched. And as the day passed, the king weakened. Then he said he would make his way north to his estate at Årstad; but when they came north to Håkhella they put ashore. By this time the king was at the point of death. Then he called his friends to him and told them how he wanted to dispose of the kingdom. He had a daughter, still a child, called Thora, but no son. He told them to send word to Eirik's sons saying they should take the throne of the country, and he commended his friends and kin to their special care.

'Even if life were granted me,' he said, 'I would leave the land and go to live among Christians, and make amends to God for the sins I have committed against Him. But if I die here among heathens, give me such burial as seems proper.' And shortly after King Hakon died there on the rock-table where he had been born. King Hakon was so greatly mourned that both his friends and his enemies wept at his death, and said that never again would so good a king come to rule Norway. His friends shifted his body north to Seim in North Hordaland, threw up a great mound and in it laid the king with all his arms and his best clothing but no other grave-goods. They held orations over his grave as is the heathen custom, directing him to Valholl. Eyvind *skáldaspillir* made a poem about the death of King Hakon, and also how he was welcomed [into Valholl]. This is how it begins: †

> The God of the Gautar sent Gondul and Skogul
> To choose among the kings;
> Which of Yngvi's race should go to Odin
> And live in Valholl.

[*Gautatýr*, 'God of the Gautar (one of the races that inhabited early Sweden)' was a nickname of Odin's. Gondul and Skogul are two valkyries, 'choosers of the slain', whose job is to find great heroes for Odin's army in Valholl.]

> They met Biorn's brother, in his armour,
> The king so glorious beneath his war-standard.
> Killing-shafts made ready, spears were waved on high,
> Then was battle begun.

[Biorn was a half-brother of Hakon, a son of Harald Finehair and the victim of one of Eirik Bloodaxe's acts of treachery – Eirik caught him when he was drinking in his home at Seim after they had quarrelled over a matter of tax-rights, and Biorn and many of his men were killed in the subsequent broil.]

> The men of Halogaland, the men of Rogaland
> The killer of earls summoned to battle.
> A good company of Norsemen followed the free-handed king.
> The terror of the Danes stood in his bronze helmet
> He threw off his armour, cast his mailcoat to the ground,
> The commander of fighters, before he took to the battle.
> He joked with his comrades – he was defending his land –
> That glad-hearted prince, clad in gilded helmet.

[Why a war-leader should cast aside his armour before battle is not immediately clear. The writer of *Nóregs konunga tal* explains: †the sun was very hot that day, so King Hakon thrust his mailcoat from him and put up his helmet. He laughed as he urged his men to the advance and encouraged his forces with his good humour.†]

> Then the sword in the prince's hand
> Bit through Odin's clothing as though thrust into water.
> Spear-shafts rattled, shield shattered,
> Swords crashed down into the skulls of men.

[Here the wording becomes metaphorical as often happens when a skald writes about battles. 'Odin's clothing' is a kenning for armour.]

> Shields, skulls were trampled down by the hilts' harsh feet
> Of the ring-God of the Northmen.
> The island rang with the clash of battle. The king stained
> The bright wall of shields with the blood of heroes.

[The metaphorical language continues. 'The harsh/hard foot of the hilt' is a kenning for a sword-blade. 'The ring-God', literally 'the Tyr of rings' is the king whose generosity is shown by gifts of arm-rings to his retinue; Tyr is the name of a god of warriors. But not all commentators are satisfied with this interpretation of the verse.]

> Wound-fires flamed in bloody gashes.
> Lombard blades sought out men's lives.
> Battle-sea surged against swords' headland.
> The spears' torrent swept down to Stord shore.

[Again a number of kennings: 'wound-fires' are swords, 'battle-sea' and 'spears' torrent' both mean blood, the 'swords' headland' is a shield.]

> Beneath the rim's heaven the red blood mingled.
> Skogul's storm-winds played against the bossed sky.
> In Odin's storm the spear-seas thundered.
> A host of men cowered before the sword's current.

['The heaven of the rim' is the circle of a Viking shield; 'the storm of the valkyrie Skogul' is battle; 'the sky of shield-bosses' is the bossed shield; 'Odin's storm' is warfare; 'the sea of spears' and 'the current of the sword' blood.]

> With drawn swords the nobles sat,
> With slashed shields and mailcoats stabbed through.
> The army was sick at heart and must
> Find its way to Valholl.
>
> Gondul spoke, leaning on her spearshaft,
> 'Our fighting-force will grow strong now the binding gods
> Have bidden Hakon to their halls with a mighty army.'

[The word translated 'binding gods' is *bönd*, a word used of the gods and literally meaning 'fetters, bonds'. It displays the gods as holding men in their power.]

> The ruler heard what the valkyries spoke,
> The glorious ones on horse-back.
> Wisely they acted. They sat there helmeted,
> Their shields raised before them.
>
> 'Why, Spear-Skogul,' said Hakon, 'did you turn the battle this way?
> Did I not deserve well of the gods?'
> 'It was I who made sure,' said Skogul, 'that you held the field
> And your foes fled.'
>
> 'Let us both ride', said the mighty Skogul,
> 'To the gods' green homes
> There to tell Odin that a great prince is coming
> Now to visit him.'
>
> 'Hermod and Bragi,' said Hroptatyr,
> 'Go to meet the great prince,
> For a king is journeying, a valiant one it's clear,
> Hither to our hall.'

[Hroptatyr is one of Odin's nicknames. Hermod is a legendary hero, Bragi a minor god.]

> The commander spoke – he was straight from the fight –
> Drenched with blood he was.
> 'An evil disposition Odin has, I think.
> I distrust his intentions.'
>
> 'You shall have sureties from all my chosen warriors.
> Come, take drink with the gods.
> Destroyer of warriors, in here you have
> Eight brothers,' said Bragi.

[Odin's temper was notoriously unreliable. He would support a hero for a time, and then betray him. Hakon very properly refuses to go to Odin without having a promise of protection. In reply he is assured that the chosen warriors, the *einheriar* who will stand by Odin in his final battle against monsters, will accept him into their community. The eight brothers (strictly speaking 'half-brothers') Hakon has in Valholl are all sons of Harald Finehair, who have predeceased him.]

'All my armour,' said the wise king,
'I will hold myself.
Secure with care helmet and mailcoat.
It's good to be well prepared.'

Then was it made clear how well this king
Had watched over their sacred places
When Hakon was given a mighty welcome
By all the gods, the governing powers.

[Hakon is shown to be the conscientious pagan king, protecting the sanctuaries of the gods. Here the gods are given two new names, indicating their power to control: *ráð* and *regin*.]

On a good day will that prince be born
Who achieves so great a heart.
His years will always be spoken of
With admiration.

Free from his bonds the wolf Fenrir
Will race through the homes of men
Before so good a man of royal race
Walks these empty ways.

Cattle die, kin die,
The land, the fields lie desolate.
Since Hakon went to live among heathen gods
Many a man lies in chains.

## A Flemish cleric describes the Vikings in action

What follows is not history but propaganda (though propaganda is an aspect of history). This is part of a Latin text called *Encomium Emmae Reginae*, 'A book in praise of Queen Emma'. The work dates from the first half of the eleventh century, probably from the English reign of Hardacnut (1040–2). It celebrates Emma, the king's mother, who was widow of Cnut the Great of England and Denmark. Emma had earlier been the wife of King Æthelred (the Unready) of England, but this liaison was conveniently forgotten by the Encomiast. The writer is fulsome in his praise of his lady, who, he says in his prologue, commissioned the book; despite this he is determined to speak the truth as a historian must. A claim we may view with some scepticism.

The Encomiast tells us he was a servant of St Omer and St Bertin; he was either a monk or a secular canon at one of those houses in Flanders. He was learned in Latin, and his text has to be seen in the light of his knowledge of Latin poetry whence he derived much of his language – his editor, Alistair Campbell (*Encomium Emmae Reginae*, Camden Society, 3. Ser. 72 [London, 1949]), has shown parallels with the wording of Virgil, Sallust, Lucan, and suggests also that he knew Horace, Ovid and Juvenal. The Encomiast's prose is rhetorical, rhythmic and sometimes rhyming, and this has to be taken into account in assessing the historical precision of the writing. Moreover, a cleric would be unlikely to have experienced Viking military or naval life at first hand, so what is said here represents, not things as they were, but things as a civilian contemporary might have supposed them to be.

1. A Viking king calls up an invasion force:

> So the king [Svein Forkbeard of Denmark], strengthened by his council of ministers and trusting in the loyalty of his army, commanded a great fleet to be made ready; and the whole of the Danish militia from every region to be given notice to muster under arms on the appointed day to hear his royal pleasure and to carry out most faithfully whatsoever they were ordered to do. Couriers had soon covered the whole area of the province at their lord's command, and made it abundantly clear to the people (at that time at peace) that no man of such a great force should fail in his duty. Every fighting-man in the land must either incur the king's wrath or rush forward at his bidding. Then what? They joined up without hesitation. Equipped with weapons of war they were presented by platoons to their king, clearly ready for danger and death if only they could fulfil their lord's wishes. And the king, seeing the huge multitude, ordered heralds to make his wishes known: that he intended to fit out a fleet against the English and to subject all that country to his authority by force or by stratagem.
>
> When this had been approved by all of them he first chose deputies to take care of his kingdom, lest in seeking a foreign one with rashness he should lose the one he held with certainty; lest reaching out for both he should hold neither. Now he had two sons of good natural abilities. The first-born of them he made a member of his guard. The younger, on the other hand, he promoted to head the government of his whole realm, attaching to him a squadron of soldiers and a small group of his ministers. They were to advise the lad shrewdly and form a wall round him in council and on the field of battle.
>
> Then, when everything had been properly organised, he mustered the partners of his expedition. Leaving his younger son on his throne he went to his fleet, encircled by an armed militia. There was no waiting. From all sides there was a rush to the shores. Scattered everywhere was a varied crop of armed men. Grouped together at last, they climbed aboard the towered ships, distinguishing by sight their individual captains on the bronze-clad prows.

The account may not be historically precise, but it contains some statements that ring true. The king has two fighting forces; his own retainers (the *comitatus, comites expeditionis*, 'the partners of his expedition') and those who were called up to fight from the whole kingdom. The former are more intimately attached to the royal person, and he is *uallatus*, 'surrounded by them as by a rampart' – they are his defensive wall, devoted to him. The latter come in troops, apparently bringing their arms with them. They are led by their individual, presumably local, captains, who command their own ships. Presumably the king has exercised his power of *leiðangr*, 'levying ships for war'. Little is known of this practice during the Viking Age, though it was usual in the later Middle Ages. There is some uncertainty how far the king's power extended – whether he could use it for offensive as well as defensive purposes. In this case Svein has sensibly consulted his council before acting.

2. A Viking armada prepares to sail:

Then King Cnut, bidding his mother and brother farewell, again sought the bounds of the encircling shore where he had already gathered a brilliant show of two hundred ships. Indeed there was so great a supply of arms there that a single one of those ships could have furnished weapons in the greatest abundance if all the rest had lacked them. For there were so many types of shields that you might have thought the hosts of all nations were at hand. Further, there was such elegant decoration on the keels that to the dazzled eyes of observers viewing from a distance they seemed made of flame rather than wood. For if at any time the sun mingled with them the radiance of its beams, here would flash the glitter of armour, there the fire of the hanging shields; burning gold on the prows, gleaming silver in the varied decorations of the vessels. In fact, so great was the magnificence of the fleet that if its commander had wished to subdue any nation, the ships alone would have terrified the enemy before their fighting-men could engage in any battle. For what adversary could gaze upon the lions, terrible in the glitter of their gold, upon the men of metal, menacing with their gilded brows, upon the dragons, flaming with refined gold, upon the bulls threatening slaughter, their horns gleaming with gold – all these on the ships – and not apprehend dread fear in face of a king of so great a fighting force? Moreover, in this great armada none among them was a slave, none a freed-man, none of low birth, none enfeebled by age; for all were noble, all strong in the power of maturity, all fully trained in any type of warfare, all of such fleetness that they despised the speed of cavalry.

If the Bayeux Tapestry (itself a piece of propaganda and made by civilians) is anything to go by, the fleet that William the Conqueror, a man of Viking descent, brought across the Channel in his mission to win England, had decorated figure-heads of beasts (including lions) and men, multi-coloured strakes and shields. But much of this may be artistic licence.

## The song of Atli

*Atlakviða* is usually thought to be one of the oldest of the heroic poems preserved in the Codex Regius, possibly from the tenth century. Its subject matter is Continental, not Norse. The sources from which the story derives do not present the simple picture of conflict between kings of two realms that the poem implies. Historically the struggle was between Burgundians (who were Germanic) and Huns (who were not), and it took place in the fifth century. Burgundians slaughtered Huns in an action in 430. Gundaharius, king of the Burgundians (represented in the poem by Gunnar Giuki's son, Wagner's *Gunther*) was defeated and killed by Huns in 437. Attila (who appears in the Norse poem as Atli) took no part in that battle. Attila died in 454, apparently from some sort of haemorrhage, on the night of his wedding to a woman whose name looks to be of Germanic origin and who some suspected of murdering him. These roughly contemporaneous events were conflated into a tale of evil and revenge in early Burgundian/Frankish tradition, and this is what the Norse poet followed. Atli's evil nature was stirred by greed for an ancestral treasure owned by Gunnar and his brothers, and this wealth was ascribed to a family or clan, the *Niflungar* (Wagner's *Nibelungen*). On all these see the introduction to the poem in Ursula Dronke, *The Poetic Edda: 1, Heroic poems* (Oxford, 1969). Thus in this and related works the Norse poets were using material several centuries old and not primarily Scandinavian. The poems are Viking only in so far as they appealed to Viking audiences – the violence, cruelty and mindless heroism they portrayed apparently struck a chord in the Viking mind. They show a vulgar delight in elaborate ornament of objects of precious metal which seems only too typical of Viking applied art. Yet in at least one respect these poems are distant from Viking Age thought. They portray national kings who have little concern for the future of their peoples, who are prepared in arrogance to go on a hopeless expedition, knowing it will leave their people leaderless and unprotected. A Viking king was supposed to bear responsibility for the safety of his nation, and this is certainly confirmed, both in kennings for 'king' (as *folkveriandi*, 'protector of people', *virða vörðr*, 'guardian of men') and in accounts of royal concern for proper government and the suppression of lawlessness.

The Codex Regius calls this poem *in grænlenzka*, 'the Greenlandic', which ought to mean that the poem was composed, or survived, in Greenland. However, it is now thought that the attribution was originally that of the poem following in Codex Regius, a related work called *Atlamál*, and was transferred to *Atlakviða* in error. There is no evidence for the provenance of *Atlakviða*, save in the content of the poem: Mrs Dronke writes: 'the mention of wolves and bears, mountains and heaths, of the halls of kings and their *dróttmegir* [courtiers, retainers], suggests that the poem was composed by a court poet of Norway or Sweden'.

At the end of *Atlakviða* is written, *enn segir glǫggra í Atlamálom enom grænlenzkom*, 'it is told even more clearly in the Greenlandic Lay of Atli'. There is no doubt that clarity is not a feature of *Atlakviða*, presumably because the audience would know the story in advance and would not need a commentary as a modern reader does. In fact the plot is clarified, by a conflation of the material in *Atlakviða* and *Atlamál*, in the later medieval prose work, *Völsunga saga* (ed. and trans. R. G. Finch, London & Edinburgh, 1965), which also sets the story within the cycle of heroic tales that record the treasure of the *Niflungar* and its disastrous effect upon successive owners. For present-day readers the following information is needed to help understand the course of *Atlakviða*. Gunnar and Hogni (Wagner's *Hagen*), princes of the Niflung clan, were owners of the great treasure which their brother-in-law Sigurd (Wagner's *Siegfried*) had won from the monster-dragon Fafnir. Their sister Gudrun, Sigurd's widow, had been married against her will to Atli, son of Budli and king of the Huns, by whom she had sons, Erp and Eitil. Atli coveted the treasure and lured the two Niflung brothers to his court by specious promises. Gudrun suspected his treachery, and sent the brothers a ring with a wolf's hair twisted round it to warn them that villainy was afoot. They understood the warning, but pride required them to accept the invitation though they feared it would lead to disaster. When they reached Atli's court, his soldiers attacked them, taking them both prisoner. Atli offered Gunnar his life in return for the treasure. Gunnar said he feared the wrath of Hogni, and would only agree if they slew Hogni first and showed Gunnar his heart as evidence. Atli at first ordered the killing of a slave Hialli instead, but Gunnar knew from the fact that the heart was quivering with fear that it could not be Hogni's. So Atli killed Hogni. Gunnar then said he was now the only one who knew where the treasure was hidden and he would never reveal it. Atli ordered him to be put bound into a pit with venomous snakes. Gudrun smuggled a harp to him there, and though his hands were tied he played it with his feet (our poem differs in this detail), which charmed the snakes to sleep, save for one that resisted and bit Gunnar to death. When Atli returned from this exploit, Gudrun pretended to be reconciled to him but in fact she plotted revenge. She gave a funeral feast after her brothers, and for the main course slaughtered her sons by Atli. She made the skulls into drinking cups, mixed the blood with wine, and roasted the flesh. When the feast was over Gudrun revealed what she had done. The king was drowsy with drink. When he fell asleep, Gudrun and Hogni's son Niflung stabbed Atli, set the hall on fire and so destroyed the king's followers. Gudrun went on to have equally horrifying experiences in her next marriage.

> **Atli's death**. Gudrun, Giuki's daughter, avenged her brothers [Gunnar
> and Hogni] as is well known. First she killed Atli's sons, and then she killed
> Atli and burned the hall and all the courtiers. This is the subject on which
> the present poem is made.

Atli sent to Gunnar an envoy
Riding, a subtle man called Knefrod.
He came to the courts of Giuki, to Gunnar's hall,
To the benches round the hearth, to the rich-tasting beer.

There the king's men drank (they hid their thoughts in silence)
Wine in that foreign hall. The wrath of the Huns they feared.
Then in a chill voice Knefrod called out,
The warrior from the south – he sat in the seat of honour –

'Atli sent me here, riding with his message,
On bit-champing steed through unknown Myrkvid,

To ask you both, Gunnar, to come to his benches
With helmets that now hang by this hearth, to visit Atli in his hall.

'There you can choose shields, ash-spears planed smooth,
Helmets gold-decked, a retinue of Huns,
Saddle-cloths of gold and silver, scarlet coats from France,
Lances pennanted and bit-champing horses.

'The field too he promises you of broad Gnitaheid,
Singing spears and gilded prows,
Sumptuous treasures, manors on the Dnieper,
That famed forest that men call Myrkvid.'

At that Gunnar turned his head and said to Hogni,
'What's your advice for us, young lord,
Since we both hear this? No gold I know of on Gnitaheid
That we together had not twice as much.

'Seven storehouses we own filled with swords,
Each of them has a hilt of gold.
I know my horse the best, my sword the keenest,
Bows fitted to the bench, mailcoats of gold,
My helmet and shield the brightest, brought from Caesar's hall.
Any one of mine beats the whole lot of the Huns.'

⟨Hogni said:⟩
'What do you think the lady meant in sending us this ring
Wound round with the heath-dweller's coat? I think she meant to warn us.
The heath-dweller's hair I found coiled round the red-gold ring.
Our path is wolfish, riding on this enterprise.'

No kin spurred on Gunnar nor neighbour either,
Privy counsellors or open advisers or men of power.
Then Gunnar called out, as a king should,
Splendid in his meadhall, in his greatness of heart:

'Stand up now, Fiornir, carry into the hall
Gold-cups fit for heroes to warriors' hands.

'The wolf shall rule the heritage of the Niflungs,
Ancient, grayhaired packs, should Gunnar go missing.
Dark-pelted bears with savage teeth will bite,
Will bring sport to the hounds if Gunnar never returns.'

A glorious host led out their ruler,
Weeping they led the valiant pair from their ancestral court.
Then said the young heir of Hogni,
'Go in good fortune and in cunning
Wheresoever your great heart leads you on.'

Swiftly over the fells the bold heroes spurred
Their bit-champing horses through unknown Myrkvid.
All Hunland shook as the savage ones rode by.
They drove their whip-shy beasts over the green plains.

They saw Atli's land, his lofty battlements,
Bikki's warband standing on the high citadel,
The hall of southern peoples, ringed with benches,
With bound shields, shining bucklers,
Lances pennanted. There Atli drank wine
In his glorious hall; outside lay guards in wait
For Gunnar and Hogni, should they seek
With singing spear to wake war against that cruel prince.

Their sister saw at once when they came into the hall,
Her two brothers – little beer had she been drinking!
'You're betrayed now, Gunnar. What can you do, king,
Against the Huns' treacherous villainy? Get out at once!

'Better it had been, brother, had you come in armour
In hearth-ringing helmet to visit Atli's hall,
Sitting in your saddle through the heat of the day
Making Norns weep for gray-faced corpses,
Letting the Huns' shield-maids learn to use the harrow.
Atli himself you should have put into a snake-pit;
A snake-pit now reserved for the two of you!'

⟨Gunnar said:⟩
'Too late it is now, sister, to call on the Niflungs.
Far distant to seek an escort of fighters,
Fearless warriors from the Rhine's golden hills.'

Gunnar they seized and put in fetters,
Lord and friend of Burgundians, they bound him firmly.

Hogni cut down seven with whetted sword.
An eighth he tumbled into the hot fire.
So should a bold man defy his enemies
As Hogni defended his brother Gunnar.

They asked the bold prince of the Goths
If he were ready to ransom his life with gold.

⟨Gunnar said:⟩
'Hogni's heart must lie in my hand
Carved bloody from the breast of the valiant knight,
Cut from the king's son with harsh-biting sword.'

They carved the heart of Hialli from his breast
Set it bloody on a dish and brought it to Gunnar.

[Hialli was a slave who happened to be convenient for this experiment.]

Then Gunnar, king of men, spoke:
'Here I have the heart of cowardly Hialli;
Unlike the heart of valiant Hogni.
See how it trembles as it lies in the dish.
It trembled twice as much when it stood in his breast.'

Hogni laughed aloud when they cut him to the heart,
Still living, that wound-smith. Cry out he would never.
They set it bloody on a dish and brought it to Gunnar.

Gunnar, mighty spear-wielding Niflung, said:
'Here I have the heart of valiant Hogni;
Unlike the heart of cowardly Hialli
See how little it trembles as it lies in the dish.
It trembled even less when it stood in his breast.

'Distant you shall be, Atli, from men's eyes.
Just as distant you shall be from my treasures.
All is hidden save from me alone,
The Niflung hoard, now Hogni lives no more.

'I was always unsure while the two of us lived.
Now I'm not, now I alone survive.
The Rhine shall rule over the treasure of strife.
The river of the gods over the inheritance of the Niflungs.
In the surging waves shall foreign rings glitter.
No gold shall gleam on the arms of Huns' children.'

⟨Atli said:⟩
'Drive out the tumbril – now the captive is fettered.'
Atli the Great, their sister's man,
Rode his ringing-maned steed, girt with blades of battle.
Gudrun [sister of the] triumphant lords
Held her tears back, weary, in the echoing hall.

⟨Gudrun said:⟩
'May your luck, Atli, be as lost as the oaths you swore
Often to Gunnar, pledged in time gone by,
By the sun to the south, by the god of victory's rock,
By the steed of the bed of rest, and by Ull's ring.'

Onward from there the bit's wearer in its trappings
Drew the treasure's warden, Odin of battle, to his death.

The bold prince, still living, they put in a pit,
That crowd of warriors, a pit crawling
With snakes within. But Gunnar alone

With hatred in his heart, struck the harp with his hand.
The strings rang loud. So must a lord,
Brave, free-handed, deny his gold to men.

Atli turned his steed, swiftly tramping the ground,
Back from the killing towards his own land.
There was a throng of steeds, a clatter in the courtyard,
The clang of men's weapons. Back from the heath they came.

Out to meet Atli Gudrun then came,
With gilt chalice to pay her debt to her lord.
'My lord, come and eat in your hall,
Enjoy from Gudrun tender morsels of creatures slain.'

Heavy with drink, Atli's beer-mugs rang
When the Huns mustered in numbers in the hall,
Long-bearded men. Eagerly the warriors entered.

Compelled to action, the monstrous queen, bright of face,
Stepped forward bearing drink for pale-cheeked nobles.
She picked dishes to eat with their ale. Then gave Atli this dread news:

'Your sons, giver of swords, their bloody hearts
You have swallowed down with honey.
Your belly is full of slaughtered human flesh, proud king,
You are eating it with your ale, passing it to the high seats.

'Never again after this will you call to your knee
Erp or Eitil, two lads cheered with ale.
Never again will you see in the midst of the floor
Those gold-giving princes shafting spears,
Or cutting manes or urging on their horses.'

A cry came up from the benches, the dread song of men,
Beneath the splendid cloaks there was terror. Hunnish children wept,
Save Gudrun alone. She never wept
For her brothers, hardy as bears, for her loved sons,
Young, innocent, whom she bore to Atli.

The swan-white woman scattered gold like seed,
Enriched the king's men with red rings.
Destiny she made grow, bright metal flow.
The lady did not respect even temple treasures.

Incautious was Atli – he was sleepy with drink –
No weapon he had, he had no fear of Gudrun.
More delightful their sport had been when often together
They would sweetly embrace before the nobles.

With weapon's point she gave the bed blood to drink.
With hellish eager hand she loosed the hounds.

Into the hall doorway – it woke the king's men –
The woman kicked a flaming log. Thus she avenged her brothers.

To the fire she gave all in the hall there
Who had come over Myrkheim after killing Gunnar.
Ancient beams crashed down, temples went up in smoke,
The stronghold of the Budlungs. Shield-maids burned too
Within there, life at an end. Into the hot fire back they sank.

All is now told. Never since then
Will a woman in armour seek to avenge her brothers so.
That bright lady lived to tell of the deaths
Of three kings of peoples before she died.

## The first lay of Helgi, killer of Hunding

The Codex Regius has two heroic poems, *Helgakviða Hundingsbana I* and *II*, about the hero Helgi, called Hunding's killer. This is the first in order in the manuscript. It is impossible to date with any certainty, but is commonly thought to be from fairly late in the Viking Age, apparently the eleventh century. It has a more artificial style than most of the early Eddic poems, containing quite a number of the sort of kennings that are more common in skaldic verses: *blóðormr*, 'blood-snake, sword', *Viðris grey*, 'Vidrir's (i.e. Odin's) hound', and *hálu skær*, 'steed of the giantess', both meaning 'wolf', *geirmímir*, 'Mimir (a god-name) of the spear, warrior', *baugbroti* or *hringbroti*, 'ring-breaker, generous prince', *ógnar liómi*, 'bright fire of the river, gold' *Kólgu systir*, 'sister of Kolga (daughter of Ægir who personifies the sea), wave', *stagstiórnmarr*, 'stay-steering-steed, ship', *giálfrdýr*, 'beast of the crashing sea, ship', *rakka hiörtr*, 'hart of the ship's stay, swift sailing-ship', *brimdýr*, 'surf-beast, ship', *hiörþing*, 'sword-meeting, battle', *benlogi*, 'wound-flame, sword', *móðakarn*, 'mood-acorn, heart', *Hugins barr*, 'fodder of Hugin (one of Odin's ravens), corpse', and several more. It also has a large number of *heiti*, particularly words for 'king, prince, battle-leader': *öðlingr, fylkir, buðlungr, lofðungr, hildingr, vísi, gramr, hilmir, iöfurr, mildingr, þengill* and others. The texture of the verse is thus rich, though its metre is simple enough; this makes the poem hard to translate with any conviction. The audience was a sophisticated one, and we may assume this work was entertainment for the upper-class Viking.

The story too is full of references that required the listener to know many of its details in advance, otherwise parts of the plot would remain obscure: Helgi's ancestry, his meeting with a posse of valkyries, the significance of some of the insults which Sinfiotli and [Gudmund] trade before the fight begins. Some of these references, indeed some of the lines, remain obscure to us today in our ignorance. However, in the thirteenth century a Norse prose-writer used this and other poems as sources for a long heroic saga called *Völsunga saga*, the tale of a King Volsung and his descendants, including Sigmund and his sons Sinfiotli and Helgi Hunding's killer. King Volsung had been treacherously ambushed and killed by his son-in-law King Siggeir, husband of Sigmund's sister Signy. The brother and sister planned revenge but Sigmund needed a helper. The only one bold enough to do this would be someone descended from Volsung on both parents' sides. Sigmund and Signy had together a son, Sinfiotli who was thus Siggeir's step-son. He turned out a savage brute, prepared to kill off his half-brothers, Signy's children by Siggeir. To toughen him up Sigmund took him into the forests where they made money as highwaymen for a time, and also had a spell as werewolves. When Sinfiotli was fully grown, he and Sigmund attacked Siggeir in his hall, and with Signy's help despatched him and his men, Signy dying with her husband to expiate her shame. Sigmund took over his father's kingdom and married one Borghild by whom he had two sons, one of them Helgi, for whom the Norns, the demi-goddesses of destiny, prophesied a great future, and to whom Sigmund gave estates, a sword, and, curiously, a *laukr*, 'leek', whatever that may have signified in the context. The prose version continues:

† It's said that while he was out on a warlike expedition Helgi came upon a king called Hunding. He was a mighty king with a large retinue and lands under his rule. A fight began between them. Sigmund pressed fiercely forward and the battle ended with Helgi gaining victory and King Hunding falling with a good part of his army. It was then thought that by laying low such a powerful king Helgi had added greatly to his distinction. Hunding's sons called up an army against Helgi, planning to avenge their father. They had a tough battle, and Helgi fought his way into the brothers' ranks, making for the standards of King Hunding's sons. He cut down these sons of Hunding, Alf and Eyiolf, Hervard and Hagbard, and so gained a splendid victory.

When Helgi was riding back from the battle, by a wood he came upon a group of women, elegant in appearance, yet one beat all the rest. They rode along in superb style. Helgi asked the name of their leader, and she gave her name as Sigrun, saying she was the daughter of King Hogni.

'You are welcome to come home with us,' said Helgi.

'We have other things to do than drink with you,' replied the king's daughter.

Helgi said, 'What is that, king's daughter?'

She replied, 'King Hogni has betrothed me to Hoddbrodd, King Granmar's son, but I have told him I would as soon marry a young crow as him. Yet the marriage will take place unless you prevent it and bring an army to get rid of him and take me away. Because there is no king I would rather set up house with than you.'

'Cheer up, king's daughter,' said he. 'I will test my courage against his rather than let you be married to him. We must first try out who gets the best of it, and I am ready to bet my life on the outcome.'

Thereupon Helgi sent messengers with gifts of money to call up men for his army, and arranged for the whole force to muster at Raudabiorg. Helgi waited there until a great regiment came to him from Hedinsey; then a huge crowd came from Norvasund with fine, big ships. Helgi summoned his commander, a man called Leif, and asked if he had counted the numbers. And he replied,

'It's not easy to count the ships that came from Norvasund, sir. There are twelve thousand men on them, but the other force is twice the size.'

Then King Helgi ordered them to turn into the fiord called Varins-fiord, and so they did. Now there came upon them a great storm, and so high a sea that, when the waves crashed against the ships' sides, it was as though huge rocks were smashing together. Helgi told them not to be afraid, not to strike sail but to hoist them higher than before. It was a close thing that they didn't founder before they made land. Then along came Sigrun, King Hogni's daughter, down to the shore with a great company and directed them to a good harbour called Gnipalund. The local inhabitants saw what was happening, and down to the shore came the brother of King Hoddbrodd who was in charge of the district there called Sva-rinshaug. He called to them, asking who was in command of such a big armada. Sinfiotli stood up. On his head he wore a helmet shining like glass, and he had a mailcoat as bright as snow, a spear in his hand with a splendid pennant, and he held gilded shield before him. He knew the way to address kings:

'When you have fed the pigs and your dogs and go to see your wife, say that the Volsungs have come here. King Helgi is here with his army ready for you to meet him if King Hoddbrodd wants to. He thought it would be fun to fight gloriously while you are kissing the maids in front of the fire.'

Granmar replied: 'You have no idea how to talk decently or speak of what has long been known if you can tell such lies about men of rank. It's more likely you were brought up out in the forests, eating wolves' food and killing your brothers. It's strange you should come here in an army of decent men when you have spent your time sucking the blood of bodies long-dead.'

Sinfiotli replied: 'You seem to forget you were once a witch on Varinsey. You said you wanted a man and chose me for the job of being your husband. Then you were a valkyrie in Asgard, and it came to a point where nearly everyone was fighting over you. In Laganess I begot nine wolves on you – I was the father of the lot.'

Granmar said, 'You tell lies all the time. I don't see how you could be anyone's father because you were gelded by the giant's daughters on Thrasness. You are Siggeir's step-son. You spent your days out in the forests among wolves, and all sorts of disasters came upon you at the one time. You killed your brothers and were notorious for your wickedness.'

Sinfiotli answered: 'Do you remember when you were a mare with the stallion Grani, and I rode you at speed on Bravoll? After that you were goat-herd to the giant Golnir.'

Granmar said, 'I'd rather cram birds full with your flesh than spend more time swapping insults with you.'

Then King Helgi said, 'You'd do better and more sensibly to fight rather than to say things that are disgraceful to listen to. Granmar's sons are no friends of mine, but they *are* men of steel.'

Then Granmar rode away to meet King Hoddbrodd at the place called Solfioll. Their horses were called Sveipud and Sveggiud. They met at the castle gate and told the king of the army's advance. King Hoddbrodd was wearing a mailcoat and had a helmet on his head. He asked who they were, 'and why are you looking so angry?'

Granmar said, 'The Volsungs have come here. They have twelve thousand men close to land and seven thousand off the island called Sok. Yet their biggest muster is off Grindir. I think Helgi is looking for a fight.'

The king replied: 'Let's send a call-up round all our kingdom and go and encounter them. Nobody who wants a fight need stay at home. Send word to Hring's sons, to King Hogni and Alf the Old. They are good men in a battle.'

The two armies met at the place called Frekastein, and there was a fierce conflict. Helgi pushed forward through the enemy ranks. Many men were killed. Then they saw a great host of valkyries, like fire to gaze on. It was the king's daughter, Sigrun. King Helgi advanced against King Hoddbrodd and cut him down beneath his banners.

Then Sigrun said, 'My thanks for this bold action. Now the lands will change hands. This is a great day for me. You will win honour and glory from killing so great a king.'

King Helgi took over the kingdom and lived there for a long time. He married Sigrun and became a famous and glorious king, and he takes no further part in this saga. †

If it tells us no more, this tells us how a slightly later reader took the text of the poem, how he interpreted its somewhat recondite wording and episodic construction. To us *Helgakviða Hundingbana I* is an indication of the tenor of life of the Viking Age, or at least one part of it – the part that saw itself as heroic. Taking risks, seeking for glory in other men's eyes, these are certainly aspects of Viking culture that tend to be missed in any more down-to-earth, economic view of the past. There is also something of the etiquette of Viking life indicated here: the relationship between lord and man which requires the great man's generosity to be matched by the lesser man's loyalty; the monetary value of a man's life which allows it proper to accept suitable compensation for the killing of a relative; taking risks that are beyond common sense (like raising sails in conditions where a wise seaman would reef them); finally the exchange of insults before battle, particularly those where you accuse the opponent of being effeminate, bestial or servile. How far this represents Viking life, how far the Vikings' ideal of what their life should be like is a different matter.

> In ancient days when eagles cried,
> The holy springs fell from Heaven's fells,
> Then was Helgi the great-hearted
> Born to Borghild in Bralund.

Night fell on the dwellings. The Norns came.
They were to shape the life of that noble child.
They bade him become most famous of battle-leaders,
Greatest of princes of royal blood.

In their power they twisted the threads of fate
. . .
They drew out golden threads
And fastened them beneath the moon's hall.

To east and west they hid the ends.
All lands between the prince possessed.
To the northern ways Neri's sister cast
A single chain, bade it hold for ever.

No single thing was grief to the Ylfing child
And to the lady who had born her beloved.
One raven said to another – it perched on a high bough
Greedy for food – 'One thing I know.

'In his coat of mail stands Sigmund's son,
Only one day old – now our day has come.
His eyes are keen as warriors' are.
He's friend to the wolf. Let us rejoice!'

The household troops judged him a true prince;
They said good times had come to men.
The king himself came from the thrust of battle,
Bringing the young heir the leek of nobility.

He gave him the name Helgi; Hringstad,
Solfioll, Snæfioll and Sigarsvellir,
Hringstod, Hatun and Himinvangar;
And a sword like a serpent to Sinfiotli's brother.

Then he grew strong in the bosom of his friends,
Noble-born, elm-tall in the brightness of fortune.
Gold he gave, paid to his followers,
The hero did not spare his blood-boltered hoard.

Not long did the leader wait for battle.
When that fighting-lad was fifteen years old
He achieved the killing of fierce Hunding
Who long had ruled over lands and men.

Thereupon Hunding's sons demanded
Money and rings from Sigmund's child,
For they claimed requital from the bold warrior
For the theft of treasure and their father's death.

No man-price the prince would pay.
The kin got nothing for their father's head.
He told them to expect a mighty storm
Of gray spears, the wrath of Odin.

The warriors went to the sword-meeting,
A meeting planned at Logafioll.
The foes tore Frodi's peace to shreds between them.
Odin's hounds roamed the isle, greedy for the dead.

The leader settled down when he had killed
Alf and Eyiolf below Arastein,
Hiorvard and Havard, Hunding's sons.
He destroyed the whole kin of the spear-prince.

Then a light glittered from Logafioll.
Out of its gleams came lightning flashes.
Then helmeted to Himinvangar
[The prince saw a crowd of women riding.]
Their coats of mail were blood-bespattered.
From their spears bright flashes gleamed.

[The sense demands a line to be supplied to this stanza, given above in brackets.]

From Ulfvid the royal prince forthwith
Asked these goddesses of the south
If they would come home that night
With the warriors. There was a clashing of bows.

Down from her horse Hogni's daughter
Said to the king – the sound of their shields was dimmed –
'Other duties we have, I think,
Than to drink beer with the ring-breaker.

'My father has betrothed his daughter
To Hodbrodd, savage son of Granmar.
But, Helgi, I once judged that king
A man as bold as any kitten.

'Within a few days that warrior will come
Unless you direct him to the battle-field
Or take his bride from that prince.'

⟨Helgi said:⟩
'Have no fear of Isung's killer.
There will be the clash of weapons first, or I shall lie dead.'

The all-powerful king sent out messengers
Through air and sea to summon a host,

Offering nobles and their men
Enough and to spare of the river's fire.

'Tell them to embark at once on their ships
And be ready to sail from Brandey.'
There the king waited until there arrived
Hundreds of heroes from Hedinsey.

From the shore of Stafnsnes
His fleet pushed out, glittering with gold.
Helgi then asked Hiorleif,
'Have you inspected these fearless men?'

And the young king replied to his comrade.
'It would be a long task to count from Troney
The long-stemmed ships with their complements
That put to sea in the Øresund.

'Twelve hundred loyal men!
In Hatun yet there are twice that number,
A royal regiment. We can look for a fight.'

The captain ordered ships' canopies lowered
And woke the generous princes' host.
Heroes saw dawn glowing red,
Noble warriors raised on the masts
The woven sails in Varinsfiord.

There was thrashing of oars, crashing of weapons,
Shield struck shield, the Vikings rowed.
Thrusting ahead beneath the princes
Rode the king's fleet, far from the shores.

Such was the noise when there came together
Kolga's sister and the longships
As if mountains and surge would break asunder.

Helgi had sails raised yet higher.
The crews did not shrink from the waves
When the terrible daughter of Ægir
Tried to swamp the ocean-steeds.

From high up Sigrun, brave in the war-host,
Helped the men and their expedition.
Out of Ran's hands with strength she snatched
The king's surge-beasts at Gnipalund.

So that by night-time the splendid ships
Were floating safe in Unavagar;
And watchmen themselves in Svarinshaug
Could spy out the fleet with hearts full of wrath.

The highborn Gudmund asked,
'Who is the captain commanding this fleet,
Bringing to our land his fearsome army?'

Sinfiotli spoke – up on the yard he slung
His crimson shield, its rim of gold.
He was watch-officer there, one to answer
And exchange insults with the enemy.

'Tonight when you set to feeding the pigs
And summon your tykes to their swill,
Say that the Ylfings have come westwards.
To Gnipalund, spoiling for a fight.

'There Hodbrodd will meet Helgi the prince,
A man who scorns to flee, amidst his fleet.
He's one who has often fed eagles full
While you were kissing kitchen-maids down at the mill.'

⟨Gudmund said:⟩
    'Your memory of old lore must be bad
    Since you accuse princes so falsely.
    It's you who once ate wolves' fodder,
    You once became your brothers' killer,
    Your chill mouth has often sucked wounds,
    Loathed by all you've haunted rocky places.'

⟨Sinfiotli said⟩
    'You were a filthy witch, a valkyrie,
    Loathsome, huge, with the Alfadir.
    The chosen warriors all would fight,
    You faithless woman, for your sake.

    'You were a witch on Varinsey,
    Full of deceit, a woman of lies.
    You said no man would ever have you,
    No mailed warrior, save Sinfiotli.

    'At Sogunes the two of us bred
    Nine wolves. I alone was the father.'

⟨Gudmund said:⟩
    'You never were father to the wolf Fenrir,
    Older than all that I can remember,
    For giant-women on Thorsnes
    Gelded you near Gnipalund.

    'You were Siggeir's stepson, you lurked beneath buildings,
    Out in the woods you came to know wolves' howling.

131

Every wicked action came to your hands
For you tore open the breast of your own brother.
You were famed for your criminal deeds.'

⟨Sinfiotli said⟩
'On Bravoll you were Grani's bride,
With gilded bit you were eager to race.
Many a long gallop I have ridden downhill
On you, worked thin, worn by the saddle.

'You were certainly thought a yobbish kid
When you milked the goats of Gullnir,
And another time, as Imd's daughter,
Scruffily dressed. Do you want more of this talk?'

⟨Gudmund said:⟩
'Rather would I feed the ravens full
On your flesh at Frekastein
Than call your dogs to their swill
Or feed your pigs. All the devils in Hell take you!'

⟨Helgi said:⟩
'More proper it would be, Sinfiotli,
To wage war and gladden the eagles
Than to hurl such vain words at each other
Though you ring-breakers share such hatred.

'I have no love for Granmar's sons,
Yet it's right for a prince to speak the truth;
They made it clear at Moinsheimar
That they had the heart to wield their swords.'

From their land they sent away
Svipud and Sveggiud to Solheimar
Galloping the dewy dales, the dark hillsides.
The valkyrie's horse shivered as the lads rode by.

They met with the prince at the castle-gate
And desperately gave the news that the killers had come.
Hodbrodd stood outside, behelmeted,
He watched the approach of his kinsmen's horses.
'Why do the Niflungs have such fearful faces?'

⟨Gudmund said:⟩
'Towards the shore are making speedy ships,
Swift as deer, with towering sails,
Shields in plenty, shaven oars,
The splendid host of Gylfi, the glorious Ylfings.

'Within the harbours hard by Gnipalund
Lie blue-black surf-beasts glittering with gold.
Fifteen companies have waded ashore
But out on the open sea are seven thousand.

'There is by far their greatest number.
Helgi will not hold back from battle for long.'

⟨Hodbrodd said:⟩
'Send the bridled horses speeding to the council-place,
Sporvitnir to Sparinsheid,
Melnir and Mylnir to Myrkvid.
Let no man stay behind
Who can handle the wounding flame.

'Call on Hogni and the sons of Hring,
Atli and Yngvi, Alf the Old.
They're always keen to get to a battle.
Let's give the Volsungs a real reception!'

In a great storming movement there came together
The iron-gray spears at Frekastein.
Always there was Helgi Hunding's killer
At the front of his force where men were fighting,
Fiercest in battle, no thought of flight.
That helmeted warrior had a savage heart.

From the heavens there came down helmeted beings
– the clatter of spears grew – they protected the king.
Then Sigrun spoke – wounding missiles flew,
The giantess's steed ate the raven's fodder –

'Hail to you, king, take heart in your men,
Staff of Yngvi, be happy in life.
Now you have cut down the dauntless hero
Who has caused many a fearful death.

'You, noble prince, have well deserved
Both red-gold rings and this noble bride.
Hail, prince, you will enjoy
Both Hogni's daughter and Hringstadir,
Victory and lands. The battle is over!'

## Parley before battle

The first of these passages comes from one of the most famous of Old English poems, *The Battle of Maldon*, written some time after the fight took place in August 991. It records a famous defeat for the English army commanded by Byrhtnoth, ealdorman of Essex. The enemy was a mixed group of Viking mercenaries led, according to one version of the *Anglo-Saxon Chronicle*, by Olaf [Tryggvason], later king of Norway. The Vikings sailed up the Blackwater estuary in Essex, landing perhaps on Northey Island. Byrhtnoth blocked their way across the causeway leading to the mainland. Rather than fight, the Vikings first tried to blackmail the English into paying them to go away, shouting their demands across the dividing stream. The poem presents this parleying between the two troops, something of the sort of 'flyting' match that Norse heroic poems describe taking place before battle is joined (above, pp. 131–2). Though it is hard to represent in translation, the English leader's reply here contains something of grim humour, suggesting it would be a pity if the Vikings missed a fight after coming all this way for one. He makes a pun on the word *heregeatu*, whose literal meaning is 'battle-equipment, arms' and which develops the meaning 'tribute, inheritance tax'. Byrhtnoth points out he will agree to pay them *heregeatu*, but only in the sense of 'weapons of war' which they will not appreciate receiving.

When the Viking demands were rejected, says the poem, they persuaded Byrhtnoth to allow them to cross the estuary and to meet the English face to face on dry land. The result was disastrous to Byrhtnoth and his force, which confirmed the English belief in the treachery to be expected of Vikings. The text is, of course, a poetic reconstruction and perhaps should not be taken too literally. After all, it is doubtful if a Viking warrior would speak such good Old English verse as the poem records here. There is a convenient translation of the whole piece in S. A. J. Bradley, *Anglo-Saxon Poetry* (London, Everyman's Library, 1982), pp. 518–28.

> On the beach there stood, calling out harshly,
> A Viking envoy; he spoke these words.
> With threats he presented the sea-rovers' demands
> To the earl, standing there on the shore.
> 'This tough crew of seamen sent me to you,
> They've instructed me tell you to send at once
> Arm-rings in return for security. It is better for you
> To buy off this surge of war with blackmail
> Than that we – rough fighters as we are – should engage in battle.
> No need for us to kill each other if you have power to agree.
> In return for such money we are willing to accept truce
> If you who are in charge here can arrange it
> To free your people from threat of attack.
> Give to the seamen, at their own assessment,
> Gold in return for quiet, and make a peace with us.
> With your money we will return to our ships,
> Put to sea and leave you in peace.'
>
> Byrhtnoth spoke, he raised his shield,
> Brandished his slim spear-shaft, spoke these words,
> Angry, determined, he gave his response.

'Sea-rover, can you hear what this people say?
They are ready to give you, as tribute-money, spears,
Killing point and tried swords,
An inheritance of arms that will do you no good in battle.
Spokesman of the seamen, report my reply.
Tell your people the much less welcome news
That here stands a nobleman, dauntless among his retinue,
Who intends to defend this his native land,
Æthelred's realm, my lord's
People and country. It is the heathen fighters
Who will fall in battle. Too great a shame it seems to me
That you should go to your ships with our property
Without a fight, seeing you have come so far
Here into our country.
Wealth will not come to you so easily.
Spear-point and sword's edge shall decide between us,
Fierce sport of warfare, before we give tribute.'

A similar form of taunting before (or rather during) fighting occurs in a famous passage from William of Malmesbury's account of the battle of Stamford Bridge, in North Yorkshire, in 1066. In this famous battle an invading Norwegian force under King Harald Sigurdarson was caught at a disadvantage by an English force under Harold Godwinson. The Norsemen were put to flight and pursued across the bridge. William was compiling his *Gesta regum Anglorum* (Exploits of the English kings) in the twelfth century, but this story must already have become a well-known episode of the battle since a version of it occurs also in Henry of Huntingdon's *Historia Anglorum* (History of the English) and in a late addition to the *Anglo-Saxon Chronicle*, both again twelfth-century compositions.

† The English got the upper hand and put the Norwegians to flight. Yet – and perhaps posterity will find this hard to believe – a victory by so many men of such quality was delayed for a long time by a single Norseman. This man stood at the entrance to the bridge called *Stantfordbrigge*, and accounted for several of our force, stopping the rest from getting across. Called on to give himself up so that a man of such valour could experience the generous clemency of the English, he laughed at those who offered it, and screwing up his face, taunted them with being men so feeble-hearted that they could not stand up to a solitary man. Nobody came nearer to him for they thought it rash to get at close quarters with someone who had desperately thrown aside all means of saving himself. One of the king's followers hurled an iron spear at him from a distance. It stuck him through as he was arrogantly making preliminary flourishes and was taking inadequate care of his safety, and he yielded victory to the English. †

The *Anglo-Saxon Chronicle*, version C, is less circumstantial:

† Then there was one of the Norwegians who stood firm against the English army so that they could not cross the bridge or achieve victory. Then one of the English shot an arrow, but it achieved nothing. Then a second one got under the bridge and stabbed him beneath his mailcoat. Then the English king Harold came over the bridge and his forces onward with him, and slaughtered a huge number both of Norwegians and of Flemings. †

## The English beat the invading Norse and their allies

This is a piece of Viking history as told by the Anglo-Saxons, a gloating poem on a decisive victory by the West Saxon army and other English levies over an invading force of Norse Vikings from Ireland and their Celtic allies. Under the date 937 one version of the *Anglo-Saxon Chronicle* has the simple entry: 'In this year King Athelstan led his defence forces to *Brunanburh*'. We do not know where *Brunanburh* was, indeed there has been much speculation; one possibility, which has impeccable place-name evidence in its favour, is Cheshire (J. M. Dodgson, *The place-names of Cheshire*, part IV, EPNS vol. 47 (Cambridge, 1972), pp. 237–40). However, under the year 937 most recensions of the *Chronicle* have a verse description of the battle that ensued. It is likely that this poem existed independently of the *Chronicle* and was inserted in the archetype of some versions because of the battle's contemporary importance. I include it in this collection for two reasons: (i) it indicates that the Vikings were not alone in recognising the heroic life – it formed part of the northern aristocratic ethic of the time: the two languages, English and Norse, even used similar clichés, as that a king is a 'ring-giver' to his retinue, and that ravens and wolves hang about battle-fields in the hope of a quick meal, (ii) if one heroic ideal was to fight 'as long as you could hold weapon', this poem shows noble Vikings taking a more practical view – they ran off, accepting the 'what good is a corpse to anyone?' attitude expressed in *Hávamál* (below, p. 141). Athelstan and his brother Edmund, sons of the great Edward the Elder, are the heroes of the conflict. The losers were captained by Anlaf (Olaf), the Dublin Norse leader, and Constantine, king of the Scots.

> Here King Athelstan, leader of warriors,
> Ring-giver to his men, and also his brother,
> The prince Edmund, fought and won
> Life-long battle-glory with the swords' edges
> At *Brunanburh*. They split the shield-wall,
> Slashed lime-wood shields with forged swords,
> Edward's sons, as it was inborn in them
> From their lineage often in warfare
> To defend against all foes their country,
> Treasure and homelands. The warlike
> Nation of the Scots fell back, doomed
> Seamen perished. The field dimmed

With the blood of heroes from the time when the sun
Rose in the morning, the supreme star
Glided over the earth, the bright light of God,
The everlasting Lord, until that noble creation
Sank to its rest. Many a fighting-man lay there
Wasted by the spear, many a warlike Norseman
Shot over his shield; Scots too,
Wearied, having their fill of fighting.
    The West Saxons for their part
For the whole day pursued their foes
With mounted forces. They cut down fugitives,
Striking them from behind with swords whetted at the grindstone.
Nor did the Mercians hold back their ferocity against any of those
Warriors who had followed Anlaf over the surging waves
In ship's bosom and attacked this land,
Doomed to die in battle. There lay dead
On the field of conflict five young kings,
Slain by swords; also seven of Anlaf's
Leading commanders, and an uncountable host
Of seamen and Scots. Put to flight there
Was the captain of the Norsemen, driven by brute force
To the stem of his ship with few followers.
The galley pushed out to sea, the king set out
On the fallow waves; he saved his life.
    Furthermore the aged Constantine
Took flight north to his homeland,
The white-haired fighting-man. No joy
He had in the swords' interchange. His kin cut off,
His friends stricken on the field of war,
Beaten down in the conflict. He left his son
On the place of slaughter, a young lad
Ground down by the wounds of battle. No boast could he make,
That grizzled veteran, about the ring of blades,
The old and crafty one; no more could Anlaf.
    With what was left of their forces they had no need
To make merry that they had the best of the battle-deeds,
At the clashing of standards on the field of war,
Of the interchange of spears, the meeting of men,
The swapping of missiles, of the sport they had
On the killing-field with Edward's sons.
    The Norsemen put out in their rivet-studded ships,
Bloodied survivors of spears, towards *Dingesmere*,
Making for Dublin across the deep,
The land of the Irish, humiliated.

Behind them they left, sharing the dead,
The dark-coated black raven
With horned beak, and the brown-coated
White-rumped eagle enjoying the meal,
The ravenous battle-hawk and the gray beast,
The forest wolf.
   No greater slaughter has there been
In this island up to now,
No army cut down by the sword's edge –
As far as books, early scholars, tell us –
Since the Angles and Saxons came ashore
From the east over the broad seas,
Sought Britain, proud battle-smiths,
Valiant fighting-men, overcame the Britons,
And seized the land.

## To be remembered with honour

Two famous verses from the complex poem *Hávamál* (below, pp. 139–40) have sometimes been interpreted as a commentary on the heroic life, the desire for lasting glory; though there is nothing in their wording that prevents them having a more general application.

Cattle die, kin die,
The man dies too.
But good fame never dies
For the man who earns it.

Cattle die, kin die,
The man dies too.
One thing I know that never dies,
The good name of the dead.

CHAPTER 6

# The unheroic life

Not all Vikings lived the heroic life. Some were too poor, others had no taste for it. There are a number of texts that point to an alternative life-style, unheroic or anti-heroic, at any rate non-heroic. The heroic life had certain ideals, among which were the obligations one social group owed to another and the rights they gained in return. There were also values such as loyalty, which were also linked to social and political relationships. There was a sense of adventure which would lead men to seek out danger and eschew prudence. And there was presumably the leisure or the wealth or the social status that allowed a man to live the heroic life. As in most medieval cultures, it is the literature of the higher social classes that is best represented in early Norse. Yet there are representatives of more humble, down-to-earth, life-styles, which I enlist in this section. There are also the examples of people who failed lamentably to hold to the requirements of their station: kings who omitted to protect their people, retainers whose ambition or greed led them to betray their lords, men who let down their comrades in need.

## The poet of *Hávamál* muses on the poor foot-traveller in Scandinavia

The collection of verses known as *Hávamál*, 'The words of the High One', form one of the most important, and baffling, of the Eddic poems. What survives is a group of separate and very different poems brought together under this one title. The problem is to determine how, when and where these poems came together, what is their common element, and when were the original versions written. Subject matter is diverse, and different metres are used in different sections. There are stanzas of popular wisdom, proverbial in mood and dealing with everyday matters like poverty and riches, hunger, shelter and comfort, how to live and die well, who to trust and who to suspect, how to gain friends and keep them, how to outwit your enemies, the temptations of strong drink and how to avoid trouble with the opposite sex. There are a couple of episodic adventure tales involving the god Odin (pp. 191–3 below). There is a group of stanzas in which someone, pronouncing in the hall of the High One, gives formal though often boring advice to an otherwise unknown Loddfafnir. And there are verses hinting at some strange adventure or ordeal that Odin went through, whose effect was that he learnt about runes and could list the magical skills he achieved presumably as a result (pp. 194–5 below).

In recent years there have been attempts to divert much of this material to the post-Christian phase of the Viking Age, and indeed to as late as the twelfth century. Many attempts have been made to reorder the *Hávamál* stanzas to make sequences that satisfy individual editor's ideas of coherence. On these see the excellent critical introduction to David A. H. Evans's edition *Hávamál*, Viking Society for Northern Research: text series vol. 7 (London, 1986). It is fairly clear, at any rate to the unbiased, that (whatever the date of its edition into a composite *Hávamál*) a good deal of the poem derives from earlier times. Also that a good deal of it illustrates aspects of the Viking Age not otherwise recorded, notably the life of the poor or underprivileged. That is how and why it is represented here and there in this book.

I give first the opening of the poem and selected stanzas with the common theme of the traveller, his needs, his reception in a strange but apparently hospitable farm and the qualities he himself must show. There is a stress on the lurking danger a wanderer must be ready for when he arrives at an unfamiliar village, his need to keep his wits about him and to pay for the hospitality shown him with conversation and gossip. The translation may seem down-to-earth and prosaic but so is much of the original verse, and so, I suspect, was much of everyday life in the Viking Age.

> All crannies and corners, before you step inside,
> Peer into them,
> Probe into them;
> For you cannot know where false friends
> May lurk in wait before you.

> Greetings, my host! A guest has come.
> Where shall he be seated?
> He must be sharp, seated by the fire,
> And demonstrate his wit.

> Warmth he needs if he's just come in,
> Chilled right to the knees.
> Food and clothes is what a man wants
> Who has tramped across the fells.

> A wash he needs when he sits to eat,
> A towel, and a hearty welcome.
> Good humour, if he can manage it,
> Converse and time to respond.

His wits he needs if he wanders far.
Dull is the stay-at-home.
He is held in scorn if his mind is blank
And he sits among the wise.

. . .

A better load none carries off
Than mother-wit can be.
In a strange town it's better than gold.
Such is the refuge of the beggar.

A better load none carries off
Than mother-wit can be.
No worse provision can you take on your way
Than a skinful of ale.

Not as good as they say it is
Is ale for the sons of men.
For the more he drinks the less he knows
Of his mind, that man.

. . .

A guest must go, he must not stay
Always in the one place.
Loved becomes loathed if he sits too long
In the home of another man.

. . .

Out in the field no man should move
A foot beyond his weapons.
For a man never knows, out on the trackways,
When he may need his spear.

## The alternative view of death

Again from *Hávamál*, a more pragmatic view of death, contrasting with the Viking ideal of defiance until the end.

Better living than not living.
Only the living hold wealth.
I saw a fire blaze up in a rich man's home,
But death stood outside the door.

A cripple can ride, an armless man herd sheep;
A deaf man fight well enough.
Better blind than burnt on the pyre.
What good is a corpse to anyone?

## Poverty

The *Hávamál* poet comments on poverty and content.

> A house of your own, however mean, is good.
> All men are heroes at home;
> Though you have but two goats and your best room's rope-thatched,
> Still it's better than begging.
>
> A house of your own, however mean, is good.
> All men are heroes at home.
> It cuts to a man's heart if he has to beg
> For his food at every meal.
>
> . . .
>
> To moot a man should ride washed and fed
> Even if he's not well dressed.
> No man should be ashamed of boots or breeches,
> Nor even of a horse that's no good.
>
> . . .
>
> I knew Fitiung's sons when they had sheep in their folds.
> Now they carry the beggar's staff.
> Wealth changes in the twinkling of an eye.
> It's the most fickle of friends.

## The *Hávamál* poet contemplates the importance of moderation

A moderate Viking would seem a contradiction in terms. Certainly it could hardly apply to the rabble who, in 1011, kidnapped Archbishop Ælfheah of Canterbury and killed him in a drunken party because: 'wine had been brought there from the south'. The end was that: 'they pelted him with bones and cattle-heads, and one of them hit him over the head with the hammer of an axe so that he sank down and his holy blood fell over the ground and he sent his holy soul to the kingdom of God'. A classic case of an undisciplined mob wasting a valuable hostage.

> A man should not hold on to the ale-cup,
> But drink moderately from it.
> Spare of speech he should be, or silent.
> No man will accuse you of ill manners
> For going too early to bed.
>
> The glutton, unless he keeps himself in check,
> Will eat himself to death.
> Often a fool's belly brings him to scorn
> When he comes among men of sense.

Cattle know when to return to the fold
And then they leave their pasture.
But a stupid man can never gauge
The full extent of his belly.

And, more thoughtfully, the danger of too much knowledge.

Medium wise should a man be
Never too wise.
The men who have the richest lives
Are those who know just enough.

Medium wise should a man be,
Never too wise;
For a wise man's heart is rarely glad,
A really wise man's, that is.

Medium wise should a man be,
Never too wise.
No man should know his fate in advance;
His heart will be the freer of care.

## The *Hávamál* poet meditates on human folly, credulity and deceit

In the outside world the Vikings had a reputation for treachery; indeed the great god Odin was notorious for his unreliability. In this section of *Hávamál* the reader is advised to suspect everything (and in the verse I put at the end, to check everything fully before believing it). There is a long list of things that cannot be trusted. Some of these are obvious – a creaking bow may break in an emergency, a rootless tree may fall suddenly, a surging breaker may hide a rock, ice one-night old may not bear you, a slave has inevitably no self-reliance and will fail you at need, the dead just killed may in fact be shamming, a house half-burnt may burst out into flames again though it seems quenched (or can this one mean that if you burn a man to death in his house, you should make sure the job is done properly in case anyone survives in the ruins?). On the other hand, I am not clear why one should be tempted to trust a raucous crow or what would be dangerous in doing so.

In woman's words shall no man trust.
Nor what a wife may say,
For their hearts were formed on a whirling wheel
And fickleness fixed in their breasts.

A creaking bow, a flaming fire,
A snarling wolf, a raucous crow,
A squealing pig, a rootless tree,
A surging breaker, a bubbling pot,

A flying javelin, a tumbling wave,
Overnight ice, a coiled snake,
A woman's pillow-talk or a shattered sword,
A bear's playfulness or a king's son,

A sick calf, a slave's self-reliance,
A fortune-teller's cheering words, new-killed dead,
A field sown early let no man trust,
Nor too young a son.
(Weather shapes the crops, good sense the son;
Both are uncertain).

Your brother's killer if you meet him in the street,
A half-burnt house, a horse too frisky,
– the beast is useless if it breaks a leg –
No man so secure as to trust all these.

Loving a woman whose heart is false
Is like driving an unshod horse over slippery ice,
A mettled two-year-old, not fully broken;
Or like handling a rudderless ship in a fierce gale,
Or like a cripple catching reindeer on the thawing fells.

Yet now I'll speak plain, I know both sides.
Men's minds are treacherous to women.
The falser our thoughts, the fairer our speech;
That deceives the wisest hearts.

Sweet talk and gifts offered
Will win a wench's favour.
Praise the lovely creature's looks.
To win you must woo.

Another man's love
You must never mock;
What the fool escapes may strike the wise –
Beauty that fires desire.

Never mock another man
For what is common to all.
Men of sense it turns into idiots,
Love mighty over all.

. . .

Don't say, 'It's been a good day' till sundown.
Don't say, 'She's a good wife' till she's buried.
Don't say, 'It's a good sword' till you've tested it.
Don't say, 'She's a good girl' till she's married off.
Don't say, 'The ice is safe' till you've crossed it.
Don't say, 'The beer is good' till you've drunk the last of it.

## Treachery

The Viking ideal of truth to one's oath was a slippery one. In the outside world the Vikings were notorious for breaking agreements. It is possible they regarded oaths sworn between closed groups, like families, bands of comrades, business partners, as sacrosanct, but were prepared to swear oaths to outside groups – for instance, representatives of foreign powers – without any real intention of keeping them. Or again, the devotion some Vikings felt to the great god Odin may have led them to adopt his characteristic untrustworthiness or deceit. Occasionally a rune-stone will record with contempt an act of treachery between comrades. Here are four examples.

1. From Uppland, Sweden: the now lost rune-stone of Söderby, known only from seventeenth-century drawings. The runes were cut on a snake that curled round the face of the stone in three concentric curves. The text must have been clear enough since the drawings coincide closely in their readings, though they have common gaps where letter groups had been lost. There are problems of interpretation of individual letter sequences. A commonly suggested text is:

> Ørikr and his kin [put up this stone in memory of] his brother Helgi.
> And Sassur killed him and [did] a contemptible act. He betrayed his
> fellow. God help Helgi's soul.

The word I have translated 'contemptible act' is *níðingsverk*, 'a deed appropriate to a *níðingr*, a strong legal term of opprobrium: traitor, apostate'. The word 'fellow' is *félagi*, literally 'one who puts down money (in a common enterprise)' and so 'business partner'; but a word that comes to include 'comrade-in-arms, fellow in an expedition' and so on. Here the oath has been broken within a closed group, which is unforgivable.

2. From Braddan, Isle of Man: a fragment of a tenth-century cross. Only part of a cross-arm remains, and with it something of the runic inscription, in two lines. The major, lost, piece of the cross-shaft presumably had a memorial text to a man treacherously killed, and the surviving fragment records the wickedness of the man who killed him. We do not know the name of the dead, but his betrayer is recorded for all time. Mark Anthony is our authority for the fact that 'the evil that men do lives after them,' and here is an example.

> Rosketil: betrayed under trust | a man bound to him by oaths.

3. From Vester Marie, Bornholm: a standing stone with a snake band and within it a second section of the text. It dates from the later Viking Age. The inscription ends with a couplet of rough verse:

> Asvaldi set up this stone in memory of Alvar his brother,
> A noble warrior | shamefully killed.
> Skogi betrayed an innocent man.

4. From Svenstrup, North Jutland: a standing slab with a running text in two sections:

> Thorgaut (or Thorgund) set up this stone in memory of his (her) father
> Asvid. Woefully he met cowardly treachery | with Ildi's sons.

There are problems with this text, partly because we are not sure of the form (or indeed gender) of the first personal name. What Asvid met (the verb is *fann*, 'found') was *argskapr*, a word usually meaning 'cowardice' but often having the connotation of effeminacy. Here it suggests that Asvid's comrades – presumably Ildi's sons – behaved as cowards and let him down in time of peril. They played an important part in the tragedy, for the rune-master took the trouble to incise a special pair of framing lines to accommodate them on the stone.

## The cost of disloyalty

This passage from *Encomium Emmæ Reginæ* (p. 115, above) is an early account of the execution of Eadric Streona, the Anglo-Saxon ealdorman of Mercia. Eadric had an unattractive reputation for treachery, and the *Anglo-Saxon Chronicle* portrays him as a turncoat. So, for instance, its annal for 1015 tells how, during a Danish attack on England:

> Ealdorman Eadric gathered his levies, as did Prince Edmund in the north.
> Then the ealdorman planned to betray the prince, and they parted with-
> out a fight and retired in the face of their enemy. And Ealdorman Eadric
> lured forty ships from the king's allegiance and then went over to Cnut.

While in that for 1016, in the midst of a battle:

> Then Ealdorman Eadric did as he had often done before – he started a
> flight among the *Magesæte* [the Herefordshire people] and so betrayed his
> lord king.

Here, after Cnut has taken the throne of England (1017), Eadric gets his come-uppance.

> As yet he [Cnut] was in the prime of youth, yet he had the power of
> indescribable shrewdness. So it came to pass that he loved those who, as he
> had heard, had fought faithfully and without deceit on Edmund's side;
> and those whom he knew to be faithless and who in time of war swung to
> either side in treacherous tergiversation he held in such contempt that one
> day he ordered many of the [English] leaders to be killed for such
> disloyalty as this. Among them was Eadric. He had fled from battle and
> when he sought some reward from the king for this behaviour – as though
> he had done it to ensure Cnut's victory – the king said rather sadly, 'Can
> someone like you who have treacherously let down your own lord be
> capable of being true to me? I will return you your reward, one so
> appropriate that this craftiness of yours will not give you much pleasure
> hereafter.' Then calling Earl Eric he said, 'This fellow here, pay him what
> we owe him. I mean, make sure he doesn't betray us. Kill him.' Eric lost no

time, brought out his double-headed axe and with a mighty blow lopped off his head. So that by this example fighting-men may learn to be loyal to their kings, not disloyal.

## Famine in Halogaland

In *Heimskringla* Snorri Sturluson tells of a disastrous famine in tenth-century Norway, when the sons of Gunnhild (widow of Eirik Bloodaxe) were joint kings of Norway. His source was a group of verses attributed to the poet Eyvind *skáldaspillir*. Whether they were part of a longer poem or were *lausar vísur*, 'free verses', is a matter of some controversy. This is how Snorri interpreted the situation. The duty a king had to protect his people comes into play, and in this Eirik/Gunnhild's sons were negligent or even corrupt.

† When the sons of Gunnhild were ruling Norway there spread a great famine which got worse the longer they held control. The peasants put the blame on the kings, the more so as the kings were grasping and made life hard for farmers. At last things reached such a state that people over a wide region were nearly out of corn and fish. In Halogaland starvation and hunger became severe for there was almost no corn growing. At mid-summer snow covered the whole land. The farm-stock were held indoors. This is what Eyvind *skáldaspillir* said – he stepped outside and a blizzard was raging. †

> Snow falls on Odin's mate.
> Like Lapps we have locked up
> Our shoot-stripping hinds
> In the depth of summer.

[Odin's mate is the goddess called *Iörð*, which also means 'earth'. The hinds who strip bark from shoots are cattle, or perhaps goats.]

† Eyvind had made up a long poem about all the Icelanders. This is how they paid him. Every free farmer gave him a penny in tribute: each one was three pennyweights of solid silver, pure white when clipped. And when the silver was paid in at the Althingi, they arranged for smiths to refine it. The silver was fashioned into a cloak-pin, less the cost of the craftsman's fee. The pin then weighed fifty marks. They sent it to Eyvind. He had the pin chopped into hack-silver and with it bought himself livestock. With spring a small run of herring came inshore at one of the outer fishing stations. Eyvind got a rowing-boat for the men of his household and his tenants, and rowed to where the herring shoal had been driven. He said: †

> Let the wave-steed kick
> With its sea-feet southwards

Towards the sharp-tailed terns
Of the long nets.
To find out, lady,
If weeds of the glacier's field,
Rooted up by wave-pigs,
Are on sale to my friends.

[The images here are far-fetched. The 'wave-steed' is obviously a ship, and its feet the oars. The herring are likened to sea-birds, distinguished by fishes' tails and caught in long nets. They are also seen as weeds growing on fields fed by glaciers (the fiords), which wave-pigs (again ships) root up.]

† But so completely had he used up all his free cash in stocking his farm that
he bartered his store of arrows for the herrings. He said: †

Last year I got a brooch
And paid it for my flocks.
The landsmen of the sea-heaven
Sent it across to me.
Later I swapped my herrings
That leap from Egil's hands
For the sea's slender arrows.
Both these the famine caused.

[An even more complexly worded verse. The 'sea's heaven' is ice; so the landsmen of this heaven are Icelanders. The second half of the stanza has two ingeniously contrasting images. Egil was an archer famous in legend. The herrings that leap from his hands are thus his arrows. Slender fish are shaped like arrow-heads, so the 'sea's slender arrows' are herrings. 'I gave the herrings of the bow for the arrows of the sea.']

The story tells a good deal about Viking economy, notably the problem of currency. Though silver may be made into a brooch, its value is a reflection of the weight of silver rather than as a work of art – hence the amount of hack-silver, jewellery of various sorts cut up in weights of bullion, that is found in Viking Age treasure hoards. Pennies were not minted in Iceland at this time, and it may be that the reference is to English (Anglo-Saxon) coins which circulated in the land. It is unlikely that Snorri's tale defines the weight of bullion given to Eyvind correctly since, according to modern calculations, this would give a total of some 12,000+ free-farmers in Iceland, which is probably too high for the tenth century. When currency and bullion ran out, Vikings clearly resorted to a barter economy.

In *Nóregs konunga tal* the story is rather different, and it is interesting to see what diverse prose tales two historians make up from the same group of verses. R. G. Poole has examined the relationship between these two accounts (*Viking poems on war and peace: a study in skaldic narrative* [Toronto, 1991], pp. 12–16). Here is the *Nóregs konunga tal* version:

† Gunnhild's sons, it is said, were baptised in their youth in England. When
they came to Norway and took the title of kings they put down temples

and the practice of sacrifice, though they did not force any man into Christianity. Indeed, there is no mention of the way they kept their faith save that anyone who wanted could be Christian, and others heathen if they so wished. The brothers – Gunnhild's sons – had many groups of retainers. Some traversed the uplands, others the sea-coast. And there was a great famine in their days because the herring stocks, indeed all sea-fisheries, declined, and the corn-harvest was a failure. The people of the country attributed this to the anger of their gods because the kings had had their sacrificial places destroyed. Eyvind *skáldaspillir* said this: †

> Snow falls on Odin's mate.
> Like Lapps we have locked up
> Our shoot-stripping hinds
> In the depth of summer.

† This is how you can tell how harsh the times were then – there was so much snow at midsummer that the cattle had all to be tended to indoors. Eirik's sons behaved insolently to the people of their land, taking no heed of the laws. It was also claimed that they hid their money in the ground like smallholders, and were reluctant to give their men their contracted pay. †

In pagan times, it is claimed, kings were responsible for the prosperity and good harvests of their people, and indeed there are stories of kings being killed for failing in this duty. The Christian historians quoted here try to rationalise this view, blaming the kings but giving as specific reasons their avarice, their lack of control over their many retainers and, more romantically, their neglect of the old gods who guaranteed fruitfulness.

# CHAPTER 7

# All sorts and conditions of men

### The origins of social class: one theory

The Vikings were – in theory at any rate – far from being a classless society. How rigidly social class groupings remained in the fluid, active and international world of the Vikings is another matter. Here, for what it is worth, is a mythological account of how the different classes of society came into being. It is a poem called *Rígsþula*, 'the rhyme of Rig'. The hero is the rather curious god Heimdall (on whom see E. O. G. Turville-Petre, *Myth and religion of the North: the religion of ancient Scandinavia* [London, 1964], pp. 147–55). The poem is preserved in a slightly unusual context, in one of the manuscripts of Snorri Sturluson's *Prose Edda* a codex from the fourteenth century. The ending is defective (though not so, according to Dumézil) and there is also a break of continuity in the middle, where the sense can be readily supplied. The poem has caused considerable scholarly controversy, both as to its date and its provenance. Datings have varied between the ninth and the thirteenth century, and there is generally thought to be Irish influence on the poem's content. However, the renowned French scholar, Georges Dumézil, has defended the Germanic form of the content of *Rígsþula* ('The Rígsþula and Indo-European social structure' in Georges Dumézil, *Gods of the ancient Northmen* (Berkeley, 1973), pp. 118–25, the article originally given as a lecture in 1958). For all that this poem must remain suspect as a statement of Viking Age thought.

> † In ancient histories men say that one of the gods, the one called Heimdall, was off on his travels. He walked out to the sea-shore, came upon a farmstead, and gave his name as Rig. This poem follows that history. †

> > Long ago, they say, the cunning god,
> > Powerful, ancient, tough, vigorous,
> > Rig came striding along the green paths.

He came to a house. The door stood open.
In he went. On the floor a fire.
An aged couple sat by the hearth.
Great-grandad and Great-grandma, in old-fashioned clothes.

Rig knew how to speak to them.
So he set himself down in the middle of the room,
And on each side, the household couple.

Then Great-grandma took up a hunk of bread,
Heavy, thick, packed with bran,
She set it in the middle of a trencher.
There was broth in a basin, she put it on the table.

Rig knew how to speak to them.
He stood upright, got ready for sleep,
So he lay down in the middle of the bed,
And on each side, the household couple.

So it went on three nights in a row,
Then off he walked along the path.
And so there passed away nine months.

Great-grandma bore a lad, swarthy-skinned,
They baptised him, called him Slave.
He began to grow and turn out tough.
On his hands the skin was roughened,
His knuckles knobbly,
His fingers coarse, his face scabby,
Crook-backed and great big feet.

Then he began to test his strength,
To bind up cord, make up bundles,
Carry back brushwood all the day.

To his home there came a knock-kneed wench,
Muck on her feet, sun-scorched arms,
Her nose down-turned, Slave-girl her name.

In the middle of the floor she sat herself down;
Next to her the son of the house.
They chatted and whispered, made their bed,
Slave and Slave-girl, night after night.

Children they had – they lived in love –

[There follows a list of boys' names, all sounding clumsy and with unattractive etymologies as far as they can be traced: names like *Drumbr*, which means 'log of rotten wood', *Kleggi* 'cleg, horse-fly'.]

They laid fences,

Carried dung afield, tended the pigs,
Watched over the goats, dug turf.

These were their daughters –

[A similar list of girls' names follows.]

From them are descended the race of slaves.

On went Rig along the straight paths.
He came to a hall. The door was latched.
In he went. On the floor a fire.
A couple sat there, busy with their work.

The man was shaping wood for a loom-beam.
His beard was trimmed, his hair across his temples.
His shirt tight-fitting. On the floor his work-box.

The wife sat there. She twirled her spindle;
Her arms outstretched, ready for weaving.
A snood on her head, a blouse across her breast,
A kerchief round her neck, brooches at her shoulders.
Grandad and Grandma kept house together.

Rig knew how to speak to them.

[Here is missing a section where Grandma makes ready a suitable meal.]

Got up from the table, got ready for sleep,
So he lay down in the middle of the bed,
And on each side, the household couple.

So it went on three nights in a row,
Then off he walked along the path.
And so there passed away nine months.

Grandma bore a lad. They gave him a name,
Called him Freeman. In linen she wrapped him,
Ruddy and clear-skinned. His eyes looked everywhere.

He began to grow and turn out tough.
He trained oxen, he made ploughs,
He put up sheds, built barns,
Made carts, turned the furrow.

Home they brought a girl, in goat-skin cape,
Keys at her belt; married her to Freeman;
Her name Daughter-in-law. A bride's veil she wore.
They lived as a couple, shared out gifts,
Spread out the bed-sheets, made a home.

Children they had – they lived in love –

[There follow two lists, of boys' and girls' names, all sounding much more up-market

than those of Slave and his wife, yet still down-to-earth: names like *Smiðr*, 'craftsman',
and *Bóndi*, 'Yeoman' for the boys, *Ristill*, 'Slender', *Svarri*, 'Serious' for the girls.]

On went Rig along the straight paths.
He came to a great house. The doors faced south.
The door leaned to. There was a ring on the handle.
In he went. The floor strewn with rushes.
A couple sat there, Father and Mother,
Looking in each other's eyes, holding hands.

The man of the household sat twisting a bow-string,
Testing a bow, shafting arrows.
The woman sat admiring her arms,
Smoothing her linen, straightening her sleeves.
Her headdress was tall, a necklet on her shoulders
A spreading skirt, a blue-coloured bodice,
Her brows clearer, her breast whiter,
Her neck brighter than new-fallen snow.

Rig knew how to speak to them.
So he set himself down in the middle of the room,
And on each side, the household couple.

Then Mother took a patterned cloth
Of white linen and spread the table.
She then took up thin-baked bread
Of white wheat and covered the cloth.

Then she carried in brimming bowls,
Silver-chased, set them on the table,
Streaky pork, roast fowl.
There was wine in a pitcher, plated goblets.
They drank and talked. And so the day passed.

Rig knew how to speak to them.
He stood upright, got ready for sleep,
So he lay down in the middle of the bed,
And on each side, the household couple.

So it went on three nights in a row,
Then off he walked along the path.
And so there passed away nine months.

Mother bore a lad, she swathed it in silk.
They baptised him and called him Earl.
His hair was blond, his cheeks bright,
His eyes piercing like a young snake's.

Up grew Earl there in those halls,
Learned to hold a shield, fit a bowstring,

Bend the bow, shaft arrows,
Hurl a javelin, thrust a spear,
Ride a horse, hunt the hounds,
Wield a sword, go out swimming.

From the thicket came Rig striding,
Rig striding; he taught him runes,
Acknowledged his son, gave him his name,
Bade him take over ancestral lands,
Ancestral lands, his ancient heritage.

From there he rode through the dusky forest,
The holy mountains, till he reached a hall.
He brandished his spear, shook his shield,
Spurred his horse and drew his sword.
He stirred up warfare, made earth red with blood,
Slaughtered men, fought his way to power.

So he soon controlled eighteen estates,
He learned to share out, grant to all
Wealth and jewels, slender horses.
He scattered rings, cut armlets into hack-silver.

His messengers coursed over sodden ways,
Came to a hall where Chieftain lived.
He had a daughter, taper-fingered,
Fair, wise. Her name was Erna.

They asked her hand, drove her back,
Married her to Earl, she wore a veil.
They lived together, content with each other,
Raised a family, had a good life.

[There follows a verse giving the names of the sons of this union. This time the names present the view of nobility, inheritance, race. The youngest is called *Konr*, whose name and epithet, *Konr ungr*, 'young Kon', will later imply an etymology for *konungr*, 'king'.]

Up grew the lads born to Earl.
They broke horses, fitted out shields,
Made javelins, swung spears.

But young Kon learned runes,
Runes of life and runes of time;
More, he learned to save men's lives,
Blunt sharp swords and still the surge,
Birds' speech, how to quench flames,
Quiet the heart and soothe all care.
He had the strength and force of eight men.

With Rig he soon shared secret lore,
Outwitted him in craft and gained more skills.
So he found strength, so he earned
The name of Rig, understanding of runes.

Young Kon rode through forest and thicket,
Shot his arrows, subdued the birds

Thus said a crow as it sat on the bough,
'Why, young Kon, must you calm the birds?
Better for you to ride your horses,
Swing your sword and slay a host.

'Dan and Danp have splendid halls,
A nobler heritage than you have.
They know well how to sail a ship,
Test the sword's edge, tear open wounds.

Here the poem breaks off (or reaches its proper conclusion, according to Dumézil).
Whether it had a more formal ending, and if so, what it was, we do not know.

## Kings

We have already seen some ways the Vikings regarded their kings. Adam of Bremen
reported that Swedish kings were of ancient race and had powers limited by the people,
so they enjoy equality at home (above, p. 43); the same applies, at least in principle, to
kings of other Viking nations. The word 'king', Old Norse *konungr*, is derived – at least
by some etymologists – from the word related to English 'kin'. So, a king is a man of
royal family, and the word need not imply rule of a country or people. Heroic verse
stresses the great king's power of command, the bonds that tie him to a loyal retinue, his
courage, initiative and preferably success in warfare. Also, though less vigorously, his
power to protect his people, to keep the laws inviolate, to secure the sanctuaries of the
gods. In these latter respects he could easily come at odds with his people, as represented
by the great free-farmers of a region. His desire to secure control might intrude on
landholders' traditional rights, and his championship of a particular religion (such as
the foreign import, Christianity) be seen as a disguised attempt to change social and
economic patterns that had existed for centuries. Certainly much Viking Age history of
Norway (where we know more than of Sweden or Denmark) could be interpreted as a
record of such conflicts.

## In praise of King Cnut

Here is a typical praise-poem written by an Icelandic skald, this time to the Danish king
Knut who became king of England and is better known to modern English historians as
Cnut and to ordinary Englishmen as Canute. The poet is Óttarr *svarti*, Ottar the Black,
an Icelander who had travelled the courts of Scandinavian kings, including those of St

Olaf of Norway and Olaf Eiriksson of Sweden. The poem is called *Knútsdrápa*, and is preserved in a composite thirteenth-century work known as *Knýtlinga saga*, 'The saga of the descendants of Knut' (though of which Knut is less clear). *Drápa* is the technical name for the more formal type of skaldic praise-poem consisting of several stanzas and with a refrain or commonly more than one. It is thought that most of this poem survives, though it is short for a *drápa* composed to honour a mighty king.

† After the death of King Svein the Danish leaders held on to the realm in England they had conquered. Fighting broke out again because as soon as King Svein was dead, Æthelred [the Unready] returned to the country and with the assistance of St Olaf took control of his kingdom, as is told in Olaf's biography in the words of the poet Ottar the Black. †

> Landward, you brought back to his land
> Æthelred, and gave him his realm.
> That close friend of warriors, strengthened
> In power, had there your help.
> Harsh was the strife when you brought
> Edmund's kinsman to his heritage.
> Of old that king of noble race
> Had ruled the region there.

[This is a verse from a poem called *Höfuðlausn*, 'Head-ransom' that Ottar composed to save his life when he had committed an offence of tact; he had made up a love-poem about Astrid, daughter of the Swedish king, who was married to Olaf Haraldsson of Norway.]

. . .

† Knut, King Svein Forkbeard's son, was ten years old when his father died. In Denmark he was chosen king over all the Danish dominions, for his brother Harald was dead. The Danish leaders who were settled in England and held land that King Svein had conquered sent a request to Denmark for King Knut to bring an army of Danes west to England to support them . . . King Knut brought his army west to England, and a powerful force he had. This is what Ottar the Black says in his *Knútsdrápa*. †

> Ship-destroyer, while not of age
> You shoved your ships to sea.
> No forward-thrusting warrior
> Left home younger than you.
> Leader of battles, you fitted out ships
> With armour, put yourself in perils.
> In fierce mood, Knut, you carried
> Bloody shields over land.

† And he says further: †

> Scornful of flight, men of Jutland
> Followed you overseas.
> The free-handed sail-deer's commander
> Armed the eager men of Skåne.
> The sail billowed above you, king.
> You veered all the ships
> West across the ocean.
> In this action your fame was made.
>
> . . .

† And as soon as Knut reached England he went ashore, harrying the countryside, killing the people and burning all the farms. This is what Ottar the Black says: †

> Mighty prince, you bore the shield
> Of battle. It gladdened you.
> No great delight, I think,
> You took in quiet, king.
> In that foray the prince of Jutes
> Slew Edgar's race.
> Son of kings, you beat them down.
> Steadfast you are called.

† And he added: †

> Before you, young as you were,
> You burned men's farms.
> You often made the farmers
> Sound the alarm for the destroyer of houses.
>
> . . .

† King Knut's first English battle was in Lincolnshire, and there was a great slaughter. Thereafter he attacked Hemingborough and killed many people there. This is what Ottar says: †

> Savage king, you waged war
> In green Lindsey.
> There the Vikings used
> Whatever strength they needed.
> Crusher of the Swedes, in your wrath
> You made Englishmen suffer
> In broad Hemingborough
> West of the River Ouse.

† After that he fought great battles in Northumberland, by the River Tees. He killed a great force there, and part of it fled and men lost their lives in a

region where there were fens and drains. Then King Knut turned his army further south and wherever he went he took the country under his control. †

. . .

† After King Æthelred's death his sons by Queen Emma were chosen as kings. The oldest was Edmund the Strong [Edmund Ironside], the second was Edgar, the third Edwig and the fourth Edward the Good [Edward the Confessor]. Now King Edmund called up an army and advanced against King Knut, and they came together at a place called Sherston, and that was the most notable battle there had ever been up to then. There was immense slaughter on both sides. King Edmund rode through the middle of the Danish force, getting so near to King Knut his stepfather [Knut had married Emma, Æthelred's widow] that he reached him with a slash of his sword. King Knut thrust his shield out over the neck of his mount, and the blow hit the shield a little below the grip. It was such a hefty stroke that the shield was split in two, and the horse chopped asunder at the shoulders, in front of the saddle. Thereupon the Danes came at King Edmund so fiercely that he turned back to his men, but he had already killed many Danes and the king had little or no hurt. But when the king had ridden out beyond all his army his men assumed he must have been killed since they couldn't see him anywhere. So a flight broke out in the army. Some saw that the king was riding away from the Danes, and all who saw it broke into flight. The king shouted loudly, telling his army to turn back and fight, but nobody claimed to have heard it. Then all the army ran off, and there was the most almighty slaughter, and the Danes chased the fleeing remnant right till nightfall. As Ottar the Black says: †

> Young fighting prince, you cut down
> The English close by Tees.
> Its deep channel covered
> The bodies of the Northumbrian dead.
> Urging on to battle, you broke into
> The sleep of the black raven to the south.
> Svein's bold son
> Forced the attack at Sherston.

. . .

† King Knut fought a second battle at a walled town called Brentford. Again there was a fierce fight; Knut won and the sons of Æthelred fled and lost many men, and the Danes broke into the town. As Ottar the Black says. †

> Breaker of shield's peace, you took
> Frisian lives, I think.
> You destroyed Brentford

> With its peopled houses.
> Edmund's noble kin
> Suffered under you.
> His men the Danish army speared.
> You hunted those who fled.

† King Knut fought a third battle against Æthelred's sons at the place called Ashingdon. Again there was a mighty fight. It lies to the north of the Danish Forest. Thus says Ottar: †

> Mighty king, beneath your shield
> You toiled in battle
> At Ashingdon. The heron of blood
> Had dark-red meats.
> With your sword, prince,
> You won a goodly name.
> North of nearby Danaskogar
> The slaughter gladdened your men.

† King Knut fought his fourth battle against Edmund and his brothers at Norwich. Again there was a great fight and a lot of men killed. King Knut won and Æthelred's sons fled. As Ottar the Black says: †

> Blithe giver of great gifts.
> You made mailcoats red at Norwich.
> Not until your death
> Will your valour fail.
>
> . . .

† Out in the river Thames there was a great fort built, and a defensive garrison established in it so that no armed fleet could come up the river. King Knut sailed straight up the river and at the fort, attacking it; and the Englishmen called up a fleet from London and elsewhere along the estuary. They opened battle against the Danes. As Ottar the Black says: †

> The day went well when you fought
> The tree of armour. Elm-bow sang loud.
> The sword dared not be blunt
> When you attacked the fort.
> No mean battle you won
> By Thames bank,
> Controller of the leaping sea-horse.
> The wolf's fangs know that.

In its content this is a typical skaldic poem of praise to a warrior king, enumerating his battles and defining him also as generous, a leader who could rely on his retainers' loyalty. How closely it confirms Snorri Sturluson's assessment (p. 17 above) that it must contain truth since nobody would dare to tell public lies in a poem like this, is quite another matter. Luckily the historical facts can be checked against the *Anglo-Saxon Chronicle's* account of these years. This chronicler does not go out of his way to praise the English resistance to Danish take-over.

According to his version, Knut was already in England when his father Svein died. Of the way he treated the men of Lincolnshire, the *Chronicle* says:

[1014] When Swegen (Svein) was dead, Cnut stayed with his army at Gainsborough until Easter. And he and the men of Lindsey came to an agreement that they should supply him with horses, and then they should all go out together and plunder. Then King Æthelred and his whole army came there to Lindsey before they were ready, and attacked and burned and killed every man they could get at. At this Cnut put out with all his ships, and so the miserable people were let down by him. And he turned south till he reached Sandwich, and put ashore there all the hostages his father had been given, and cut off their hands, ears and noses.

Of the battles of Sherston and Brentford it reports:

[1016] And he [Edmund] fought a second battle after Midsummer at Sherston and there was great slaughter on both sides, and the armies went their own ways from the fight of their own accord ... And then for the third time he gathered his army and went to London and relieved the garrison and dispersed the Viking army to its ships. Then two days afterwards the king crossed over at Brentford, and fought against the army and put it to flight. And there a large number of the English drowned through their own lack of care – they had gone ahead of the main army to gather in plunder. After that the king turned back to Wessex and collected his levies. At that the Viking army went straightway to London and besieged the city, and attacked it in force by sea and by land, but Almighty God saved it.

Of the battle of Ashingdon and its consequences the Chronicle says:

[1016] When the king heard that the Viking army had come inland, he collected all the English forces for the fifth time and pursued them. And he overtook them in Essex, at the hill called *Assandun* and there they clashed together fiercely. Then Ealdorman Eadric [a notorious English turncoat, above, p. 146] did as he had so often done before, he started to run off along with the *Magonsæte* [the men of Herefordshire] and so abandoned his king and lord and all the people. And there Cnut had the victory, and with it he gained control of all Anglia. And there was killed Bishop Eadnoth and Abbot Wulfsige and Ealdorman Ælfric and Ealdorman Godwine, and Ulfcytel of East Anglia, and Æthelward, son of Ealdorman Æthelsige, and all the best men of England.

But this is not the end of the story.

After this battle Cnut turned inland to Gloucester with his army since he had learned that King Edmund was there. Then Ealdorman Eadric and the members of the council who were assembled there advised the kings to come to terms. Hostages were exchanged. And the kings met at Alney, and there formalised their friendship with pledges and oaths. They arranged a payment to the Danish army, and then separated on these terms. And King Edmund took Wessex and Cnut Mercia.

## A court poet tells a Norwegian king some home-truths

This poem declaimed before a Norwegian king is completely different in tone and content from *Knútsdrápa*. A Scandinavian king did not have absolute power. He was constrained by the law which he must both uphold and obey. The free farmers of the individual regions were wealthy, powerful and often firm in their traditional outlook, and they could and sometimes did take an independent line and oppose a king by force if they disliked his policies.

Snorri Sturluson tells this story of the eleventh-century Norwegian king Magnus. Magnus was the son of (St) Olaf Haraldsson who had tried to bring Christianity forcefully to Norway; this caused such uproar that he was obliged to flee the country, and was killed in battle at Stiklestad, near Trondheim, in 1030 trying to regain his throne. When he became king, Magnus began avenging himself on his father's enemies (as Kalf of Egge), and stealing the ancestral property of those who had died in the struggle against him (as Hrut of Vigg and Thorgeir of Kvistad). This led to serious trouble for the king, and his loyal retainers used the court poet, the Icelander Sigvat Thordarson, to give him some unpalatable advice; a court poet, who to some degree stood outside the common group of king's men, was not infrequently used for this duty (see above, p. 20). Sigvat fitted his advice into poetic form, and the result is the *Bersöglisvísur*, 'The plain-speaking verses'.

There are variant versions of the prose in the various thirteenth-century histories, and indeed different texts preserve different selections of Sigvat's verses. For a short discussion of the point see R. G. Poole, *Viking poems on war and peace* (Toronto, 1991), pp. 8–10.

I do not attempt the form of Sigvat's verses, which are in the complex *dróttkvætt*. Far from being plain-speaking the verses use difficult language and interlaced sentence structures. Yet when the poet wants to get a clear message across he uses simple speech order: the sentence 'My lord lays hands on the family lands of his servants' (v. 9 below) is in prose order though it has the rhymes, rhythms and alliteration of verse, *Minn dróttinn leggr sína eign á óðöl þegna*.

Since my purpose is to give the content of the verses, I render them here virtually in prose. Sigvat begins by declaring his personal loyalty to Magnus. Then he adduces the examples of earlier great kings of Norway in announcing and holding to the law that is promised to the freemen. This is the approved royal response to his election by his subjects. If the king fails in it, the freemen are relieved of their duty to acknowledge him as king. Finally there is the typical Norwegian stress on their *óðöl*, the inherited lands which belong to a family and are inalienable.

Snorri takes up the story.

† King Magnus seized hold of Vigg (which Hrut had owned) and Kvistad (which Thorgeir had owned); also Egge and all the property Kalf had left behind there. To the royal estates he added many other great properties that had been held by men who had fallen in the [rebel] yeoman army at Stiklestad. Further, he handed out severe punishments to many of the men who had opposed King Olaf in that battle. Some he expelled from the country; of others he confiscated much of the property; of others again he slaughtered the livestock. The free farmers began to mutiny, saying one to another, 'What does this king think he's doing, breaking our laws that King Hakon the Good instituted? Doesn't he realize we have always refused to tolerate encroachment on our rights? He seems to have the same temperament as his father and the other great men we put to death when we couldn't stand their arrogance and contempt for the law any longer.' This murmuring was widespread in the land.

The men of Sogn had gathered in arms, and they made it clear that if King Magnus went there they would meet him with force. At this time Magnus was in Hordaland. He had been there a long time with a great army and it looked as if he intended to march north to Sogn. The king's friends came to know of this. Twelve of them met together and made an agreement to draw lots to decide which of them should tell the king of this grumbling. As things happened the lot fell to the court poet Sigvat.

Sigvat composed a poem, a *flokkr*. It is called 'The plain-speaking verses'. It begins by saying that they thought the king was hesitating too long in opposing the free farmers who were threatening armed revolt against him. He said: †

> I'm told Sigvat restrained
> His bold prince from testing the men
> Of Sogn in a battle of great armies.
> If it comes to fighting, I'll be there.
> Let's get on our armour
> And valorously defend our king
> And his land with our swords.
> How long till that meeting?

† In the same ode are these verses: †

> Hakon who fell at Fitje
> Was called the most noble of men.
> He was a bulwark against the rapine
> Of evildoers. Men loved him.
> Thereafter the nation held firmly
> To the laws of the gracious foster-son
> Of Athelstan. And the free farmers
> Are loath to give up remembered benefits.

[Hakon the Good, youngest son of the great tyrant Harald Finehair, took the kingship of Norway from his unpopular brother Eirik Bloodaxe in the 930s. He had been brought up at the court of Athelstan of England, and so is nicknamed his foster-son (above, pp. 31–4). He was brought up in a Christian context and traditionally tried to introduce that religion to Norway, with limited success. In thirteenth-century sources he is credited with founding the laws of the Gulathing and the Frostathing, two of the regional assemblies of medieval Norway (see above, p. 34)]

> I think the freemen and nobles
> Made wise decisions,
> For the two Olafs had respect
> For the possessions of men.
> Harald's most trusted heir
> And Tryggvi's son held secure
> The leek-straight laws
> The people received from these namesakes.

[In theory the people of the Norwegian regions elected their kings. Two of the greatest of Norse kings – obviously sound elections, thinks Sigvat – were both called Olaf: Haraldsson and Tryggvason.]

> You must not, my king, be angry
> At your advisers' blunt speech.
> The licence you give us to speak
> Will lead to your honour, prince.
> Unless the men of this nation lie,
> The freemen say they have worse laws,
> Other laws than you promised men
> Some time back in Ulfasund.
>
> Who urges you, prince
> Firm in your hatreds,
> To retreat from your promises?
> Often you test sharp steel.
> To prosper a king of a nation
> Must hold true to his word.
> It can never be worthy of you
> To break your vows, my war-leader.
>
> Who urges you, battle-joiner,
> To slaughter your servants' cattle?
> Tyranny it is for a prince
> To do that within his own land.
> No-one before can have advised
> A young prince to act so.
> Your men grow weary of this plundering.
> Your army grows restless, king.

Destroyer of thieves,
Take heed of the rumour
That now is current here.
Hold back your hand in caution.
A true friend he is
Who offers warning. Listen,
Gladdener of the raven,
To what your landmen seek.

Dangerous is the threat.
I hear that all your tried men
Will move against their prince.
Take action against it in time.
Terrible it is when your lieges
Sink their heads,
Hide their faces in their cloaks.
Silence falls on your supporters.

One thing there is that all are saying.
'My lord lays hands
On the family lands of his servants.'
The nobles turn their backs on you.
Plunder he will call it who has to
Hand over his heritage
To a king's officers
On some specious pretext.

† After this rebuke the king amended his behaviour. Many others also repeated this warning to the king. So it came about that the king held a conference with his wisest men and they amended their laws. Then Magnus had a legal code written out, one that is still in use in Trøndelag and is called *Grágás*. King Magnus came to have many friends and to be loved by all his people. That is why he was called Magnus the Good. †

## Peace between warring kings

Here is another case of the people controlling their kings. In *Heimskringla* Snorri tells of a peace-treaty arranged between Danish and Norwegian kings because people of both nations were tired of the continuous active hostility between the two lands. The kings in question are Harald Sigurdarson of Norway and Svein Ulfsson, sometimes called after his mother Svein Estridsson, of Denmark. Snorri's source is a small group of verses by an unnamed poet. Whether they were part of a longer poem or were occasional verses is unknown. From their fairly meagre information Snorri builds up this story. It gives some idea of the realities of life in the Viking Age which diplomacy had to respond to, of the limitation of royal control by the people's will, of an oral society where agreements were sealed by oath and confirmed by witnesses.

&dagger; That winter ambassadors and messages passed between Norway and Denmark. Bound up with this was the fact that both sides, Norwegians and Danes alike, wanted to conclude an agreement and peace treaty together. They requested their kings to accept, and the exchanges looked to favour a settlement. In the end what happened was that a peace conference was arranged, to be attended by Kings Harald and Svein at the Götaälv River. When spring came each of the kings called up a huge army and a fleet for this expedition. The poet speaks in a *flokkr* of the expeditions of these two kings. &dagger;

> With his longships' stems the fierce king,
> The raven-feeder encircles his land,
> Encloses it from Øresund in the north.
> He spurned the harbour bar with his ships' heels.
> Prows, glittering with gold,
> Cut keenly through the crashing sea
> West of Halland, transporting the troops,
> The washboards shiver.

> Firm in his word, Harald often
> Walls round his land with ships.
> Svein cuts through the island sound
> To meet the other king.
> No mean force of the Danish people
> Has that king, eager for fame, called out.
> With his ships the raven-pleaser
> Blockades all the southern bays.

&dagger; It says here that these kings kept the appointment made between them. Both came to their land-boundary, as it says here: &dagger;

> South you sped, bold prince,
> As all the Danes demanded of you.
> No less is the likelihood
> Of the planned conference.
> Svein journeys north
> Close to the land-boundary.
> To a meeting with Harald.
> The wind blew fiercely off the broad lands.

&dagger; And when the kings met, men began a discussion of terms of settlement between the kings, and as soon as this matter was raised, many of the people complained of the losses they had incurred from the raiding, thieving and killing. This went on for a long time, as it says here: &dagger;

> When the fighting-men meet,
> Sturdy farmers from both sides

Complain at the tops of their voices,
Words that raise great anger.
Those who never cease
From quarrelling are slow
To accept arbitration.
The princes grow in arrogance.

If there's to be a settlement
There's peril in the kings' wild anger.
Men skilled in arbitration
Weigh up both sides of the case.
It's important to tell both kings
Just what is wanted here.
If men part worse friends
Selfishness is to blame.

† Then the noblest and the most experienced put in their oars. A settlement
was concluded between the kings on the following terms. Harald should
have Norway, Svein Denmark up to the ancient land-boundary between
Norway and Denmark. Neither side should pay reparations to the other.
Cross-border raiding that had been endemic should cease, and each
should keep the advantages that had fallen to them. This agreement
should last as long as they both were kings. The settlement was formally
bound by oaths. Then the kings exchanged sureties, as it says here: †

This I heard: Harald and Svein
Each readily gave the other
Pledges against attack.
That is God's doing.
Let them keep their oaths
And the full terms of peace
So neither side breaks it.
Witnesses saw the peace concluded.

† King Harald took his army back north to Norway, and King Svein went
south to Denmark. †

The mention of the 'ancient land-boundary' between Norway and Denmark shows that
at this date the Swedish coasts opposite Sjælland and North Jutland were part of the
Danish king's dominions, which spread north to the Göta River. Norway extended
further south than it now does, including the present Swedish province of Bohuslän.

## King and retainer

Two rune-stones, found close to the great fortifications that surround the Viking Age
trading-town of Hedeby (Haddeby) in South Jutland, now North Germany, commemorate a king and his retainers.

1. A plain granite slab has four lines of text on its face, and completes the epitaph with a line on one side.

> King Svein set | a stone in memory of Skardi | his retainer who had | travelled in the west and now | met his death at Hedeby.

2. A more carefully worked granite pillar with its inscription divided between its two faces. There are three straightforward lines of text on the front. The back has three clear lines but also a section harder to make out because it is written in 'same-stave runes' (that is, several runes combined on a single stave).

A. Thorulf raised this stone, | Svein's retainer, in memory of | Erik his comrade who met his
B. death when fighting-man | besieged Hedeby | and he was a ship's captain, a man [this is the bit in 'same-stave runes'] | very good.

Some of the words used in these inscriptions are technical ones that require care in translating. The word rendered 'retainer' is in each case **himþigi**, literally 'one receiving a home', so the king's man is seen as being looked after, as a beneficiary of the king who could therefore trust him to be faithful – a contractual relationship between lord and man. The word 'fighting-men' is **trekiar**, in normalised spelling *drengiar*, a notoriously difficult word to render because it was used in several senses on the rune-stones. The men who besieged Hedeby were presumably out on active service with King Svein, free-men who held some duty towards or office from the king: *drengiar* is then used in a technical sense. But Erik is also called **tregʀ harþa kuþr**, *drengr harða góðr*, where the sense may be looser, 'jolly good chap', though personally I think it unlikely. Even the word *góðr* is ambiguous since it may refer to Erik's qualities or his status – a man of good family perhaps. The word I have translated 'comrade' is **filaga**, a form of *félagi* whose primary meaning was 'partner', literally 'one who put money' into an enterprise. So Thorulf and Erik may have been in business together. Or the word here may be used in a more general sense, 'comrade-in-arms', 'member of the same unit'.

The king's action in setting up the memorial stone to someone killed in his service may be his acknowledgement that he accepted responsibility for the death, and so for paying compensation to the dead man's kin: something of a legal declaration. Similarly, a man who erected a memorial to his business partner may be informing the public that he took responsibility henceforth for the joint enterprise: cf. the Berezan' stone (above, p. 97).

## The accomplishments of a gentleman

Including this piece involves a bit of sleight of hand. It apparently refers to the early twelfth century, just after the end of the Viking Age. I add it here because it defines an aspect of late Viking culture that is worth recording. Vikings were not ignorant ruffians; they had their distinctive cultural activities which an educated man was expected to take part in. Here, Rognvald Kali, later to be a great earl of the Orkneys, defines the *íþróttir*, 'accomplishments, skills', that he commands. The passage is taken from a latish source, the early-thirteenth-century *Orkneyingasaga*. 'History of the men of Orkney'. However, the textual tradition of the verse is confused; its second half is elsewhere ascribed to King Harald *harðráði*, so the authenticity of this tale cannot be assured.

> † Kol lived on his farms in Agder [in southern Norway] as was written earlier, and was the shrewdest of men. He never went back to the Orkneys. His son Kali grew up there [in Agder], and was a most promising lad, of medium height, well-developed, as strong of limb as any man, light chestnut of hair. He was a man of many friends, more accomplished than practically anyone else. He made up this verse: †

> > Artful I am at chess;
> > Nine special skills I own;
> > Not likely to forget runes;
> > Often at book or smithy;
> > I know the art of skiing.
> > I shoot and row well enough;
> > Two more I keep in mind;
> > Strike the harp, indite a verse.

In *his* verse Harald *harðráði* was more modest and his skills were more practical. The first half reads:

> > Eight arts I know;
> > To brew the drink of Ygg;
> > I'm fast and skilled to horse
> > Sometimes engage in swimming.

Ygg is a name for Odin, so his drink is the mead of poetry; thus Harald's verse boasts first of his skill at versifying.

That a knowledge of runes was a proper accomplishment for a gentleman is also implied on a rune-stone at Ågersta, Uppland, Sweden. This granite boulder has a most elaborate pair of intertwined serpents on which the runes are cut. One of the interpretations of its text (of course, disputed by some) is:

> Vidhugsi had this stone put up in memory of his good father Særæif. He lived | in Ågersta.

> > Here will stand the stone between the townships
> > Let the man who is skilled in runes
> > Read the letters that Balli cut.

If this interpretation is correct, the word I have translated 'man' is *drengr*, a status word implying standing and worth.

## Rank, office and condition on rune-stones

As is the case in later epitaphs those on rune-stones give a variety of details about the human condition, and often define the position a man or woman held in society. Here are a few examples from various Viking regions.

1. Tuna, Småland, Sweden: two lines of text cut vertically up the edge of a tall pillar, the whole inscription surmounted by an incised cross. The stone stands close by a Viking Age grave-field.

> Tummi raised this stone in memory of Assur | his brother who was
> ship-mate of King Harald.

The word translated 'ship-mate' is *skipari* which can certainly have that meaning, though at some dates it can mean 'ship's commander'. The Swedish runic corpus hedges its bets here by paraphrasing, 'who served under King Harald as a fighting seaman'. There are a number of possible candidates for Assur's royal ship-mate. The most likely is the Anglo-Danish Harald Harefoot, son of Cnut the Great, who for a short time controlled the Danish territories in England.

2. Sävsjö, Småland, Sweden: a fragment of a rune-stone, its complete text known from an early drawing. It stood by the roadside near a bridge. The runes are cut on a snake-like band that follows the edge of the boulder's face.

> Tofa raised this stone after her father Vrai, marshal to Hakon | earl.

The word for 'marshal' is *stallari*. Both these words had an original meaning 'stable-man', and both came to designate a high officer of the court. There are several known Hakons who qualify for the title *jarl*, 'earl'. The current favourite for Vrai's patron is a nephew of Cnut the Great who was drowned in the Pentland Firth in 1029. He was related to the great earls of Lade, near Trondheim, Norway. Vrai's link with western enterprise is shown in a second rune-stone from this Swedish parish. Vrai put it up. It reads:

> Vrai set this stone in memory of Gunni his brother. He met | his death in
> England.

3. Egå, Jutland, Denmark: a granite boulder with, following the edge of the face, two lines of text and a few extra runes squeezed into the centre field. It was dug out from a mound or hill near a bridge.

> Alfkel and his sons raised this stone in memory of | their kinsman Manni
> who was bailiff to Ketil the | Norwegian.

Again a technical word is hard to translate. I have used 'bailiff' for *landhirðir*, 'guard (literally perhaps shepherd) of the land'.

4. Bro, Uppland, Sweden: a large granite slab with an elaborately arranged inscription on two snake-like bands, set round an ornamental cross. The stone was taken from the wall of the church, but originally marked a 'bridge', which in this terrain probably means a raised causeway across marsh-land.

> Ginnlaug, Holmgæir's daughter, Sigraud and Gaut's sister, had this
> bridge made and this stone set up after her husband Assur, | son of Earl
> Hakon. He was guard against Vikings with Gæitir. Now may God help his
> spirit and soul.

Assur's title was *vikinga vörðr*, literally 'watchmen of Vikings'. In early Norse the word
*víkingr* did not necessarily have our specific sense of 'Viking', but tended to be a more
general pejorative word, 'robber, pirate'. Assur was presumably leader of a local defence
force that could be called up against any raider (perhaps 'shipborne raider') who
attacked the settlement.

5. Bjudby, Södermanland, Sweden: an elaborate stone with a large central cross
surrounded by a serpent on which the first part of the text is cut. The rest is scattered
round the face and one side.

> Thorstæin and Øystein and Nattfari raised the stone in memory of Finnvid
> and Olæif, Thorkel, their brothers. | All | Viking's sons were | men born to
> land. They had the stone put up. | Stæinkel cut the runes.

The central part of the epitaph, which is in a sort of rough verse, contains the word
*landbornir* (or *lændbornir*), translated literally above, but presumably a status or rank
term, 'men whose birth entitles them to hold land'.

6. Hørning, Jutland, Denmark: a granite boulder with a well laid-out inscription
surrounding a central cross. The rune-stone stood by a river crossing.

> Toki the smith raised the stone in memory of | Thorgisl Gudmund's son
> who gave him | gold and his freedom.

If this is correctly translated – and the version given here has been disputed – this comes
from a different social group, that of the freed slave. Toki expressed his gratitude to his
former master who had given him capital for his job as smith (though the word may
have the rather wider meaning 'craftsman') as well as setting him free. The milieu is
Christian.

7. Dynna, Hadeland, Norway: a very tall pillar-slab of a sandstone which must have
been brought from some distance. It has a group of line-carvings on the face (including
an Epiphany scene of the three magi, star and angel), and the runic inscription carved
along one edge. It was once set up over a mound at the farm at Nordre Dynna.

> Gunnvor, Thrydrik's daughter, made the bridge in memory of her daugh-
> ter Astrid. She was the handiest maid in Hadeland.

This is obviously a sumptuous monument put up by a woman of wealth and authority.
The adjective used of the dead girl, *hannarst*, is literally translated above. It presumably
means 'most skilled'. It has been suggested that the monument's decoration derives
from or represents woven or embroidered designs; so might indicate in what way Astrid
was 'most dexterous'. For a fascinating commentary on this and related material, Dag
Strömbäck, *The epiphany in runic art. The Dynna and Sika stones* (London, 1970).

8. Stenkumla, Gotland: a fragmentary runic memorial stone, details of which are uncertain, though some bits can be supplied from earlier drawings.

> Botmund and Botræif and Gunnv[ar, they raised this stone ... ] and he
> lived in the south, engaged in the fur-trade, and he died at Ulfshale ...

The epitaph actually says that the man commemorated on the stone **sunarla sat miþ skinum**, literally, he 'sat in the south with skins'. Gotland had a thriving trade in furs in Viking times and later, sending wares to Continental Europe, perhaps through Hedeby.

9. Sigtuna, Uppland, Sweden: a standing stone re-used in the foundations of the thirteenth-century Dominican monastery. Its original site is unknown.

> The brethren of the Frisian guild had this stone erected in memory of
> Thorkel their guild-brother. God help his soul. Thorbiorn cut ⟨the runes⟩.

This is one of four guild-memorials from late Viking Age Sweden. The members listed here and on a second, fragmentary, stone at Sigtuna, are called the *Frisa gildar*, presumably Swedish merchants trading into Frisia who formed a society for mutual protection and help. The two other guild-stones are from Bjälbo and Törnevalla, both in Östergötland. They give no names for their guilds but probably also indicate mercantile associations.

## Friendship

Friendship was a social bond like kinship. It was seen less as a sentimental tie, more as a contractual one, bringing advantage to both sides and sustained by visits, gift-exchange and acts of support. It involved clear obligations as well as benefits. A man owed no duty to anyone who was not loyal to him. The distinction between true amity and false was a topic the poet of *Hávamál* kept returning to. Here are a few of his pronouncements, some of them sounding to us cynical comments on friendship.

> To a false friend's house it's a wasted journey
> Even if he lives just by the road.
> But to a good friend's home all paths are worth walking
> However far off he's gone.
>
> ...
>
> I never met so generous a man, so free in entertaining
> Who did not delight in some return.
> No man so liberal of his wealth
> That receiving was unwelcome to him.
>
> ...
>
> Friends should please one another, giving weapons and clothing.
> Experience makes that clear.

In giving and taking friendship endures
If it succeeds in turning out well.

To his friend a man should be a friend,
Repaying gifts with gifts.
Men should repay laughter with laughter
And deceit with deceit.

To his friend a man should be a friend,
And to his friend's friend.
But no man should be friend
Of his foe's friend.

Know this. If you have a friend you trust freely
And want some benefit from him,
Open your heart to him, exchange gifts,
Go to see him often.

But if you have another you hardly trust,
Yet still want some benefit from him,
Speak sweetly to him however falsely you think.
Repay one lie with another.

Moreover, if you have one you hardly trust
And you suspect his intentions,
Smile at him but don't speak your thoughts.
Gifts should be repaid in kind.

I was young once. I walked alone.
Soon I went off my path.
Rich I felt when I found a friend.
Man is man's delight.

. . .

The fir-tree standing on the heath withers;
Neither bark nor leaf can sustain it.
So is it with the man no-one loves.
Why should he go on living?

Hotter than fire love will burn
For five days between false friends.
When the sixth day comes it dies down
And all the friendship fades.

Don't think to give only lavish gifts.
Respect can be cheaply bought.
With half a loaf and a near-empty bottle
I have gained a comrade.

CHAPTER 8

# Law

I have already written (pp. 34–5, above) about the importance of law to the Norsemen and the difficulties of finding legal texts appropriate to the Viking Age. Here are a few passages, mainly from later or overseas sources.

## The introduction of law to Iceland

*Íslendingabók* and *Landnámabók* give related accounts of how the Icelanders accepted a legal code. *Íslendingabók*'s version is succinct, but details are expanded in *Landnámabók*.

1. From *Íslendingabók*:

> When Iceland had been widely settled a Norwegian first brought law into this country from Norway. He was called Ulfliot – so Teit told me – and this was known as Ulfliot's law. He was the father of Gunnar from whom the Diupdal family of Eyiafiord are descended. In the main the laws were worded according to those of the Gulathing [in western Norway] or as Thorleif the Wise Horda-Karason advised in so far as laws had to be added, removed or amended.

2. From *Landnámabók*, H:

> † When Ulfliot was sixty he went to Norway and stayed there three years. There he and his uncle Thorleif the Wise established the law that has since been called Ulfliot's law. And when he came back to Iceland the Althingi was established, and ever after there has been a single law in this land.

At the beginning of that heathen law it says that men should not have ships with animal figure-heads at sea, but if they had them, they should unship them before they came in sight of land, and not sail near the land with figure-heads with jaws gaping wide or grinning muzzles, which would terrify the 'land-spirits'.

A ring of at least two ounces [of silver] should lie on the altar of every main temple. Every 'priest' should have such a ring on his arm at all legal moots that he had to inaugurate himself. First it must be reddened in the blood of the cattle that he himself had sacrificed there. Every man who needed to take part in pleading before the court must first swear an oath on the ring and give the names of two or more witnesses. 'I name witnesses to this,' he must say, 'that I swear my oath on the ring, an oath at law. So help me Freyr and Niord and the Allpowerful God that I shall pursue this case – or defend it – or bear witness – or give verdict – or pass judgment, as I know to be most just and most true and most in accordance with the law. And all matters that come under my jurisdiction I shall determine lawfully as long as I am at this meeting.'

Then the land was divided into Quarters. And there should be three legal assemblies for each Quarter, and three main temples in each *thing*-district. Men were elected for their wisdom and righteousness to keep the temples. They had the duty of naming judges at the assemblies and ordering the legal cases. So they were called *goðar*. Everyone must pay a temple tax as now they pay tithes to the church. †

The word *goði* (plural *goðar*) is an important one in Icelandic social history, but it is hard to translate. The etymological sense is 'priest', and this passage shows them with priestly functions. But they also came to have temporal power, and indeed in much of the saga literature of Iceland it is the temporal rather than spiritual power of the *goði* that is apparent. The word occurs outside Iceland too, but rarely. Important is an example from a Danish rune-stone, that of Glavendrup in Fyn – and it would be even more important if we were clearer about the meaning of some bits of its inscription. It is a memorial stone to a man Alli, and formed part of an impressive stone setting which ended in a natural mound whereon the stone stood. Alli was not under it, nor, as far as we can tell, nearby. The Glavendrup rune-stone is a natural granite boulder, with vertical lines of runes inscribed upon it. They read:

A. Ragnhild se | t this stone in memory of | Alli godi of the Saulvir | the honourable thegn of the *vía*-men |
B. Alli's sons made | these monuments in memory of their father | and his wife in memory of | her husband, and Soti cut these run | es in memory of his lord. | May Thor bless these runes.
C. May he become a *rati* who this stone | damages or hauls away for [a monument to] someone else.

Alli was a *þegn*, 'thegn', which seems a worldly word of rank, status or office, yet he is a *goði*, 'priest' of ? a people called the Sølvir, and he is connected with a *lið*, which usually means a warlike band, but here it is a *vía-lið*, and *vía* ought to mean 'of the sanctuaries'. There is a further sign of religion in the appeal to Thor to *vígia*, 'hallow', the runes; not to mention the sinister curse upon anyone who tries to steal the memorial stone for reuse to commemorate someone else – he shall become a *rati*, which seems to mean 'pervert'.

## Legal practice in early Iceland

Even in early times, as Ari Thorgilsson has told us, Iceland had a sophisticated legal system based on the participation of its free farmers. A legal meeting was called a *thing*, and the great common moot for the whole of Iceland was the *Althingi*, held each summer at Thingvellir, 'Thing-plains', a watered plain bounded by a great rock face some 50 km north-east of Reykjavík (British place-names such as Dingwall in Cromarty, Thingwall in Cheshire and Tynwald in the Isle of Man have the same meaning, and are lexical borrowings from Norse). At the Althingi the free farmers met to record, form and administer the common law of Iceland, civil, criminal and administrative. Its presiding officer was the *lögsögumaðr*, 'lawspeaker', an elected official who served for a number of years.

Here is Ari's record of two problems to come before the Althingi, one administrative and one criminal, and how the Icelandic people solved them.

**About the calendar**.
It was when the most learned men in Iceland were counting 364 days in two half-years – that makes 52 weeks, or twelve 30-day months and four days over – it was then they realised that summer was moving back towards spring. But there was nobody who could tell them that this was because there was one day more than tallied with the whole weeks of a year, and that was the reason.

There was a man called Thorstein surt. He came from Breidafiord and was the son of Hallstein, son of Thorolf Mostrarskegg who was one of the original settlers, and of Osk, daughter of Thorstein the Red. He had a dream. He was at the Law-rock [where formal speeches were made at the Althingi] when the Althingi was well attended, and was standing there awake while everyone else was fast asleep. Then he fell asleep when everyone else woke up. Osvif Helgason, maternal grandfather of Gellir Thorkelsson, interpreted the dream in this way: that everyone would stay silent while Thorstein was speaking at the Law-rock, and when he came to an end everyone would applaud what he said. And both these were very clever men.

Then when men assembled for the *thing* Thorstein took his place at the Law-rock and put forward the plan that they should add an extra week every seventh summer and see how that worked. And it was just as Osvif had interpreted the dream. Everyone was impressed with the idea, and it was immediately put into the law on the advice of Thorkel mani and other learned men.

**About the division of Iceland into Quarters**.

There arose a great legal dispute at the *thing* between two people, Thord gellir, son of Olaf feilan from Breidafiord, and Odd, known as Tungu-Odd, who came from Borgarfiord. Odd's son Thorvald had taken part with Hœnsa-Thorir in the burning of Thorkel Blundketil's son in Ornolfsdal. Thord gellir was the prosecutor in the case because Herstein, the son of Thorkel Blund-Ketilsson, was married to his niece Thorunn ... The defendants were prosecuted at the *thing* held at the place which was later called Thingnes in Borgarfiord, because it was then the legal requirement that homicide cases should be pursued at the *thing* that was nearest the spot where the killing occurred. But the two sides fought there, and the *thing* could not be conducted according to law. There Thorolf 'fox', brother of Alf of the Dales, was killed; he was in Thord gellir's party.

Later they brought the case before the Althingi, and there the two sides fought again. In this broil men from Odd's party fell: moreover Hœnsa-Thorir was outlawed and later killed, and others too who had taken part in the burning.

Then Thord gellir made a speech about it at the Law-rock pointing out what problems men had if they must go to unfamiliar *things* to bring suits for homicide or injuries done them, and he spoke of what he had had to go through before he could bring this case to law and the various troubles that would arise if no solution could be reached.

Then the land was divided into Quarters, so that there should be three *things* in each where members of the same *thing* could bring their lawsuits; except that in the Northern Quarter there should be four because the northerners were not prepared to accept anything else – those who lived north of Eyiafiord were not willing to attend the thing there, nor those who lived to the west go to Skagafiord. Yet the nomination of judges and the appointments to the legislative council should be the same from that Quarter as from each of the others. And after that the Quarter-*things* were established. This is what the lawspeaker Ulfhedin Gunnarsson told me.

Setting fire to a house and burning a man in it to death was a well-known way of getting rid of an enemy in medieval Iceland. The case involving Hœnsa-Thorir and Thorvald Tungu-Odd's son became the subject of a later saga, *Hœnsa-Þóris saga*, translated into English as 'Hen-thorir' by Gwyn Jones, *Eric the Red and other Icelandic sagas* (Oxford, 1961), pp. 3–38. Curiously, in that saga the man burnt to death is Blund-Ketil, not his son Thorkel; which emphasises the danger of using *Íslendinga sögur* as historical sources.

## Two Viking peace-treaties

1. The *Anglo-Saxon Chronicle* records much of Alfred the Great's struggle against the Viking incomers. Two of the events mentioned are relevant to this passage. The first, in

the year 878, reports how he defeated a Danish force, beseiged it and made it surrender. Thereafter he came to terms with the Danish leader:

> The Viking army gave him [Alfred] hostages and swore great oaths that they would leave his kingdom. They also promised that their king would receive baptism, and they kept their promise too. And three weeks later that king, Guthrum, came to him at Aller (which is near Athelney) with thirty companions chosen from those who were of highest rank in the force. And the king sponsored them in baptism there, and the unbinding of the chrism was performed at Wedmore. And he stayed with the king for twelve days, and the king honoured him and his comrades with generous gifts of money.

The second relevant entry is for 880:

> In this year the Viking force left Cirencester for East Anglia, and they settled in that land and divided it between them.

The treaty given below prescribes the terms on which Englishmen and Norsemen could work together in neighbouring lands, and produce something of a common market. The treaty survives in two texts, both in the same manuscript, Corpus Christi College, Cambridge, 383, a manuscript notorious for the incompetence of its scribe. The two texts are not identical, and I give here the more complete version. It was probably drawn up after 886 when Alfred took control of London: 'and the whole English people submitted to him save those who were under the Danish yoke.'

> This is the treaty that King Alfred and King Guthrum and the council of all England and the whole people that is in East Anglia have declared and have confirmed with oaths on behalf of themselves and their dependants, both born and unborn, who count on the mercy of God and ourselves.
> 1. About the boundaries [of the two countries]: up the Thames and then up the Lea, along it as far as its source, then in a straight line to Bedford, then up the Ouse to Watling Street.
> 2. If anyone is killed, we account an Englishman and a Dane of exactly equal worth, eight half-marks of pure gold, except for a freeman who lives on leased land and their [? the Danes'] freedmen – they are of equal worth, both at 200 shillings.
> 3. If a king's thegn is accused of manslaughter, if he dare to assert his innocence he must do it with the support of twelve king's thegns. If a man is accused who is of lower rank than a king's thegn, he must clear himself with the support of eleven of his equals and one king's thegn. The same applies to any case that involves more than four mancusses. If he dare not, he must pay three-fold compensation according to assessment.
> 4. Every man is to know his warrantor when buying men, horses and oxen.

5. We all agreed at the time we swore oaths that neither slaves nor freemen could join the Viking forces without leave, any more than a Dane could join ours.

6. Should it happen that through necessity any one of them wants to do business with us or we with one of their men in a matter involving cattle or property, it is to be allowed on this condition, that hostages be given as a pledge of fair dealing and as a clear indication of the fact that no false dealing is intended.

Though this is a document in English it must incorporate thinking appropriate to both English and Scandinavian races, otherwise it could not have been acceptable to both. Certainly some ideas are common. In a proto-literate society much of what we now establish by written documents was done by swearing a statement before witnesses. The witnesses must have appropriate social standing so that their oaths had validity. A man of higher rank also had higher social responsibility than one of lower. His oath would be more highly regarded; but he would also have to produce higher warranties for his innocence if he were accused.

Anglo-Saxon law was in some ways more advanced than modern English (and European). If a man was murdered, the loss to his family was recognised and the culprit must pay compensation to the kin, the man's *wergild*, which in England depended upon his status. Provision 2 of this treaty thus gave security to the mixed Anglo-Danish community of East Anglia as well as the Dane who came among the West Saxons and the West Saxon in the Danelaw – they would have no family near to demand the *wergild*, but this provision makes clear it was legally payable, presumably to the king if the family could not follow up the case. A *wergild* of eight half-marks of gold was probably equivalent to 1200 shillings, the higher assessment of *wergild* for an English freeman. The lower assessment, 200 shillings, applied to both English lease-holder and Danish freedman. The 'mancus' mentioned in provision 3 is a unit of account worth thirty silver pennies.

2. For the year 991 the *Anglo-Saxon Chronicle* (versions CDE) records:

Here Ipswich was attacked and very soon after that Ealdorman Byrhtnoth was killed at Maldon. And in this year it was first suggested that tribute be paid to the Danes because of the great distress they were creating along the sea-coast. At first it was ten thousand pounds. Archbishop Sigeric was the first to advise this course of action.

The treaty given below dates from some time after that. The Anlaf involved was probably Olaf Tryggvason, later king of Norway.

The agreement survives in a late Old English version in MS Corpus Christi College, Cambridge, 383, and in a post-Conquest Latin version in the legal collection known as *Quadripartitus*. Again we must assume that the treaty records views of life acceptable to both Englishmen and Danes: that a man's life could be given a monetary value, fixed by law and dependent on status – his *wergild*; that both societies had slaves whose value in financial terms was much less than that of freemen (perhaps that of a piece of household or farm equipment); that men must accept responsibility for criminal actions of their kin; that it was possible to make, even with an illiterate enemy, a treaty that would cover political and commercial matters, to ensure mutual security.

These are the terms of peace and the conditions which King Æthelred and all his council have agreed on with the Viking army that Anlaf and Iustin and Gudmund Stegitan's son served with.

1. First, that an agreed treaty should exist between King Æthelred and all his people and all the Viking army to whom the king gave money, on the conditions that Archbishop Sigeric and Ealdorman Æthelwerd and Ealdorman Ælfric proposed when they were authorised by the king to buy a peace for those regions where they exercised authority under the king.

2. And if any sea-borne army attacks England we shall have the assistance of all the Viking army, and we shall provide them with food as long as they serve with us. And any of the lands that have an agreement of mutual help with those who attack England shall be treated as enemies by us and by the whole of the Viking army.

3. And every merchant vessel that comes into a harbour-mouth shall have security, even if it is a ship from a community that has no treaty with us, as long as it was not driven in by storms. And even if it is driven in by storm and takes refuge in some treaty port and the crew break into the port, yet they and the goods they bring with them shall have security. And any men covered by this treaty shall have security, both on land and sea, both within the harbour-mouth and without it.

4. If any of Æthelred's subjects covered by this treaty comes into a place outside the treaty and the Viking army comes there, his ship and all his possessions shall have security. If he has dragged his ship ashore or built a shelter or pitched a tent, he and all his goods shall have security there. And if he brings his goods into a building alongside the goods belonging to men outside this treaty, he shall forfeit his goods, but the man himself shall have security and life if he makes himself known. But if that man runs away or fights and will not make himself known, he shall not be compensated for if he is killed.

5. If a man is robbed of his goods and he knows by which ship's company, the skipper shall return the goods, or with four comrades (he himself being the fifth) shall testify that he took the goods lawfully as is agreed on above.

6. If a free Englishman kills a free Dane he must pay compensation of twenty-five pounds (or the culprit must be handed over). And the same applies to a Dane who kills an Englishman. If an Englishman kills a Danish slave he must pay one pound in compensation. And the same applies to a Dane who kills an English slave.

7. If eight men are killed, that amounts to a breach of the treaty whether

it takes place within a town or without. For fewer than eight men full *wergild* must be paid. If the breach of the treaty occurs within a town, the townsfolk themselves must take action and seize the killers, alive or dead, [or] their nearest relatives, head for head. If they are un- willing to do this, the ealdorman must take action. If he is unwilling, then the king. If he is unwilling, the region the ealdorman governs is to be excluded from the treaty.

8. All killing, rapine and damage that was done before this treaty came into force shall be dismissed. No man shall avenge it or seek compensation.

9. Neither we nor they shall receive into the community a slave, thief or enemy of the other.

10. And if a man of our country is charged with stealing cattle or with killing a man, and a Viking and a man of this country bring the charge, then he is not entitled to deny it [but must undergo the ordeal].

11. And if their men kill eight of ours, they shall be declared outlaws both by them and by us, and they will be entitled to no compensation [if they are killed].

12. Twenty-two thousand pounds in gold and silver were paid to the Viking army from England for this treaty.

## From one class to another

Even in the structured society of the Vikings it was possible to move from one class to another, but this had to be recorded formally so that a man or woman's worth in monetary terms could be surely known. There is little information on this coming direct from the Viking Age, but it is possible to use post-Viking legal material – cautiously – to give some idea of the practices of the earlier period. Here are two examples from the thirteenth-century *Frostuþingslög*, the law of the Frostathing which controlled a group of smaller districts in Trøndelag, Norway. They may, according to some legal his- torians, represent earlier practices; indeed the requirement that legal changes be attested by witnesses and accompanied by some formal ceremony (to aid memory) is commonplace in semi-literate societies. Moreover the public ceremony ensures that no arrangements are made in secret, that all who may be affected have opportunity to reveal their approval or disapproval; and that a man's new social status is made known to all.

† On adoption into the family.
It serves as full legitimation if a father brings his child into the family and it is accepted by those who are direct heirs to the man who introduces him. Three measures of ale must be brewed, and a three-year-old ox slaugh- tered, the skin flayed from the right hind-leg of the ox above the knee- joint, and a shoe made of it. The father shall make the child to be

legitimised put his foot into the shoe, and then take his sons who are not yet of age on to his lap, while those sons who are of age shall also put their feet into the shoe. And if he has no direct heir, then those who are closest to him in inheritance shall put on the shoe. And then the child to be legitimised shall be taken to the bosom of the man and woman of the house. Women may bear witness to the child equally with men, as can the shoe they put on, if it be preserved. A thrall-born son shall be brought into the family by whoever has given him his freedom, and it should be the father or the brother who gives it, or whoever it may be who is nearest in line to the inheritance, whether young or old. And consent must be given by those who are nearest in line to the one who wants to bring the man into the family. And the son of a free-born woman should be brought into the family just like the son of a bond-woman. In this way too free-born kinsmen on the father's side should bring a man into the family where there is no father or brother available. †

† On freedom-ale.
If a thrall comes to own land or set up his own farm, he shall give his freedom-ale – each man nine measures [of malt]. He shall slaughter a wether. A free-born man must cut off its head and the thrall's owner shall take his neck-ransom from its neck. If the owner is prepared to let him make his freedom-ale, then the thrall must request him in the presence of two witnesses to let him make his ale and must invite him with five others to the celebration at which he gives his freedom-ale. Otherwise he shall do it anyway, and let the high-seats of the master and his wife lie vacant. And if the master has doubts about whether he made his freedom-ale, the former thrall shall bring forward witnesses who were there and drank the ale, and have the evidence presented at the thing. If their testimony is convincing enough to satisfy the law, so be it. From then on let it be published every tenth year, and let the former thrall have the services of those witnesses whenever he needs it. And it will remain valid even if it is not published every ten years, as long as witnesses who heard the evidence can testify to it at the thing. †

The 'neck-ransom', *hálslausn*, is the final instalment of money that buys a slave's freedom. The feast of the 'freedom-ale' is a formal one, with master and mistress sitting in the 'high-seats' that represent their authority as heads of a household. If they do not turn up, the seats are left vacant to symbolise them. Slaughtering a sheep may be a remnant of pagan sacrificial practice.

 CHAPTER 9

# Myth, religion and superstition

Sources for Norse myth are plentiful; as usual the difficulty is in evaluating them. Primary must be some of the poems of the *Poetic Edda* and Snorri Sturluson's thirteenth-century *Prose Edda* explication of them (above, pp. 12–13, 17). Dates of composition of the Eddic poems are established only within broad limits of time and plausibility; so, though we use their texts, we do it with caution and recognition of the limitations. The poems are some encyclopaedic, containing esoteric information, as *Vafþrúðnismál, Grimnismál* and *Völuspá*, some episodic, as *Þrymskviða* and *Skirnismál*; some platitudinous, as much of *Hávamál*. Most need extensive annotation to bring out their implications, a thing not possible here. Indeed, I give only a tiny selection of the rich mythological material of the *Poetic Edda*. And only a single example, though an important one, from skaldic poetry. For a short introduction to this aspect of Norse culture see my *Norse myths* (London, 1990).

On religious practice information is scattered and diverse in trustworthiness, and it is likely that customs varied considerably in the different regions and at different dates within the Viking world. Both Constantine Porphyrogenitos and the *Russian Primary Chronicle* preserve occasional observations of interest, while Arabic writers, notably the tenth-century Ibn Fadlan, tell of infidel practices among the Rus of the Volga region, which may, or may not, reveal Scandinavian attitudes (included in P. G. Foote and D. M. Wilson, *The Viking achievement* (London, 1970), pp. 408–12). The runic evidence is disappointing, considering it comes largely from memorial stones. On the analogy of Christian epitaphs we might expect rune-stones to refer often enough to the gods. All we get is an occasional request for a blessing on a stone, as þur:uiki, *Þórr vígi*, 'Thor hallow ⟨the stone, the runes⟩' at the end of a memorial to one Ogmund, on a standing pillar at Väne-Åsaka, Västergötland, Sweden. An important source, which cannot be cited in detail in this sort of book, is place-names, which can indicate local patronage of gods, sites of cult-places, relationship between god and community.

# What Vafthrudnir said

*Vafþrúðnismál* is another of the poems of the *Poetic Edda*. manuscripts, Codex Regius and (a large part of it) MS AM 74 individual stanzas quoted by Snorri Sturluson in the first sometimes supplying lines not in the two major texts. The reach derives from these three. Snorri wrote his *Prose Edda* thirteenth century, so that by then the poem was already ext The Codex Regius and AM 748 4° texts are from *c*.1270 and the end of century respectively, and their closely related versions of *Vafþrúðnismál* appear descend from a common exemplar written abut Snorri's time. But this does not date the composition of the poem itself. For this dating there is no direct evidence, but a common opinion puts it in the tenth century, and so at the centre of the Viking Age. How far the present version represents accurately a poem preserved by oral delivery several centuries earlier is again a matter for discussion. Some scholars regard parts of the present text as interpolations. There are also clear cases where parts of verses have been lost (stanzas 27, 40). On all these matters see the discussion in the introduction to the edition by T. W. Machan, *Vafþrúðnismál*, Durham Medieval Texts 6 (1988).

*Vafþrúðnismál* is a debate/contest poem of a type quite common in medieval literature, and found elsewhere in Norse. However, it is rather different from the 'flyting' in *Lokasenna* (p. 195 below). Two figures compete with one another in knowledge. Here they are Odin, god of, among other things, wisdom; and a giant Vafthrudnir, who being a giant is of immense age and therefore immensely learned in ancient history. Odin takes upon himself the name *Gagnráðr*, literally 'one who gives helpful advice'; and the poem also attributes to him other nicknames (*heiti*), *Heriaföðr*, 'Father of warbands', *Aldaföðr*, 'Father of men', *Yggr*, 'Terrible'.

*Vafþrúðnismál* is almost entirely in speech form, hence its title, 'The sayings of Vafthrudnir' (though that is not a particularly accurate indication of the poem's contents). The speakers are indicated only sporadically in the manuscripts, but can be deduced from the contents. Within Old Norse mythology gods and giants are traditional enemies; so this contest becomes one to the death. Odin's wife, Frigg, who appears at the beginning of the poem, is apprehensive of the outcome of the meeting between the antagonists, but all turns out well – at any rate for Odin. In the course of the debate a good deal of information on Norse mythology is bandied about; indeed, this poem is one of our major sources for that subject. Unfortunately the wording is not always as explicit or informative as we would like. It tends to be allusive, and though the original hearers may have followed the allusions, we cannot always do so. It lists many names, but says little about their owners. Snorri Sturluson expounded much of this and related information in his *Edda*, and we are grateful for his early interpretations, which must be based on a closer knowledge of the traditional Icelandic version of the mythology than we can have.

⟨Odin says:⟩
> 'Advise me now, Frigg, since I'm so eager
> To go to meet Vafthrudnir.

I'm curious to debate ancient lore
With that most learned giant.'

⟨Frigg replies:⟩

'I wouldn't hold back the Father of Hosts
In the halls of the Gods.
Though no giant, I think, is as powerful
As Vafthrudnir must be.'

⟨Odin says:⟩

'Much have I travelled, much have I tried,
Much have I tested the Gods.
One thing more I have to know – how it is
In Vafthrudnir's halls.'

⟨Frigg retorts:⟩

'Go out in luck, come back in luck,
Be lucky in your comrades.
Your wit assist you, Father of Men,
If you must exchange words with the giant.'

Off went Odin to test the word-skills
Of that most learned giant.
He came to a hall – Im's father's it was –
In went Ygg at once.

[Of *Imr*, apparently Vafthrudnir's son, nothing more is known than this. *Imr* is also a wolf-name, and seems to mean 'the gray one'.]

'Hail now, Vafthrudnir! To your hall I come
To meet you in person.
First I must know just how wise you are,
If you know all there is to know.'

'Who on earth can it be who addresses me like this?
And in my own hall too!
Never will you get out again
Unless you speak with more care.'

'I'm called Gagnrad. From my travels I come
Thirsting into your hall.
A long way I've come. I need a welcome,
And your warmest hospitality, giant.'

'Then why, Gagnrad, do you speak from down there?
Take up a seat in the hall.
Then we can find out who knows most,
The stranger or the old know-all.'

[The visitor speaks 'from down there', that is from the body of the hall, not the raised platform on which the head of the household sits. The text reads *á golfi*, literally, 'on the floor'. The word I have translated 'know-all' is *þulr*, for which we have no modern equivalent. It is used as a title in one Danish rune-stone. It may also imply esoteric knowledge and poetic skill.]

> 'The poor man, visiting the rich
> Should be sparing of speech or silent.
> Too much talk has a sad result
> If you're up against the cold-blooded.'

[The word translated 'cold-blooded' is *kaldrifiaðr*, literally 'cold-ribbed', a compound that occurs only here. Various connotations have been supplied for it: 'malicious, hostile, cunning'.]

> 'Tell me, Gagnrad, since down there
> You plan to test your wits,
> What's the name of the horse that draws the days
> Across the world of men?'

> 'Skinfaxi's his name who draws bright day
> Across the world of men.
> The Hreidgotar judge him the best of beasts.
> His mane is always a-glitter.'

[*Skinfaxi* means 'shining-mane'. *Hreiðgotar*, literally 'glory-Goths', is a tribal-name, used here generally for mankind.]

> 'Tell me, Gagnrad, since down there
> You plan to test your wits,
> What's the name of the steed who westward draws
> Night over the glorious gods?'

> 'Hrimfaxi's his name who draws the nights
> Over the glorious gods.
> Each morning he dribbles down flakes of foam.
> That brings dew upon the dales.'

[*Hrímfaxi* means 'frosty-mane'.]

> 'Tell me, Gagnrad, since down there
> You plan to test your wits.
> What's the name of the river that divides the lands
> Of the kin of giants and the gods?'

> 'Ifing's its name; it divides the lands
> Of the kin of giants and the gods.
> Ever will it run unchecked.
> No ice forms over that river.'

> 'Tell me, Gagnrad, since down there
> You plan to test your wits.

What's the name of the plain where battle must join
Between Surt and the splendid gods?'

⟨Odin said:⟩
'Vigrid's its name where battle must join
Between Surt and the splendid gods.
Each way it spreads a hundred leagues
As anyone who knows it will tell.'

[These two verses refer to the final battle between gods and monsters on the day of Ragnarok. *Surtr*, a fire-giant, is one of the leaders of the enemy host, and when the gods are defeated, he will hurl fire over the whole world and destroy it. Here there may be a hidden reference to the volcanic fires Icelanders experienced.]

⟨Vafthrudnir said:⟩
'You're a wise one, stranger. Come to the giant's bench.
Let's sit together and talk.
We'll wager our heads here in the hall
Against our knowledge, stranger.'

⟨Odin said:⟩
'Tell me first, if your wit is sound
And you know it all, Vafthrudnir,
Where did earth come from, or the heaven above,
On the first day, clever giant?'

⟨Vafthrudnir said:⟩
'From Ymir's flesh the earth was shaped,
And from his bones the rocks;
Heaven's vault from the skull of the ice-cold giant,
And the sea from his blood.'

[Snorri clarifies this verse for us. At the beginning of all things there was the great void, Ginnungagap, its northerly part chill and frosty, the southerly hot. Where these two met, the frost melted, the drops quickened in the heat and formed a being, Ymir, who was the ancestor of all frost-giants. Odin, Vili and Ve, three brothers, killed Ymir, and his blood created a great flood in which all the frost-giants were drowned except one called Bergelmir, who floated off on a *lúðr*, a word of uncertain meaning here though sometimes translated 'cradle' (see verse 35 below). Then the brothers: † dragged Ymir to the middle of Ginnungagap and created the earth out of him; from his blood the sea and lakes. The land was made of his flesh; the mountains of his bones; stones and scree they made of his teeth and molars and bits of broken bone ... Then they picked up his skull and made it into the heavens, setting it over the earth with four corners under each of which they put a dwarf. †]

⟨Odin said:⟩
'Tell me second, if your wit is strong
And you know it all, Vafthrudnir.

Where did the moon come from – it soars over the earth –
And the sun as well?'

(Vafthrudnir said:)

'He's called Mundilfœri, the moon's father,
And the sun's as well.
Every day they must sweep the skies
To measure the years for men.'

(Odin said:)

'Tell me third, since they call you clever,
And you know it all, Vafthrudnir.
Where does day come from – it moves over men –
And night with the dying moon?'

(Vafthrudnir said:)

'He's called Delling. He is day's father.
Night was born to Nor.
New and old moons the great gods made
To measure the years for men.'

(Odin said:)

'Tell me fourth, since they call you wise
And you know it all, Vafthrudnir.
Where did winter first come from and summer warm
Among the wise gods?'

(Vafthrudnir said:)

'He's called Vindsval, winter's father,
And Svasud, the summer's.'

(Odin said:)

'Tell me fifth, since they call you wise
And you know it all, Vafthrudnir,
Whether the kin of the Gods or that of Ymir
Was born first of old.'

(Vafthrudnir said:)

'Countless years before earth was shaped,
Then was Bergelmir born;
Thrudgelmir was his father,
And the grandfather Aurgelmir.'

(Odin said:)

'Tell me sixth, since they call you clever
And you know it all, Vafthrudnir.
Where did Aurgelmir come from to giants' kin
In the first place, wise giant?'

⟨Vafthrudnir said:⟩
   'Out of Elivagar dripped poison drops.
   So they grew till they formed a giant.
   From there came all our race together.
   That's why we are so sinister.'

⟨Odin said:⟩
   'Tell me seventh, since they call you clever
   And you know it all, Vafthrudnir.
   How did that fierce giant beget children
   When he had no giantess to sport with?'

⟨Vafthrudnir said:⟩
   'Beneath that frost-giant's arm, they say,
   A boy and girl both grew.
   The wise giant's one foot begot on the other
   A six-headed son.'

⟨Odin said:⟩
   'Tell me eighth, since they call you wise
   And you know it all, Vafthrudnir.
   What's the first you recall? How far back do you go?
   After all, you're a clever giant.'

⟨Vafthrudnir said:⟩
   'Countless years before earth was shaped,
   Then was Bergelmir born.
   The first I recall was that wise giant
   Being placed in a cradle.'

⟨Odin said:⟩
   'Tell me ninth, since they call you clever
   And you know it all, Vafthrudnir.
   Where does the wind come from – it blows over oceans –
   Yet no man ever sees it?'

⟨Vafthrudnir said:⟩
   'He's called Hræsvelg, he sits at heaven's end,
   A giant in eagle's guise.
   From his wings, they say, the wind comes
   Over every man.'

⟨Odin said:⟩
   'Tell me tenth since, Vafthrudnir, you know
   All the exploits of the gods.
   How did Niord come to live among the Æsir?
   Temples and shrines he rules in hundred,
   Yet he was not brought up among the Æsir.'

⟨Vafthrudnir said:⟩

'In the Vanir's land the mighty powers made him
And gave him as hostage to the gods.
At the end of time he'll return again
Back to the wise Vanir.'

[Here there is a reference to the two distinct groups of gods in Norse mythology, the larger one, the *Æsir*, and the smaller, the *Vanir*, below, p. 203]

⟨Odin said:⟩

'Tell me eleventh, in what courts heroes
Fight together each day?'

⟨Vafthrudnir said:⟩

'The mighty heroes of Odin's courts ·
Fight together each day.
They choose who shall die, ride out of battle,
Then sit together in friendship.'

⟨Odin said:⟩

'Tell me twelfth, why, Vafthrudnir, you know
All the exploits of the gods.
Of the secrets of giants and all the gods
Tell me the whole truth,
Most learned giant.'

⟨Vafthrudnir said:⟩

'Of the secrets of giants and all the gods
I can tell the truth,
Since I have travelled every land,
Nine lands I have reached below Niflhel
Where heroes die out of death.'

⟨Odin said:⟩

'Much have I travelled, much have I tried,
Much have I tested the gods.
What men will live on when the Dread Winter
Passes over mankind?'

[The Dread Winter, Old Norse *fimbulvetr*, literally 'monster-winter', will presage Ragnarok, the final day of the old gods. Snorri Sturluson defines it: † Snow will drive in from all directions. There are fierce frosts and biting winds. There is no heat from the sun. Those winters go three in a row with no summer in between. †]

⟨Vafthrudnir said:⟩

'Lif and Lifthrasir – they will hide
In the forest of Hoddmimir.
Morning dew they have as their food.
From that will mankind be nourished.'

⟨Odin said:⟩

> 'Much have I travelled, much have I tried,
> Much have I tested the gods.
> How did sun come back to the spacious heavens
> After Fenrir had caught up with it?'

[Fenrir, the great wolf who will invade the world of the *Æsir* at Ragnarok, here destroys the sun. Snorri tells a rather different tale. According to him the force that makes sun and moon circle the earth is terror, each running away from a wolf that is trying to devour it. After the Dread Winter: † Then something that might be thought important news happens. The wolf will swallow the sun, and men will think that a great loss. The other wolf will catch the moon, and he won't be much of a help either. †]

⟨Vafthrudnir said:⟩

> 'Alfrodul will bear a single daughter
> Before Fenrir catches her.
> When the gods are dead, that daughter will ride
> The paths of her mother.'

⟨Odin said:⟩

> 'Much have I travelled, much have I tried,
> Much have I tested the gods.
> Who are those maids who fly across the sea?
> Wise in mind they journey.'

⟨Vafthrudnir said:⟩

> 'Three of maiden's race will fly over
> The lands of Mogthrasir.
> They alone will be guardian spirits of the world
> Though they were raised among the giants.'

⟨Odin said:⟩

> 'Much have I travelled, much have I tried,
> Much have I tested the gods.
> Which of the Æsir will rule the gods' lands
> When the flames of Surt die down?'

⟨Vafthrudnir said:⟩

> 'Vidar and Vali will hold the gods' shrines
> When the flames of Surt die down.
> Modi and Magni shall own Miollnir
> And wield it in battle.'

[Vidar and Vali are to be heirs to Odin; Modi and Magni to Thor, whose great hammer Miollnir they take over.]

⟨Odin said:⟩

> 'Much have I travelled, much have I tried,
> Much have I tested the gods.

What will bring about Odin's death
When the gods are torn apart?'

⟨Vafthrudnir said:⟩
'Wolf Fenrir will gulp down the Father of Men.
Vidar will avenge him.
He will rip apart its chill jaws
In battle with the wolf.'

⟨Odin said:⟩
'Much have I travelled, much have I tried,
Much have I tested the gods.
What did Odin say in his son's ear
When he laid him on the pyre?'

⟨Vafthrudnir said:⟩
'To none is it known what you of old
Said in your son's ear.
My mouth was doomed when I related old lore
And spoke of the world's end.
It was Odin with whom I shared my skill.
You'll always be wisest of all.'

[Here, as elsewhere, Odin asks the trick question which could only be answered by Odin. So Vafthrudnir at last realises who Gagnrad really is, and how he has been beaten in the contest. Odin's son is the god Baldr, killed by a ruse at Loki's instigation.]

## Odin deceived and deceiver

This is one of the narrative sections – two separate episodes – of *Hávamál*. From the context we know the speaker is Odin, a god notorious for his treacherous behaviour. In his first adventure (the first eight verses below) he is outwitted by what in former days would have been called a coquette or flirt, though our robust modern age prefers a more direct description. The story is known only from this extract; luckily the narrative line is relatively clear. The second episode, in which it is Odin who behaves deceitfully, is told allusively, as though it were a well-known tale which would have been familiar to the audience. Luckily for us Snorri Sturluson produced a more explicit version in his *Prose Edda*, so we can use this as at any rate a learned thirteenth-century author's understanding of the events.

Only the mind knows what dwells close to the heart.
Alone it knows its moods.
No sickness plagues a wise man more
Than having no means of content.

This I found when I lurked in the rushes
Waiting for my beloved.

Body and soul was that girl to me.
Yet I could not win her.

Bright as the sun, Billing's girl
I found abed asleep.
No greater delight could I think for man
Than to live with that lovely creature.

'Not before nightfall, Odin, must you come
To declare your love to me.
Not decent if more than you and I
Together know of our doings.'

Back I turned, thinking to enjoy her,
Quite beyond my senses.
Indeed, I believed I had gained her heart
Utterly, all her love.

When next I came there was a stalwart band
Of guards, all on watch,
With flaming torches of wood on high.
My journey was a bitter one.

Close to dawn I came again,
The watch were all asleep.
But on the bed of that crafty woman
Was a bitch tied up.

Many a good lass – when you get to know her –
Proves fickle towards men.
That I found when I tempted her,
That wise girl, to folly.
Every way she cunningly humbled me,
And in the end I didn't get her.

. . .

The ancient giant I sought; now I'm back again.
Little I got by silence there.
Many a word I spoke in my own praise
In Suttung's halls.

On the golden throne Gunnlod gave me
One drink of the mighty mead.
An ill return I made to her
For her true heart, for her troubled spirit.

With Rati's mouth I made myself space
And gnawed through the rock.
Above me and beneath stood the giants' paths.
So I risked my neck.

I made good use of my feigned appearance –
The clever have few wants –
Because now Odrerir has come to light
Within the bounds of man's holy places.

Doubt there is that I would have returned
From the cities of the giants
Without the help of Gunnlod, that noble lady,
Whom I took into my arms.

. . .

Odin, I think, swore his oath on the holy ring.
How can his truth be trusted?
He left Suttung tricked of his mead,
And Gunnlod in tears.

Snorri's *Prose Edda* version explains the story as part of his discussion of the origin of poetry – Odin as patron of skalds. Beginning with the tale of how the giant Suttung got hold of the mead that gives man poetic power, put it into three cauldrons called Odrerir, Bodn and Son, and hid it within a rock, guarded by his daughter Gunnlod, he continues:

† There is this tale about it. Odin left home and reached a place where nine thralls were mowing hay. He asked if they wanted him to whet their scythes. They said yes. So he took a whetstone from his belt and sharpened the scythes. They thought the scythes cut much better, and asked him for the whetstone. This is how he settled it; anyone who wanted to buy it should give what was appropriate. But they all said they wanted it, and asked him to sell it them. He threw the whetstone up in the air and as they all tried to grab it, they ended up cutting one another's throats with their scythes.

Odin sought lodging for the night with a giant called Baugi, Suttung's brother. Baugi said he was in a difficult position. His nine thralls had killed one another, and he admitted he didn't know where he could get labourers from. Odin gave his name as Bolverk. He offered to do nine men's work for Baugi, stipulating in return one drink of Suttung's mead. Baugi said he had no control over the mead since only Suttung had that, but he would go with Bolverk and see if they could get the mead.

Bolverk did nine men's work for Baugi over the summer, and when winter came he asked Baugi for his pay. So they both went to Suttung. Baugi told his brother Suttung of the bargain he had made with Bolverk, but Suttung flatly refused a single drop of the mead. Then Bolverk said to Baugi that they must try a bit of cunning to get at the mead, and Baugi agreed it was a good idea. Bolverk pulled out a gimblet called Rati, and told Baugi to bore through the rock if the gimblet could cut it. So he did. Then Baugi said that he had pierced the rock, but Bolverk blew into the hole and the bits flew back at him. So he spotted that Baugi was planning to trick him, and he told him to bore right through the rock. Baugi continued boring, and when Bolverk blew a second time the bits flew inwards. Then Bolverk turned himself into a snake and crawled into the gimblet-hole, and Baugi stabbed at him with the gimblet, but missed.

Bolverk went on till he reached where Gunnlod was. He slept with her for three nights, and she allowed him three gulps of the mead. The first gulp emptied Odrerir, the second Bodn, the third Son, so then he had all the mead. Then he put on his eagle's skin and flew off as fast as he could. And when Suttung saw the eagle flying he also took on his eagle-skin and flew after him. And when the Gods saw Odin flying, they put out their buckets into the courtyard. And when Odin came within Asgard [the land of the Æsir – the Gods] he spewed the mead out into the buckets. But it was a close shave – Suttung nearly got him – and he squirted out some of the mead backwards, and that was not saved. Anyone who wanted it could have it – we call it 'the jingle-writers' share'. But the real mead Odin gave to the Gods, and to anyone who had the gift of poetry. So we call poetry 'Odin's plunder' or 'discovery' or 'his drink' or 'his gift' or 'the Gods' drink.' †

## Odin sacrificed

This episode, again from *Hávamál*, is one of the most mysterious of Old Norse mythological literature. It is given here in its entirety – that is, in so far as we can tell where this section ends, and as far as the episode is preserved since it could be an extract from a longer and more explicit poem. The context makes clear that the speaker is the god Odin himself, and he is engaged, apparently willingly, in some sort of test or discipline which endows him with abnormal power, the sort of self-torment that in other cultures shamans undergo to achieve occult wisdom. There is also a disturbing similarity to aspects of Christian myth: a god hanging on a tree, pierced by a spear, thirsting.

> I know that I hung on the windy tree
> Nine whole nights, wounded with the spear,
> Given to Odin, myself to myself,
> On the tree that sprang from roots
> No man knows of.

> They gave me neither bread, nor drink from the horn.
> I peered down.
> I took up runes, howling I took them,
> And then fell back.

> Nine monstrous songs I learnt from the glorious
> Son of Bolthor, Bestla's father.

And one draught I took of the glorious mead
Poured from Odrerir.

Then I began to quicken, to become fertile,
To grow tall and to thrive.
From a word, one word led to another.
From a deed, one deed led to another.

## Loki speaks his mind

This is a poem called *Lokasenna*, a title commonly translated 'The flyting(s) of Loki'. 'Flyting' is not a word much used in present-day demotic English (though it would do very well to describe what passes for debate in our modern legislative assemblies). The *Oxford English Dictionary* defines it as a Scottish word meaning 'a kind of contest . . . in which two persons assailed each other alternately with tirades of abusive verse.' This is certainly something like what goes on in the poem, and the practice is found elsewhere in Norse literature, notably in a heroic poem like the First Lay of Helgi, killer of Hunding, describing warriors' behaviour before battle (above, pp. 131–2). Whether it was a genuine aspect of Viking behaviour rather than a literary one is a different matter, though verse contests of this sort continued into modern times in Norway under the title *stevjing*.

*Lokasenna* is one of the poems of the *Poetic Edda* (contained only in Codex Regius, though Snorri quotes from it in his *Prose Edda*), so its date is conjectural. A common (though not universal) modern view is that it is an early piece, from the Viking pagan period. Its irreverent picture of the gods is then not a sceptical, satirical Christian view, but a genuine reflection of Viking attitudes to the supernatural forces they cultivated. The poem has a prose introduction, and the relationship of this to the verse dialogues that follow and to the prose epilogue is also disputed. *Lokasenna* displays considerable knowledge of the more scandalous aspects of the lives of the pagan gods, and would require an equal knowledge in its audience so that its references could be followed up. The ambiguous god Loki appears here in his most demoniacal guise, as father of the monstrous wolf Fenrir, as the enemy of the other gods and their opponent at Ragnarok, the final day of this world.

The speakers of the individual verses are only tentatively indicated in the manuscript. I add them here for clarity.

**About Ægir and the gods**.
When he had got hold of the great cauldron – as I have just told – Ægir (whose other name was Gymir) made up a brew of beer for the gods. To that party came Odin and his wife Frigg. Thor was not there because he was on one of his journeys to the east. Sif, Thor's wife, was there, and Bragi and Idunn his wife. Tyr was there. He had only one hand; the wolf Fenrir bit his other hand off when it was put in fetters. Niord and his wife Skadi came, Freyr and Freyia, and Vidar, Odin's son. Loki was there, and Freyr's servants, Byggvir and Beyla. Many of the gods and elves were there too.

Ægir had two servants, Fimafeng and Eldir. A glittering gold ring took the place of firelight. The beer served itself. The hall was under the laws of sanctuary. Everyone was full of praise for Ægir's servants. Loki couldn't stand that and killed Fimafeng. Then all the gods shook their shields, howled at Loki and drove him out to the woods, while they went about their drinking.

Loki came back and met Eldir outside. Loki spoke to him:

Tell me, Eldir, before you go one foot further.
What are the sons of the glorious gods talking of over their drinking?

⟨Eldir said:⟩ The sons of the glorious gods are boasting of their weapons and their prowess in war.
Of all the gods and elves here in this hall, none has a good word for you.

⟨Loki said:⟩ In I'll go to Ægir's halls to look at this feasting.
Hatred and bitterness I'll bring to the gods. So I'll mix malice with their mead.

⟨Eldir said:⟩ Let me tell you, if you go into Ægir's halls to look at this feasting,
Bespatter the noble gods with slander and calumny and they'll wipe themselves off on you.

⟨Loki said:⟩ Let me tell you, Eldir, if we two are to wrangle with cutting words
My retorts will be sharper than yours if you speak too freely.

Then Loki went into the hall. And when everyone there saw who had arrived they all fell silent.

⟨Loki said:⟩ I'm Lopt. It's been a long journey here. I'm thirsty enough
To ask one of you gods to serve me a welcome drink of mead.

Why don't you speak out? Swollen with pride? Have you nothing to say?
Either find me a seating-place at your feast or send me out.

⟨Bragi said:⟩ Never will the gods find you a seating-place at their feast;
The gods know well what sort of man they provide such drink for.

⟨Loki said:⟩ Do you remember, Odin, how in days of old we mingled our blood together?

⟨Odin said:⟩      Then you said you never would taste ale unless we were both served it.

⟨Odin said:⟩      Move out, Vidar, and let the wolf's father sit down to our feast,
Else Loki will speak slander about us in Ægir's halls.

Then Vidar got up and poured out drink for Loki. Before he drank he addressed the gods:

     Hail gods, hail goddesses, and all the holy powers,
Except for one of you – Bragi, who sits at the inner end of the bench.

⟨Bragi said:⟩      A horse I'll give, a sword from my wealth. Bragi will reward you with rings,
If you'll only restrain your malice to the gods. Don't rouse their anger at you.

⟨Loki said:⟩      Both horses and arm-rings you'll always be poor in, Bragi.
Of all the gods and elves in here, you've always been careful to avoid battle,
Most terrified of shot.

⟨Bragi said:⟩      Let me tell you if I were outside Ægir's hall, as now I am in it,
I would carry away your head in my arms. I'll pay you back for that lie.

⟨Loki said:⟩      You're brave enough seated inside here. You just couldn't do it, Bragi.
You're only a bit of bench-decoration.
Come out if you really are angry. Brave men have no fear.

⟨Idunn said:⟩      I beg you, Bragi, by our kinship, by all our loving family,
Not to find fault with Loki in Ægir's halls.

⟨Loki said:⟩      Silence, Idunn! You I know to be the most lecherous of women,
Since, fresh and bathed, you clasped in your arms your brother's killer.

⟨Idunn said:⟩      I'll not find fault with Loki in Ægir's halls.
I'll calm Bragi though he's flushed with ale. You two mustn't fight in your wrath.

⟨Gefion said:⟩      Why must you two gods squabble so savagely in here?

    Loki won't realise he's been outwitted, and that all
      the gods hate him.

⟨Loki said:⟩      Silence, Gefion! Why don't we talk of the lad who
      seduced your heart.
      That fair-haired boy who gave you a brooch so you
      laid a leg over him.

⟨Odin said:⟩      You're mad, Loki, out of your wits, to make an
      enemy of Gefion,
      It's my belief she knows all the fates of men just as
      well as I do.

⟨Loki said:⟩      Silence, Odin! You never could judge fairly between
      men in battle.
      Victory you've often given to the undeserving, to
      cowards.

⟨Odin said:⟩      Let me tell you, if indeed I gave victory to the
      undeserving coward,
      You lived eight years in the underworld, a milch-
      cow, a woman,
      There you bore children – that I reckon a pervert's
      act.

⟨Loki said:⟩      As for you they say you cast witch's spells, practising
      sorcery on Samsø;
      Arrayed like a wizard you strode through the world –
      that I reckon a pervert's act.

⟨Frigg said:⟩      You two should never speak openly about your ways
      of life,
      What the two of you got up to in days of old. Men's
      former exploits are best forgotten.

⟨Loki said:⟩      Silence, Frigg. You are Fiorgyn's daughter. You've
      always been a lecherous one.
      After all – though you were Vidrir's wife – you took
      both Ve and Vili into your arms.

⟨Frigg said:⟩      Let me tell you, if I had a son like Baldr in Ægir's
      halls,
      You'd never get out from among the gods. You
      would have been beaten up in your fury.

⟨Loki said:⟩      Do you want me to keep on telling you, Frigg, what
      misery I caused you?
      I it was made sure you would never again see Baldr
      riding home.

⟨Freyia said:⟩      Mad you are, Loki, to insist on telling your wicked, loathsome deeds.

                           Frigg, I think, knows all our fates, though she herself says nothing.

⟨Loki said:⟩      Silence, Freyia! I know you well. You are not exactly free from fault.

                           All the gods and elves in here, all have been lovers of yours.

⟨Freyia said:⟩      Your tongue is treacherous. Soon it will bring you to disaster, I think.

                           Gods and goddesses all are furious with you. You'll go home with your tail between your legs.

⟨Loki said:⟩      Silence, Freyia! You're a wicked creature, filled to the brim with evil,

                           For the glorious gods surprised you with your own brother. You farted with fear then, Freyia.

⟨Niord said:⟩      No trouble it is if women take on husband, lover or both.

                           A stranger thing when we come upon an effeminate god who has himself borne children.

⟨Loki said:⟩      Silence, Niord! You are here with the gods only because you were a hostage sent from the west.

                           Hymir's daughters used you for a chamber-pot and pissed in your mouth.

⟨Niord said:⟩      Though I was sent far away as a hostage to the gods, I have this consolation,

                           I begot a boy disliked by none. He is a prince of gods.

⟨Loki said:⟩      Stop that now, Niord! Hold back a bit! I'll not keep this quiet any longer.

                           That boy you begot on your own sister. Which is no more than I would expect of you.

⟨Tyr said:⟩      Freyr is the boldest of all fighters in the courts of the gods.

                           To no maid, to no man's wife does he bring wretchedness. He frees captives from their chains.

⟨Loki said:⟩      Silence, Tyr! You could never bring peace between two foes.

                           What about that right hand of yours that the wolf Fenrir bit off?

⟨Tyr said:⟩      I miss my hand, you miss your son. Both suffer bitter loss.

The wolf too is desolate. It must lie in fetters until the final day.

⟨Loki said:⟩ Silence, Tyr! What happened to your wife? She bore a son to me.

Not a bit of stuff, not a penny piece did you get in compensation, you poor wretch.

⟨Freyr said:⟩ I can see the wolf lying by the river's mouth until the great powers are torn to pieces.

Unless you shut up, you fount of all evil, you will be chained next to it.

⟨Loki said:⟩ You had Gymir's daughter bought for gold. That's what you gave your sword for.

When Muspell's sons ride across the Dark Wood, how are you going to fight, you wretch?

⟨Byggvir said:⟩ Let me tell you, if I had Ingunar-Freyr's lineage and his worldly state

I would beat this crow into a pulp and break every bone in his body.

⟨Loki said:⟩ What's that snapping little thing I see, fawning like a dog?

He always seems to be at Freyr's side, twittering like a girl grinding meal.

⟨Byggvir said:⟩ Byggvir's my name. All gods and men call me a brisk fellow.

I'm proud to be here where all Hropt's kin are drinking beer together.

⟨Loki said:⟩ Silence, Byggvir! You couldn't even carve up food for men.

You hid in the straw of the hall-floor and couldn't be found when men were fighting together.

⟨Heimdall said:⟩ You're drunk, Loki, out of your wits. Why don't you put a stop to it?

Too much to drink affects a man so he doesn't know what rubbish he's talking.

⟨Loki said:⟩ Silence, Heimdall! In days of old an ugly life you led.

With soaking back you must stand for ever and keep watch to guard the gods.

⟨Skadi said:⟩ You sound merry, Loki, but you won't run around free for long.

The gods will bind you to a sword with the guts of your rime-cold son.

⟨Loki said:⟩ Let me tell you, even though the gods bind me to a
sword with the guts of my rime-cold son,
I took the leading part in the killing when we laid
hands on Thiazi.

⟨Skadi said:⟩ Let me tell you, if you took a leading part in the
killing when you laid hands on Thiazi,
From my lands, from my temples, chill counsels will
reach you.

⟨Loki said:⟩ You spoke more fairly to Laufey's son when you took
me to your bed.
All that will come into the open if we number up our
follies exactly.

Then Sif came up, offered Loki mead in a crystal cup and said:
Hail now, Loki! Take the crystal cup full of mature
mead.
Better admit one woman alone among the sons of
the gods is faultless.

He took the horn and drank.
You would be alone in that, if indeed you were wary
and careful with men.
Only I know – it seems to me – that you were
unfaithful to the Thunderer,
And your seducer was the cunning Loki.

⟨Beyla said:⟩ The mountains are quaking. I think the Thunderer is
on his way.
He'll silence the one here who is slandering all gods
and men.

⟨Loki said:⟩ Silence, Beyla. You're Byggvir's woman and full of
wickedness.
No greater disgrace came among the sons of gods:
you're full of filth, you slave.

Then Thor arrived and said:
Silence, you pervert! My mighty hammer, Miollnir,
will stop your talk!
From your neck I'll cut the rock of your shoulders,
and that will be the end of you.

⟨Loki said:⟩ So, Earth's son has now come in. Why are you rant-
ing like that, Thor?
Will you dare be so bold when you have to fight the
wolf and he swallows Sigfadir whole?

| ⟨Thor said:⟩ | Silence, you pervert! My mighty hammer, Miollnir, will stop your talk! |
| | I'll throw you in the air to the eastern ways. You'll never be seen again. |
| ⟨Loki said:⟩ | You should never mention your eastern travels among men. |
| | You huddled in the thumb of a glove, you great fighter, and then you didn't look much like Thor. |
| ⟨Thor said:⟩ | Silence, you pervert! My mighty hammer, Miollnir, will stop your talk! |
| | With my right hand I'll hit you with Hrungnir's killer and break every bone in your body. |
| ⟨Loki said:⟩ | I expect to live a long life even though you threaten me with your hammer. |
| | You thought Skrymir's leather straps so tough that you couldn't get at your pack, |
| | You nearly starved to death. |
| ⟨Thor said:⟩ | Silence, you pervert! My mighty hammer Miollnir will stop your talk! |
| | Hrungnir's killer will send you to your doom, down beyond the gates of death. |
| ⟨Loki said:⟩ | To the gods, to the sons of gods I have spoken what my heart urged me to say. |
| | Only you can send me away for I know you're a killer. |
| | You have brewed ale, Ægir, but never again will you set out a feast. |
| | All that you have – you in here – may the fire blaze over it, and scorch your backsides for you. |

**About Loki**. After this Loki hid in the waterfall Franangr, taking on the form of a salmon. There the gods caught him. He was tied up with the entrails of his son Nari. His other son, Narfi, turned into a wolf. Skadi caught a venomous snake and tied it above Loki's face. Poison dripped from it. Sigyn, Loki's wife, sat by, holding a basin under the poison. But when the basin was full she had to carry the poison away and in the mean time it dripped on to Loki. At that he shuddered so hugely that it made all the earth tremble. What we now call earthquakes.

It is worth examining this poem to see some of the things it tells about, or hints of, the Norse gods. Luckily the thirteenth-century Icelandic writer, Snorri Sturluson, explained much of this and related material in his *Prose Edda*, a work intended to educate his contemporaries, particularly those who aspired to writing poetry, in the mythology of their predecessors.

Loki, Laufey's son, also called Lopt, plays a confused part in this mythology, sometimes being the rather mischievous companion of Thor and the friend of Odin (who must have been his blood-brother, for they 'mingled their blood together'). But Loki is also a figure of evil, father of the terrible wolf Fenrir who at Ragnarok would swallow up Odin (nicknamed Sigfadir, 'father of victory'). To postpone this the gods had shackled Fenrir, capturing him by a trick. To gain the wolf's confidence the god Tyr had placed his right hand in Fenrir's mouth, and when the wolf found itself deceived, it bit off Tyr's hand. The gods took the shackled wolf and tied it to a group of rocks. There it will remain till the last day.

Loki also boasts in this poem of his greatest crime, his responsibility for killing Baldr (though another hand did the deed), the beloved son of Odin and Frigg. Baldr travelled down to the underworld, and will return, according to some sources, only after Ragnarok.

Odin is the ambiguous and treacherous god of wisdom, magic and victory, who would support a great warrior for some time and then allow him to be killed in fight so that he could join Odin's army for the final battle against Loki, Muspell's sons and the armies of destruction. So Loki accuses him justly of sometimes supporting the wrong side in battle. Odin was also sexually ambiguous, for he engaged in the magical practice of *seiðr* which gave knowledge and power but also effeminacy, a quality the Vikings abhorred. Hence the charges and countercharges of perversion between Odin and Loki – Loki was also sexually ambiguous, and in one of his guises, a mare, had given birth to the great stallion Sleipnir.

*Lokasenna* also makes clear there are two groups of gods. The majority are of the type known as *Æsir* (singular *Áss*) but there is also a foreign group, the senior of which is Niord, who live as hostages among the *Æsir*. These other gods, the *Vanir*, had different customs from the *Æsir*. For instance, Niord's mate was his own sister, and by her he had his famous son Freyr and also his lovely daughter Freyia (who mated with her brother). These were gods of wealth, fertility and sexual love. Freyr fell in love with a giantess, Gymir's daughter, and to woo her sent his servant Skirnir, bribing him with a splendid sword which fought by itself. (The tale of this is told in the Eddic poem *Skírnismál*). It is this sword that Freyr will miss when Ragnarok (and the army containing Muspell's sons) comes. Freyia was, as the goddess of sexual desire, notorious for her affairs and to some degree for her covetousness.

Thor, *Iörð*'s (that is, Earth's) son, the god who above all protected his fellow-gods by his strength and ferocity, was often away on journeys in the east, returning at the critical moment as he does here. Loki attempted to humiliate him by recounting episodes where Thor had failed. On one of his journeys, when Loki was with him, Thor found himself out in the woods overnight. He took refuge in what he thought was a hut with a side room, and only in the morning realised he had slept in the thumb-piece of a mitten belonging to the giant Skrymir. Skrymir, Thor and his companions packed all their provisions together in Skrymir's backpack, and Skrymir tied it up. When Thor tried to open the pack to get at his supper, he couldn't undo the straps (which later turned out to be iron bars). In his retort to Loki Thor points out that his hammer is 'Hrungnir's killer' – Thor had destroyed a giant Hrungnir by throwing his hammer at him.

The only other major god in *Lokasenna* is Heimdall, watchman of the gods and a very cryptic creature who had some connection with the sea – his 'soaking back' here may refer to this, or may indicate that as watchman for the gods he had to be out in all weathers. But there are references to a group of minor and little-known creatures and to a number of goddesses, most of whom are accused of unchastity. How far these accusations were justified, how much they indicate Loki's spite is unknown. Bragi is a god of poetry, and hence, apparently, not a fighter; so he becomes an object of Loki's scorn. He cannot have any wealth because he hasn't fought for it. Byggvir is a little-known and minor figure, and shown here as a coward and an incompetent. Skadi, a giantess, is the wife of Niord. Her father, Thiazi, had been killed by the gods, and the match with Niord was her compensation, though not a satisfactory one. Loki boasts he has led the attack on Thiazi but Skadi gets her own back in the epilogue. Even Snorri does not tell us all the stories of the gods referred to in the poem – the indelicate episode of the daughters of (presumably the giant) Hymir, for instance. Nor do we know for certain whether my translation of Frigg as 'Fiorgyn's daughter' is correct. It has Snorri's approval but some have suggested that he was mistaken here, that *Fiörgynn* is another of Odin's names (like *Hroptr* and *Viðrir*) and the translation should be 'Fiorgyn's wife'.

## The wise woman's prophecy

Perhaps the most famous, certainly the most haunting, and in general the most complex and baffling of mythological poems of the *Poetic Edda* is *Völuspá*, about the beginning and end of the world as recounted by a *völva*, a word hard to translate and frequently rendered by the archaic word 'sybil'. She is being interrogated by *Valföðr/Valfaðir*, 'father of the slain', a name of the great god Odin; and many scholars believe she has been called back from the grave to assist him with his enquiries.

The poem contains a wealth of information on Norse myths, on how the world was created, and how and why it will end. And what will happen then. It was natural for Snorri Sturluson to make great use of this poem in his *Prose Edda*, and we are indebted to him for clarifying much of what is mysterious to us or confused in the tale. But though Snorri certainly knew more of early myth than we do, we must keep in mind that he wrote over two centuries after Christianity had been formally accepted by the Icelanders. To that extent he was parted from a complete or sympathetic understanding of pagan thinking. *Völuspá* is usually dated to *c*.1000, that is to the time when Vikings were moving towards (in some cases had achieved) Christian belief, and scholars have seen the penetration of pagan by Christian in some of the poem's motifs. There are, moreover, gaps, confusions and inconsistencies in the story it tells, and the two major versions of the poem, one in Codex Regius, one in the early-fourteenth-century manuscript called *Hauksbók*, do not always order their verses in the same way.

A guide to some of the complexities of the poem is Sigurður Nordal's 'Three essays on *Völuspá*', *Saga-book of the Viking Society* 18, parts 1–2 (1970–1), pp. 79–135.

Because of the problems of interpretation and of sequence of thought, I do not attempt a complete translation here. Instead I give extracts, each of them coherent in itself though its link to what precedes and follows may be hard to trace.

The world begins and has its Golden Age.

A hearing I seek from all holy peoples,
Great and small, of Heimdall's kin.
You bid me, Valfodr, recount to you
Ancient myths of men, back to the depths of memory.

I remember giants born at the beginning of time,
Who fostered me in distant days.
Nine worlds I remember, nine roots of the mighty tree
That bounds the world, as yet beneath the earth.

It was in distant times when nothing was;
Neither sand nor sea nor chill waves,
No earth at all, nor the high heavens;
The great void only; growth nowhere,

Until Bur's sons raised up lands,
They created glorious Middle-Earth.
From the south shone the sun on the rocky beds.
Then the ground greened with growing grasses.

From the south the sun, moon's comrade,
Thrust her right hand over heaven's rim.
The sun did not know where her dwellings were,
The stars did not know what stations they must hold.
The moon did not know what force he possessed.

Then ruling powers took their thrones of fate,
Mighty, holy gods, held council together.
Names they gave to night and its children,
Morning they named and Midday,
Afternoon and Evening, numbering the years.

The Æsir met on Idavoll,
High they built up altars and temples
They set up forges, crafted rich treasures,
Invented tongs, created tools.

Chess they played in the meadow, they were merry,
Not the least shortage they had of gold
Until three came, giant-women,
Monstrous, from Giantland.

[The first section of the poem ends here. What the giant-women did to bring the Golden Age to an end we do not know. The word I have translated 'played chess' is *tefla*, literally 'played *tafl*, tables'. *Tafl* (also *hnefatafl*) was played on a squared board, but the rules were quite different from chess, with one side occupying the centre of the board, the other its edges. At the beginning of the game the king (*hnefi*) stood at the centre, and his aim was to reach one edge. The game has cult significance for the Golden Age. At the rebirth of the world at the end of *Völuspá*, the lost *tafl*-pieces will be rediscovered. The poem now continues with the creation of the race of dwarfs. Then follows abruptly how three gods made mankind from pieces of driftwood found on the sea-shore.]

> Until from that host there came three
> Mighty, great-hearted Æsir to the sea-strand.
> Washed ashore they found two of little strength,
> Ask and Embla; beings without destiny.

> Breath they had none, soul they had not,
> No flow of blood, no voice, no colour.
> Odin gave breath, Hœnir gave soul,
> Lodur gave blood and healthy colour.

[Then comes an account of the great world-tree, and the Norns, the demi-goddesses of man's destiny, who live beneath it.]

> An ash stands, I know; its name Yggdrasil,
> A lofty tree sprinkled with bright water.
> Thence come the dews that fall on the dales.
> Evergreen it towers over the well of Urd.

> From it come three maids, filled with wisdom,
> From the hall that stands beneath the tree.
> One is called Urd, the second Verdandi
> (Runes of fate on twigs they cut), Skuld the third.
> They laid down laws, they allotted life
> To men's sons, destiny to warriors.

[There follows a brief and obscure allusion to warfare between the two main groups of gods, the Æsir and the Vanir, strife that began somehow with the appearance of a witch Gullveig among the Æsir. They tried unsuccessfully to destroy her and then demanded (or received a demand for) compensation. The war was inconclusive; we know from other sources that it ended with each side giving hostages to the other. This explains why some Vanir live among the Æsir (above, pp. 188–9, 199.]

> She remembers the first war between nations
> When they had spitted Gullveig with spears
> And burned her in the hall of the High One,
> Thrice burned, thrice reborn,
> Again and again – yet she lives on.

> They called her Heid when she came among men,
> With deep powers of foresight she cast spells.

Witchcraft she practised wherever she could,
Enchanted the mind,
Ever the delight of evil women.

Then ruling powers took their thrones of fate,
Mighty, holy gods, held council together.
Whether the Æsir must suffer loss
Or all the gods should claim compensation.

Odin cast his spear, hurled it into the army;
This indeed was the first great battle on earth.
The shield-wall of the Æsir was shattered.
Foreseeing battle's outcome, Vanir trod the field of war.

[The next allusion was luckily explained by Snorri Sturluson. It refers to the trouble the Æsir got into when they hired a giant to build a defensive wall round their territory. He required as payment the sun, the moon and the goddess Freyia, wife to an obscure deity Od. The gods agreed, thinking he could not fulfil the contract in time, and when he looked like doing so it took all Loki's trickery to rescue them. Then Thor came back from one of his adventures and put paid to the giant. But the Æsir had betrayed their oaths guaranteeing his safety; a shocking breach of Norse morality.]

Then ruling powers took their thrones of fate,
Mighty, holy gods, held council together.
Who had filled the whole sky with treachery.
Who had given Od's mate into the power of giants?

Swollen with wrath, Thor alone fought there.
He seldom sits quiet when he learns of such things!
Oaths were trodden underfoot, word of honour, sworn
    pledge,
All the mighty bonds made between them.

[A few verses tell of the powers of the gods. Heimdall who had keen hearing had perhaps to pledge one of his ears to get this power in the other. Odin, also known here as Yggiung, certainly had to leave one eye as a pledge in the well of Mimir in return for supernatural insight and wisdom.]

She knows the hearing of Heimdall hidden
Under the holy tree beneath the clear heavens.
A stream she sees tumble, a muddy fall,
From Valfodr's pledge – would you know more than this?

Alone she sat outside when the ancient came,
Yggiung of the gods. He looked her in the eye.
'What are you asking? Why are you testing me?
I know it all, how you hid your eye
In the famous well of Mimir.'
Every morning Mimir drinks mead
From Valfodr's pledge – would you know more than this?

The Father of Battle brought rings and necklets.
She learned wise lore and power of prophecy.
Far and wide she saw over all worlds.

[There is a passage on the valkyries; then an allusion to the tragedy of the beloved god Baldr, accidentally shot by a mistletoe shaft launched by the blind god Hod. Loki had plotted it, and in punishment was bound to three rocks, where he must remain till the final day. Only his faithful wife Sigyn gives him solace there.]

I saw the fated end of Baldr,
Odin's child, bloodied god.
There it grew, high over the meadow,
Slim, very fair, the mistletoe.

From that shaft that seemed so slender
Was made a killing dart, Hod hurled it.
Quickly after was born Baldr's brother,
One-day-old, he began to fight.

He neither washed hands nor combed hair,
Before he brought Baldr's enemy to burn on the pyre;
But Frigg mourned in Fensalir
Valholl's woe – would you know more than this?

A captive she saw lying below Hveralund
Like to the evil-driven Loki himself.
There sits Sigyn, but in great grief
For her man – would you know more than this?

[There are places of punishment for the evil – more a Christian than a pagan concept, I suspect. The greatest wickedness would seem to be breach of trust, of which after all the gods were guilty.]

A hall she saw standing far from the sun
On Nastrond. The door faces north.
Drops of poison drip through the roof-lights.
The hall is thatched with serpents intertwined.

There she saw wading through heavy streams,
Men whose oaths are false, wolfish killers,
Men who have seduced others' lovers.
There Nidhogg sucks the dead corpse dry,
The wolf tears men asunder – would you know more than this?

[The final section of the poem is the only one that properly qualifies as prophecy. It tells of the future fall of the gods. And what will follow. The final day is to be signalled by the baying of the wolf Fenrir, called first Garm and later Loki's son, who has been shackled but will now escape to lead the attack on the gods' kingdom. It is joined by a heterogeneous group of destroyers: the giant Hrym, the serpent Iormungand (also called Midgardsorm, the World Serpent) who had been banished to the ocean depths, the sons of Muspell on their ship Naglfar, with Loki steering; the fire-giant Surt. The course of battle is not made clearer by the poet's allusive way of referring to the combatants. Loki is called also Byleif's brother and Hvedrung. Beli's killer is the god Freyr. Thor is known as son of Hlodyn (his mother) and of Odin, as well as Midgard's preserver and Fiorgun's lad. Hlyn is another name for Frigg, Odin's wife. She had already suffered a bitter grief in the loss of her son Baldr. Odin's heroic death in battle is the second. The poet also uses the occasional kenning: 'wood's destroyer' for 'fire'. For those who still find the story hard to follow, I append Snorri's prose version.]

Garm howls loud before Gnipahellir.
His fetter will snap, the wolf run free
Many secrets she knows; farther I can see
To the terrible fate of the gods of war.

Brothers will fight, will kill each other.
Kin will break the bonds of kin.
A harsh world it will be, whoredom rampant,
An axe-age, a sword-age, shields shattered,
A wind-age, a wolf-age before man's age tumbles down.
No man will spare his neighbour.

. . .

Heimdall blows loudly, horn raised aloft.
Odin consults with Mimir's head.

The ash Yggdrasil stands yet.
The ancient tree quivers. The giants break loose.

. . .

What of the Æsir? What of the elves?
All Giant-land is in uproar.
The Æsir gather in council
Dwarfs groan outside their stony doors,
Those who know well the rocky walls.
Would you know more than this?

Garm howls loud before Gnipahellir.
His fetter will snap, the wolf run free.

Hrym drives west, his shield before him.
Iormungand twists in giant-rage
The serpent kicks up waves. The eagle screams.
Pale of beak it tears corpses. Naglfar floats free.

The ship drives westwards. Muspell's sons
Cross the ocean, Loki at the helm.

All the monstrous kin advance with the wolf.
Byleif's brother is in their company.

Surt advances north with wood's destroyer.
The sun shines bright on the giants' swords.
Crags clash together, the trolls stumble,
Heroes walk the path to death, the heavens split open.

Then comes Hlin's second grief,
When Odin goes to fight the wolf,
And Beli's bright killer against Surt.
Frigg's beloved will fall.

Then the mighty son of Sigfodr,
Vidar, comes to fight the killer-beast.
His hand thrusts the sword to the heart
Of Hvedrung's son. His father is avenged.

Then goes the glorious son of Hlodyn,
Odin's son, to fight the snake.
Midgard's preserver kills it in his wrath.
All mankind must depart this world.
Fiorgun's lad walks away nine feet,
His strength at its end, fearing no reproach.

The sun blackens. The earth sinks into the sea.
The brilliant stars dash down from the skies.
Fire flares up against fire.
Intense heat plays as high as the heavens.

Garm howls loud before Gnipahellir.
His fetter will snap, the wolf run free.

[The poem ends with a new age of hope, the dead god returning, but, in a last stanza, punishment for the wicked.]

She sees, rising again out of the ocean,
The earth, eternally green.
The cataracts fall, above flies the eagle,
Hunting fish upon the fells.

The Æsir meet again on Idavoll,
And speak of the terrible world-snake,
And call to mind the great events
And the ancient judgments of the Great Seer.

The splendid playing-pieces, all of gold,
Will once again be found, in the grass,
Those they owned in ancient times.

Fields unsown will flourish,
All ills will be cured. Baldr will return.
Hod and Baldr will dwell together
In the sanctuaries of the gods, in Hropt's ancient dwelling.
Would you know more than this?

. . .

She sees a hall standing, brighter than the sun,
Gold-thatched, on Gimle.
There shall dwell those of noble life,
And throughout all ages live in joy.

There the mighty king will come to his great judgment,
Descending in power, who rules all things.

There will come the dusky dragon flying,
The glittering serpent, down from Nidafioll.
Nidhogg bears the dead on his wings, flies across the fields.

Now the seeress must sink back.

[Snorri's prose version of the final day of the Æsir, Ragnarok, derives in part from *Völuspá*, but does not follow it in all details. Snorri writes:

† Then the wolf Fenrir will get free. The sea overswims the land because the World Serpent is writhing in its giant rage and pushing ashore. The ship called Naglfar is also freed. It is made up of dead men's nails, so it is worth noting that if a man dies with his nails uncut, he will supply a lot of material for the ship Naglfar, and both men and gods want that to be completed as slowly as possible. In this surging sea Naglfar floats. The giant at the helm is called Hrym.

And the wolf Fenrir will advance, mouth wide open – its upper jaw touches the heavens and its lower the earth; he would gape wider if there were space. Fire flames from its eyes and nostrils. The World Serpent spews out such venom that it infects all the sky and sea; and it is terrifying. It runs along on one side of the wolf.

In this uproar the heavens split open and Muspell's sons ride out of them. In front rides Surt, with burning flames both before and behind him. He has a superb sword – it glitters brighter than the sun. And when they ride over [the bridge] Bifrost, it shatters, as I said above. Muspell's kin advance to the plain called Vigrid, and the wolf Fenrir and the World Serpent will come there too. Also Loki and Hrym and all the frost giants with him, and with Loki all the company of Hel . . .

When all this happens Heimdall will rise and blow strenuously on the Giallarhorn, and wake up all the gods who take counsel together. Odin rides to Mimir's well and seeks advice from Mimir, both for himself and his men. The ash-tree Yggdrasil quivers, and nothing in heaven or earth is free of fear.

The Æsir and all the chosen slain will take up their arms and advance on the plain. In front rides Odin with his helmet of gold, his splendid mail-coat and his spear called Gungnir. He engages the wolf Fenrir. Thor advances by his side but can be of no help to him because he has all on to fight the World Serpent. Freyr fights Surt, and there is a tough contest before Freyr falls. This will bring about his death – he misses the great sword that he gave to Skirnir. Then runs free the great hound Garm who had been tied up in front of Gnipahellir. He is an evil monster. He has a duel with Tyr and each kills the other. Thor destroys the World Serpent, steps back nine paces and then falls dead to the ground, killed by the venom the snake spewed over him. The wolf will gulp down Odin, and that is the end of him. At once Vidar steps forward; he puts one foot on the wolf's lower jaw. (On that foot he wears a shoe that has been collected together throughout all ages. It is made of the slips of leather that men trim from their shoes, at toe or heel. So if you want to be a help to the Æsir, throw those bits away.) With one hand he grabs the wolf's upper jaw and rips his mouth in two, and that will be the end of the wolf. Loki engages Heimdall, and each kills the other. Then Surt will sling fire over the earth, and burn the whole world up †

## Spells

The final section of *Hávamál* is commonly called *Ljóðatal*, 'The catalogue of chants', a summary of eighteen magical spells the speaker, presumably Odin, could command. It is likely to have been an independent group of verses that became incorporated into *Hávamál* because Odin was master of magic. In the first section of *Heimskringla* Snorri Sturluson lists some of the god's successes in this field:

> † He knew such skills that he could change his shape and complexion in whatever way he wanted ... He could also ensure that his enemies in battle were struck blind or deaf or with terror, and their weapons were no more cutting than canes ... Odin changed his shape. Then his body lay as though asleep or dead, and he became a bird, animal, fish or serpent, and in a flash travelled to far-off lands on his own or other people's business. Furthermore, with a single word he could put out a fire, calm the sea and turn the winds in whatever direction he wished ... And sometimes he brought dead men to life out of the earth or would sit down under men who were on the gallows. And so he was called 'Lord of the Dead' or 'Lord of the Hanged' ... All these skills he taught through runes and the chants called *galdrar* ... There was one skill he knew that commanded the greatest power – he practised it himself – it is called *seiðr*. By means of it he could foresee men's futures, things that had not yet happened; he could

bring men death or misfortune or ill-health; also take wit or strength from one man and give it to another. †

Many of these details Snorri probably cribbed from the *Ljóðatal*.

> These chants I know. No noble wife knows them
> No man's son neither.
> The first is called 'Help'. It will help you
> Against strifes and troubles and every sort of misery.

> The second one I know, which children of men
> Need if they are to live to be doctors.

> This third I know. If I have real need
> To hold my foes in check.
> I blunt the blades of my adversaries.
> Their weapons and cudgels cannot harm.

> This fourth I know. If men put
> Shackles on my limbs,
> My chant will let me walk free.
> The fetter springs from my legs,
> The handcuff from my arms.

> This fifth I know. If I see, shot in enmity,
> An arrow flying in battle,
> It will not speed so surely that I cannot stop it,
> If once I get my eye on it.

> This sixth I know. If a fighting-man wound me
> By the roots of a strong young tree,
> Then the man who means evil towards me
> He it is the peril strikes, not me.

[This is a strange stanza. One interpretation is that the man who 'wounds me by the roots of a tree' is an enemy carving malicious runes on a tree-root to bring evil on the speaker. This makes sense but is not very convincing.]

> This seventh I know. If I see a great hall
> Blazing over bench-mates,
> The fire cannot spread so far that I can't save it.
> That charm I can chant.

> This eighth I know, important
> For everyone to know how to use it.
> If hatred grows between a prince's sons
> I can clear that up at once.

> This ninth I know. If it is imperative for me
> To save my ship at sea,
> The winds over the waves I can tame
> And calm the whole ocean.

This tenth I know. If I see witches
Riding through the skies,
I can so contrive it that they go astray
From their proper shapes
From their proper minds.

[This too is a strange verse. The word translated 'witches riding' is *túnriður*, literally 'fence-riders, yard-riders', though the word occurs only here. It fits a group of compound nouns referring to supernatural women who 'ride', perhaps sit astride fences or house-tops. The word given as 'proper' is *heim*, 'home', which does not help much. Perhaps it is best to leave this verse unexplained, and simply say that it shows how the charm can overcome supernatural menace.]

This eleventh I know. If to battle
I must take old friends,
I chant spells beneath our shields; and in strength they go
Safe into battle,
Safe out of battle,
Every time they come back safe.

This twelfth I know. If in a tree-top I see
A noosed corpse,
I cut and paint runes
So the man will walk
And talk with me.

This thirteenth I know. If I get to
Sprinkle a young lad with water,
He will never perish if he goes into battle,
That fighter will never fall to the sword.

[Old Norse literature has other references to a heathen practice of sprinkling a child with water in some ceremony similar to Christian baptism. Whether this was truly pagan (it is, I think, not found elsewhere in early Germanic religion) or whether there is Christian influence here is disputed.]

This fourteenth I know. If before a group of men
I have to count up the gods,
I know something about all Æsir and elves.
No ignorant man can do that.

[This verse and the following do not fit the sequence of thought. They are verses of knowledge rather than magic. Yet they are needed for the numerical sequence.]

This fifteenth I know which the dwarf Thiodeyrir
Chanted before Delling's doors.
Strength he chanted to the Æsir, success to the elves,
Intellect to Hroptatyr.

[Hroptatyr is one of Odin's nicknames. Thiodeyrir is not otherwise known. Delling is a known dwarf-name. But what the verse refers to is a mystery.]

> This sixteenth I know. If a prudent girl's thoughts and delights
> I want to possess utterly,
> I can sway the mind of that white-armed lass
> And completely change her heart.
>
> This seventeenth I know so that a young maid
> Will be reluctant to leave me . . .

[The second part of this verse seems irrelevant to its opening, and may not properly belong here.]

> This eighteenth I know which I shall never tell
> To maid, to man's wife –
> Better it is if only one knows;
> It is the last of my chants –
> Except for she who holds me in her arms,
> Or perchance my sister.

[The catalogue ends abruptly with a hint at some special skill but no more than a hint. Odin has supreme wisdom, his wife Frigg (who 'holds him in her arms') also knows fates and futures, he has no sister. So there is no reason for him to reveal his final secret.]

## Egil Skalla-Grimsson grieves for his sons

Egil Skalla-Grimsson (or Egill Skalla-Grímsson, to give him his Icelandic form) was the greatest of the medieval Icelandic poets whose works have survived attributed. Of him a thirteenth-century writer composed a biography *Egils saga* which, however, is probably more historical novel than history (above, p. 25). It tells of his birth at Borg in western Iceland to a family traditionally at odds with the Norwegian monarchy, his turbulent youth, his adventures both at home and abroad, and his death as an embittered old man some time towards the end of the tenth century. In the course of this tale the writer quotes a number of verses that he attributes to Egil, some of which are generally accepted as genuinely by that poet. Many of these verses are individual stanzas describing his reaction to his contemporary circumstances, *lausar vísur*, 'free verses'. There are, however, three longer poems. I give here a translation of Egil's *Sonatorrek*: 'The grievous loss of my sons'. The prose that explains the composition of this work is quoted from the thirteenth-century saga and so has no historical validity. It is used here simply to explain how the poem came to be written – if the later tradition has any truth behind it.

> † Bodvar, Egil's son, was by this time growing up. He was a most promising young lad, good-looking, big and strong, just like Egil or Thorolf [Egil's brother] had been. Egil was very fond of him, and Bodvar too was attached to his father. It happened one summer that a ship came into

Hvita river where there was a trading centre. Egil had bought a load of timber there and was having it freighted back by boat. His men came to fetch it with the eight-oared boat Egil had.

One time Bodvar asked to join in so they let him. He rowed along the fiord to Vellir with the workmen, six of them together in the eight-oared boat. And when they were due to return, there was a flood-tide late in the day and they had to wait for it. So they set out late at night. Then there sprang up a fierce south-westerly with the ebb-tide running against it. Conditions grew rough in the fiord as often happens, and the end was that the ship capsized beneath them and all hands were lost. And the next day the bodies floated ashore. Bodvar's body came up at Einarsnes, further in along the fiord; others to the south of the fiord where the boat drifted too – that was found off Reykiarhamar.

Egil heard the news the same day and rode off at once to search for the bodies. He found Bodvar's body washed ashore. He picked it up, set it across his lap and rode with it out to Digranes to Skalla-Grim's burial mound. He had the mound dug open and set down Bodvar there next to Skalla-Grim. The mound was closed again; this took till sundown. After that Egil rode home to Borg. When he got home he went straight to the bed-closet where he used to sleep. He lay down pushing the latch to. No-one dared to speak to him . . .

The next day Egil refused to open the bed-closet. He took neither food nor drink and lay there all that day and the following night. No-one dared to talk to him. Then on the third day, at daybreak, Asgerd [Egil's wife] told a man to grab a horse and ride as furiously as he could west to Hiardarholt and tell Thorgerd [Egil's daughter] all that had happened. It was about three in the afternoon when he got there. He added that Asgerd had sent word for her to come south to Borg as quickly as she could.

Thorgerd had her horse saddled at once and took two men to escort her. They rode through the evening and night till they got to Borg. Thorgerd went straight into the main room. Asgerd welcomed her and asked whether they had supped. Thorgerd said loudly, 'No supper have I had, nor will I have any until I dine with Freyia. I know no better way of behaving than my father's. I have no desire to live after my father and brother.'

She went to the bed-closet and called, 'Open the door, father. Let the two of us travel the same road.'

Egil pulled back the latch. She stepped up on to the raised floor and latched the door behind her. Then she lay down on the other bed there. 'You have done well,' said Egil, 'wanting to go with your father. Deep love you have shown me. Who could expect me to want to live on after such a loss?'

Then they lay silent a while. Then Egil said, 'What are you up to, lass? Chewing something?' 'Samphire', she said, 'I expect it will make me sicker than I was before. Otherwise I am afraid I may live too long.'

'Is it bad for you?' asked Egil.

'Very bad,' she said; 'do you want some?'

'What does it matter?' he said.

A bit later she called out and asked for something to drink; water was brought for her. Then Egil said, 'That's what comes of eating samphire. You are all the more thirsty.'

'Do you want a drink, father?' she asked.

Egil reached for the horn and took a swallow. Then Thorgerd said, 'We've been cheated. This is milk.'

Then Egil took a great bite out of the horn, as far round as his teeth could compass, and threw the horn down.

'What shall we do now, father?' asked Thorgerd. 'This plan of ours has been spoiled. For my part I would hope we could continue our life together until you have composed a memorial ode to Bodvar. Then I will engrave it on a piece of wood, and then we can die if we both still want to. It will be a long time, I think, before your son Thorstein makes such a poem for Bodvar, and it is not decent that he shouldn't be commemorated, though I don't think we shall be at his wake.'

Egil said it was not to be expected that he would be able to write a poem even if he tried – 'but I can make an effort.'

Egil had had another son called Gunnar, and he too had died a short time before. This is the opening of his poem: †

> Reluctant I am to stir my tongue,
> Or raise on high my weight of song;
> No promise of gain from Vidrir's thieving,
> Can I readily draw from my heart's secret places...
>
> . . .
>
> For the line of my kin has come to its close
> Like the rotten stump of a forest tree.
> Bitter it is for a man to bear
> His children's bones down from his halls.
>
> Yet first I will speak of my mother's death,
> Of the fall of my father;             .
> The piers of my praise, foliate with words,
> I carry away from the temple of speech.
>
> Harsh to me was the breach the wave broke
> Through the encircling dyke of my father's line.
> My son's loss, the gash cut by the sea,
> Stands, as I know, open and unhealed.

Savagely has Ran handled me,
I am stripped of the friends I loved.
The main has slashed through the bonds of my kin,
The tight-spun thread of the man himself.

Know that if I could settle this feud with the sword
The end would come for the gods' ale-smith . . .

. . .

But, I thought, I had no way to find
Power to pursue my son's killer.
Only too clear to all men's eyes
An old fellow has no following to aid him.

Cruelly the sea has plundered me.
It is bitter to count the fall of kin.
Since the shield of my race departed lifeless
To travel along the paths of desire.

In my heart I know it – within my son
Sprang naught of the stuff of a man of evil;
Had he only been granted to grow in ripeness
Until the hands of the warrior-god seized him.

Ever he heeded his father's sayings
Though the whole world took another path.
In my own house he upheld me,
And was a steadfast support to my strength.

Often for me my brother's death
Enters the fair wind of the moon-wolf.
When battle swells, my thoughts engage it,
I look round for him and realize this:

What other fighting-man so valiant
Would stand beside me in angry strife;
One I often miss amidst my enemies?
As my friends diminish I become as a wounded bird.

Hard it is to find one to have faith in
Among all the peoples under the world-tree.
For there are killers of kin, deathly evil,
Who would sell a brother's corpse for rings of gold . . .

. . .

Moreover it's said that no-one can look
For recompense for his son; unless himself he fathers
Another child who to others shall be
A man born in his brother's stead.

To me there is no pleasure in man's company
Though each in his degree hold trust.
My boy has entered Odin's halls,
My wife's son, to seek his kin.

And, as I thought, the lord of malt
Still stood against me, unyielding in temper.
I cannot hold upright the hooded land,
The chariot of my understanding,

Since the flame of sickness, vengeful in act,
Seized my son from this world,
A lad, as I know, watchful against weakness,
Who guarded his tongue from slanderous speech.

This I yet remember – when the Goths' companion
Raised aloft to the home of the gods
The ashtree of my race which sprang from me,
The branch of the tree of my wife's kin.

I lived in friendship with the lord of the spear,
I felt secure, I trusted him;
Until the prince of chariots, ruler of victory,
Cut asunder our comradeship.

Not readily do I give sacrifice
To the rampart of the gods, Vilir's brother.
Yet judging more fairly, Mimir's friend
Has made me gifts that console my griefs.

Wise in warfare, the wolf's adversary
Gave me a skill that knows no fault,
And such an understanding that could reveal
Clear enmity that hid behind deceit.

Now things go hard with me. On the headland
Stands the sister of Odin's enemy.
Yet serene, in good heart, undismayed
Shall I meet death face to face.

The diction of this poem of Egil's is comparatively simple, yet there are a number of points that need explanation for the modern reader. The theme is clear enough: Egil rails against Odin who has taken from him the members of the family who should support his old age, yet recognises that Odin, giver of poetry, has been his patron through the years. But he expresses much of this elliptically. Odin is referred to as Vidrir (whose theft is the mead that gives poetic skill), he is the warrior-god, the Goths' companion, the lord of the spear, the prince of chariots. Vilir's brother, the rampart of the gods, Mimir's friend, the wolf's (i.e. Fenrir's) adversary. The sea is referred to in personified terms as Ægir who is called the ale-smith (since he brewed ale for the gods, as above, p. 195), the lord of malt; and as his wife Ran. The sister of Odin's enemy is Hel, goddess of death, sister of the wolf Fenrir. These are mythological metaphors, but there are others, not always easy to interpret. 'The fair wind of the moon-wolf' is a metaphor for thought, though why is not clear. 'The hooded land', 'the chariot of understanding' signifies the head. Even to get thus far involves a good deal of emendation of the manuscript readings. It is clear that this sort of verse was difficult even for Norsemen to get right, and it implies a sophisticated approach to poetry, which is a Viking characteristic that is not always realised by those who take their view of Vikings from simplistic sources.

From his journeys abroad – so his saga tells us – Egil had come into contact with Christianity; yet his poem shows only a pagan view of death and the afterlife. Bodvar 'has entered Odin's halls' (where all the greatest fighters shall be gathered together in readiness for the final battle of the gods against the demons); similarly Gunnar has been 'raised aloft to the home of the gods'. The values Egil celebrates here are Viking Age ones. He regrets he cannot take vengeance on or get compensation from his son's killer. He regards his family as a source of political strength, a surrounding dyke that protects him, and the loss of a member is a weakening of that protection.

## Adam of Bremen describes the great temple at Uppsala

I have already drawn attention to the fourth book of Adam of Bremen's *History of the archbishops of Hamburg-Bremen, Descriptio insularum aquilonis,* 'A description of the northern isles', with its geographical and anthropological material on the regions of Scandinavia. In its chapters 26 and 27 (and Adam's accompanying notes) there is this famous description of the heathen temple at Old Uppsala, by which archaeologists have tried to interpret the meagre finds from excavations under the church there. Nothing suggesting Adam's elaborate building has yet been found, but this has not stopped enthusiasts from reconstructing, by imagination or at best interpretation, a variety of possible sanctuaries on the site. See here Olaf Olsen's *Horg, hov og kirke* (Copenhagen, 1966, English summary, pp. 277–88). How much we need to believe Adam's account is uncertain, but even the sceptical must accept there could be truth behind some of it. Adam cites one eyewitness of at any rate the temple grove, which is like to have been a prominent feature of any major Germanic temple.

> Now let us say a bit about the superstitions of the Swedes.
>
> That nation has a most famous temple which is called Uppsala [Ubsola], not far distant from the town of Sigtuna [Sictona; another text adds or Birka]. In that temple, which is all fitted out in gold, the people honour the statues of three gods. The most powerful of them, Thor, has his seat in the centre of a triple throne. On either side Wodan and Fricco take their places. These are the significations of the three. 'Thor,' they say, 'has dominion over the atmosphere.' He is the one who governs thunder and lightning, winds and pouring rain, fine weather and fertility. The next is

Wodan, which is to say 'Fury'. He wages war and gives a man courage in the face of the enemy. The third is Fricco, distributing peace and sensual delight to mortals. His image they portray with a huge erect penis. Wodan, on the other hand, they sculpt in armour, as our carvers usually portray Mars. And Thor with his sceptre looks very like Jupiter. They also pay reverence to gods derived from men, to whom they ascribe immortality because of their heroic deeds ...

So for all their gods they have priests appointed to offer the peoples' sacrifices. If plague or famine is nigh the sacrifice is to the idol Thor; if war, to Odin; if a marriage is to be solemnised, to Fricco. In addition every nine years a communal celebration involving all the Swedish provinces is held at Uppsala. No-one is granted exemption from that particular festival. Kings and peoples, one and all, send their gifts to Uppsala; what is crueller than any penalty, those who have already turned to Christianity have to buy themselves out of those ceremonies. The sacrifice is like this. Of every living creature that is male, nine heads are offered, with whose blood it is the custom to placate the gods. The bodies are hung in the grove which lies near the temple. To the pagans that grove is so sacred that each individual tree is thought divine by virtue of the death or corruption of the creatures sacrificed. There they hang dogs and horses side by side with men. A certain Christian informed me he had seen seventy-two miscellaneous bodies suspended there. For the rest, the trivial songs that they use in this sort of sacrificial rite are many and shocking, so it is best to keep quiet about them.

*Note 1*. Near this temple is a huge tree, its branches spreading far and wide. It is always green, winter and summer alike. Nobody knows what species it is. There is also a well there where they have the practice of holding pagan sacrifices. A living man is plunged into it. If he does not surface again, the people's desire will be fulfilled.

*Note 2*. A gold chain surrounds the temple, hanging from the gables of the building. It shines far afield to those who approach it since the said shrine is set on a plain and has hills round about it in the form of an amphitheatre.

*Note 3*. These feasts and sacrifices continue for nine days. Each day they offer a man with the rest of the beasts, so that in nine days that makes seventy-two creatures offered up. This sacrifice takes place about the vernal equinox.

CHAPTER 10

# The conversion to Christianity

Christianity reached the Viking peoples at different times, in different places, probably in different guises and certainly for diverse motives. Inevitably stories told by missionary groups will give their particular slant on events, and are likely to stress the conflict between Christian and pagan religions, with particular emphasis on the miraculous way in which Divine Grace imposed itself on obstinate unbelievers. In practice, of course, it is likely that political as well as religious considerations were significant in determining whether a leader received Christianity and whether he could induce his followers to agree. Cnut the Great is an obvious example of a great Viking ruler who recognised that widespread political success would depend on his acceptance by Christian rulers abroad, which in turn required him to confirm his own Christian faith. It seems that Viking traders sometimes found it helpful to business to profess a nominal acceptance of Christianity.

Settlers in countries already converted were likely to become converted themselves, particularly if they mated with natives. Norsemen who martyred St Edmund of East Anglia in 870 were issuing a memorial coinage in the saint's name by the end of the ninth century. Another striking case is that of the Isle of Man. The tenth-century rune-stones of this island are usually in the form of a cross, of a design that is local to the Irish Sea area. Yet some of them also incorporate scenes from pagan myth. Their inscriptions show a mixed society. The texts are in Norse, though in some cases a bastard dialect that suggests a mixed language community. The script is runic, but the Celtic ogam also occurs, though rarely. The memorials record families that have, some only Norse names, others only Celtic, and yet others part Norse, part Celtic. So, Andreas II has:

Santulf the Black [Norse] put up this cross in memory of his wife Arinbiorg [Norse];

the Bride stone reads:

> [D]ruian [D]ubgall's son [Celtic] put up this cross in memory of his wife Athmiu[l] [Celtic];

while Braddan IV has:

> Thorleif hnakki [Norse] put up this cross in memory of his son Fiac [Celtic], Hafr's [Norse] nephew.

Some of the settlers of Iceland came from mixed communities like this, and brought with them their form of Christianity. *Landnámabók* (SH) has the passage:

> † Men who know say that some of the first settlers – those who colonised Iceland – had received baptism. Named among them are Helgi the Skinny, Ørlyg the Old, Helgi biola, Iorund the Christian, Aud the Deeply-Wealthy, Ketil the Daft, and others too who had sailed from the western colonies [the British Isles or Ireland]. And some continued in their Christianity right to their deaths. But that did not spread in the families, because the sons of some of them put up temples and carried out sacrifices, and the land was completely heathen for a hundred [if the numeral is used precisely, this should mean 120] years. †

Thus the conversion of the Viking nations was no simple and comprehensive business as some missionary stories imply. For a long time there were mixtures of paganism and Christianity. Indeed, as late as *c*.1200 it was possible for a Norwegian in Bergen to cut on a stick: †hæil:seþu:ok:ihuhum goþum | þor:þik:þig:gi:oþen þik æihi † 'may you be in good health and spirits: Thor receive you, Odin possess you.'

Here is given a small sample of differing approaches to the conversion of the Vikings.

## Denmark converted to Christianity: the official version

At Jelling in central Jutland is one of the most impressive of Viking Age monuments: for details see Else Roesdahl, *The Vikings* (London, 1991), pp. 162–5. It consists of two great mounds, one of which once contained a burial chamber. They are set either side of a church – now a later medieval one, but beneath it excavators have identified earlier buildings. They have also traced lines of standing stones connected somehow with the site, while at its centre, on an alignment with the tops of the mounds, are two rune-stones (one still standing where it was first set, the other brought here from elsewhere). The earlier and smaller of the two was put up by a King Gorm in memory of his wife Thorvi. The later is the most impressive single runic monument in Scandinavia. It is made from a granite erratic boulder, elaborately carved with a monstrous beast on one uneven face, and a crucifixion on another, both liberally supplied with interlace ornament. The texts inscribed on the three sides of the stone constitute a major historical source. They read:

A. King Harald ordered to be made | these monuments in memory of his father Gorm | and of his mother Thorvi. This | Harald it was who won for himself Denmark

B. all and Norway

C. and made the Danes Christians.

The complex is a public assertion designed to enhance the fame of a dynasty of kings. The Harald mentioned is known from other sources. He is the great king distinguished by his nickname *blátönn*, 'bluetooth'. Harald ruled in Denmark in the second half of the tenth century, and his conversion to Christianity occurred *c*.960. He died *c*.985. Later Norse sources show him involved in Norwegian politics during the long, confused struggles of the tenth century. A contemporary skaldic verse claims he summoned the great Earl Hakon of Trøndelag south to help him defend the border of Jutland so there is some justification for his boast of having won Norway. All this suggests a ruler determined to assert and extend his authority. His acceptance of Christianity may have been another aspect of this.

## A Viking king confirmed in Christianity in England

This account of the year 994 appears in several of the recensions of the *Anglo-Saxon Chronicle*, the C, D, E versions. It shows a mixed Viking force under the leadership of Olaf Tryggvason (*Anlaf*) of Norway and Svein Forkbeard (*Swegen*) of Denmark. The English try to split the alliance by luring Olaf to their side and reintroducing him to Christianity, and for once their diplomacy seems to work.

994. This year Anlaf and Swegen came to London with ninety-four ships on the Feast of the Nativity of St Mary, and they set about attacking the city vigorously and tried to set fire to it as well. But there they suffered greater casualties and injury than they ever thought any garrison could do to them ... Then they went off and did the greatest damage any invading force could do, burning, ravaging and killing both along the coast and in Essex, Kent, Sussex and Hampshire. In the end they seized horses, rode as widely as they wanted and kept on doing indescribable damage.

Then the king and his councillors determined to send to them and offer them blackmail money and supplies on condition they gave up the devastation. That they accepted, and all the Viking army came to Southampton and took up winter quarters there, and they were victualled from the whole of Wessex. And they were paid 16,000 pounds in cash.

Then the king [Æthelred the Unready] sent Bishop Ælfhere and Ealdorman Æthelweard to fetch Anlaf, and meanwhile hostages were handed over to the Viking ships. And then with great formality they conducted Anlaf to the king at Andover. And King Æthelred stood sponsor for him before the bishop and endowed him royally with gifts.

And Anlaf promised him that he would never return to England in hostility – and he kept his word too.

Olaf Tryggvason is known in Norse tradition as a convinced and proselytising Christian, so much so that he offended the traditional farming aristocracy of some of the Norwegian provinces and eventually lost his realm. He reigned from 995 to 1000 (according to the traditional dating), and much of that time was spent in gaining and controlling a recalcitrant kingdom. It may be this that prevented Olaf from returning to England 'in hostility', but the Chronicler implies it was his confirmation in Christianity that caused this change of behaviour.

A rune-stone, from Kuli in Møre and Romsdal, Norway, adds an interesting footnote to history. It is a simple pillar with a two-line text, badly weathered and so in part conjectural. There may be letters lost at the end of each line.

A. Thorir and Hallvard erected this stone in memory of Ulf...
B. Twelve years had Christianity been in Norway...

This is likely to refer to Olaf Tryggvason's determined mission and so to the date the local assembly accepted Christianity, perhaps under threat from the king.


## How Christianity returned to Iceland

Olaf Tryggvason tried to bring Christianity to Iceland too, but his missionary, one Thangbrand, failed because of his difficult temperament. When Thangbrand reported back Olaf was fiercely angry and planned to do harm to all Icelandic men he caught within his dominions. Two leading Icelanders, Gizur the Fair and Hialti Skeggiason, persuaded the king to let them make a new attempt to convert the pagans in Iceland. Ari Thorgilsson takes up the tale in his *Íslendingabók*.

> The next summer they came west to Iceland, bringing with them a priest called Thormod, and they landed in the Vestmannaeyiar [islands off the south coast of Iceland] when it was ten weeks into summer and had had a good voyage. This is what Teit said was told him by a man who had been there. The previous summer it had been enacted that men should attend the Althingi when it was ten weeks into summer; up to then they had come a week earlier.
>
> They went straightaway to the mainland and on to the Althingi, but they prevailed upon Hialti to stay behind at Laugardal with eleven men because the previous year at the Althingi he had been sentenced to outlawry for blasphemy. And the case against him was that he had recited this couplet at the Law-rock:
>
> > Blasphemy is not for me,
> > But what a bitch must Freyia be.
>
> Gizur and his companions travelled as far as a place near Olfossvatn called

Vellankatla, and from there sent word to the *thing* for all their supporters to come and join them because they had heard that their enemies would try to keep them away from Thingvellir by force of arms. And before they journeyed on who should come riding up but Hialti and the men left behind with him.

So they rode on to the *thing* but not until their kinsmen and friends had come to meet them as they had begged them to. But the heathens gathered together fully armed, and it looked a close thing whether they would fight or not. And the following day Gizur and Hialti walked up to the Law-rock and declared their message; and the record tells how remarkably well they spoke. But this was the effect, that one man after another named witnesses, and the two sides, Christians and pagans, declared themselves to be out of law with one another. And so they left the Law-rock.

Then the Christians asked Hall of Sida [one of Thangbrand's converts] to declare publicly for them a law that would be conformable to Christianity. But he excused himself, making a bargain with the law-speaker Thorgeir to declare the law despite the fact that he was then still heathen. After that, when they had all returned to their huts, Thorgeir set himself down and spread his cloak over him, and lay there all that day and the following night, and not a word did he say. And the next morning he sat up and sent round for everyone to go to the Law-rock.

When they had all arrived he began his speech. He said that, as he judged it, men's affairs would get into an impossible state if they should not all have the same law in this land, and he argued in various ways that that could not be allowed to happen. He said it would lead to so much dissension as to make certain that there would be such fighting between men that the land would be devastated. He told how the kings of Norway and Denmark had waged war and battle against each other for a long time until the people of those lands made peace between them though they had no wish for it. That plan worked out so well that they were soon sending gifts, one to the other, and what's more the peace continued as long as they both lived.

'So it seems advisable to me', he said, 'that we should not leave decisions in the hands of those who are most fiercely opposed to one another. Let us mediate between them so that both sides get some part of their case, and we all have the same law and the same religion. For it will turn out to be true that if we cut law asunder, we cut peace asunder too.' His speech ended with both sides agreeing that they should all have the one law and that should be what he declared.

Then it was promulgated by law that everyone should be Christian and accept baptism if they were still unbaptised in this land. But the old law should stand as regards exposure of [unwanted] infants and eating horse-flesh. If they wished men could sacrifice in secret; but suffer the sentence of outlawry if witnesses to it could be produced. But a few years later these aspects of paganism were abolished like the rest. These were the circumstances under which, Teit told me, Christianity came to Iceland.

What is interesting here is that, though both sides felt deeply about religion, the final decision was made not on the grounds of religious truth but of political and legal unity; to the extent that practices that must have been repugnant to Christianity were allowed to continue, at least for a time. To leave an unwanted or unviable infant outside to die was a method of controlling population in an age that had not yet developed a safe method of killing them before birth as in our more enlightened times. The link between eating horse-meat and practising paganism is a curious one, but it persists in the Germanic consciousness for centuries (on this see my inaugural lecture, *Anglo-Saxon aptitudes* [Cambridge, 1981], pp. 15–19). On the whole subject of this passage Dag Strömbäck has written in *The conversion of Iceland: a survey*, Viking Society for Northern Research: Text series vol. 6 (London, 1975).

## Two attempts at converting the Swedes

These two reports are taken from Rimbert's *Vita Anskarii*, 'Life of St Ansgar'. Rimbert, who became Archbishop of Hamburg-Bremen in 865, wrote the life of his predecessor, the Apostle of the North, at some time between 865 and 876. Ansgar made two missionary journeys to what is now Sweden in 829–31 and the early 850s, though their early successes did not lead to lasting conversion since the country remained largely pagan until towards the end of the Viking Age. The scene of these two episodes is Birka, a great international trading-town on an island (Björkö) in Lake Mälar in central Sweden. Excavations of the site in the nineteenth and twentieth centuries have confirmed the town's commercial importance.

Rimbert's account gives useful information on the organisation and control of such a trade centre, and also stresses the limitation of royal power by popular will as expressed in formal assemblies of the people held at specific times and on specific sites. The first of these extracts records Ansgar's first journey to Birka at the request of Swedish envoys to the imperial court, who had conveyed their king's invitation to a Christian mission to teach such of his subjects as wanted to convert to Christianity.

> 1. So they travelled the immense distances on foot with the greatest of hardship, and where it was appropriate crossed the intervening seas by boat. At length they arrived at a port in the kingdom of the Swedes called Byrca. Here they were graciously received by the king, whose name was Bern. His envoys had informed him why the Christians had made their journey.
>
> When he learned the object of their mission he took counsel with his faithful people about it, and with their unanimous approval and agreement gave them permission to stay there and preach the gospel of Christ. Freedom was granted to anyone who wanted it to seek out their teaching. So the servants of God, seeing their affairs had turned out favourably and

to their wish, began with eager hearts to proclaim the word of salvation to the people living in the town.

Many there were who looked with favour on their mission and freely heard the Lord's doctrine. There were even a number of Christians held captive among them, who were glad to be able to participate in the holy mysteries at last. So it demonstrated the truth of all that the Swedish envoys had declared to the Serene Emperor. Numbers of them earnestly sought the grace of baptism. Among these was the prefect of the town, a man called Herigar, member of the royal council and much loved by the king. He received the gift of holy baptism and continued very firm in the Catholic faith. Soon afterwards he built a church on his family estate and devoted himself assiduously to the service of God ...

When they had spent another half-year with the Swedes and had demonstrated the success of their mission, the aforesaid servants of God returned to the Serene Emperor with letters in the king's own hand, formed according to the Swedish practice.

The Christian mission did not long survive Ansgar's return to Germany and election to the see of Hamburg. A replacement, Gautbert, was driven out by a pagan mob, and for some seven years Birka remained without a priest, though Herigar and his comrades remained faithful, supported by one Ardgar, 'a certain anchorite'. Eventually Ansgar was allowed to make a second attempt.

2. Completing the journey he had undertaken, Ansgar reached Byrca after nearly twenty days on board ship. There he found the king and most of the people confused with grievous error. At the instigation of the devil, who had quite foreseen the arrival of this blessed man, there happened to come there one who said he had been at a council of the gods who were thought to be owners of this land, and had been sent by them to make this representation to the king and people.

'You, I say, have long found us gracious towards you. With our support you have held this most fertile land – your dwelling-place – in peace and prosperity for many years. On your part you have performed sacrifices and rendered us your votive offerings. Your allegiance has been pleasing. But now you are withholding your customary sacrifices and becoming slack in your voluntary offerings. What displeases us even more, you have raised up an alien god over us. So if you want us to continue gracious to you, augment the neglected sacrifices and offer greater votive gifts. Reject the cult of another god whose teaching is contrary to ours. Do not turn to his service. In any case if you want to have more gods, if we are not adequate to your purposes, we are ready to admit to our society Eric, once your king, so that he may take his place among your gods.'

Now this announcement of the devil's, publicly proclaimed at the lord bishop's arrival, disturbed the minds of everyone, and even greater error and confusion seized men's hearts; for they had established a temple in honour of the said king (who had died a little before this), and had begun to render him votive offerings and sacrifices as though he were a god.

So, on his arrival the lord bishop began to question the friends he had made there earlier, asking how he might approach the king on this subject. They spoke against it with all their force, asserting that his embassy could achieve nothing at this time; but if he had brought anything of value with him, he should give it the king and so escape with his life . . . Since he was placed in a position of great uncertainty he eventually accepted this advice and invited the king to partake of his hospitality. While giving this entertainment he brought out such gifts as he could, and set forward the terms of his embassy . . . Delighted by his loving kindness and generosity the king replied that for himself he would be glad to accept what the other had proposed. 'However,' he said, 'in the past there have been clerics who were thrown out, not by royal command, but by popular insurrection. That is why I cannot – indeed I dare not – support this mission of yours before I have consulted our gods by lot-casting, and also determined the people's will in this matter. Let your envoy join me at the next legal assembly and I will speak to the people on your behalf. And if, with the gods' approval, the people consent to your wishes, what you have asked for will be fulfilled. If not, I will let you know. It is, you see, our practice for all public business to remain in the hands of the people as a whole, and not in the king's' . . .

When the day of the assembly (which, as was customary, was to take place in the aforesaid trading centre of Byrca) drew near, the king made a proclamation to the people through the mouth of a spokesman, announcing the purpose of their mission. When they heard it, so confused were they by their previous errors that they began to quarrel with one another and to lose all restraint. They made a great uproar, whereupon one of them, an older man, stood up in the midst of the crowd and said.

'Listen to me, king and people! About the worship of this god. Many of us know already what great help can come to anyone who puts his trust in Him. Indeed, many of us have discovered this often when in peril on the sea and in various other straits. So why should we reject what we know is both necessary and useful to us? Any of us who have been at one time or another in Dorestad [a famous commercial centre in the Low Countries] will have recognised that this form of religion was beneficial and will have embraced it spontaneously. Now the journey there is beset by so many ambushes and by danger of pirate attacks. Why then don't we take to ourselves what is offered now, since we have already sought it so keenly from afar? . . .'

When he had finished his speech, the whole crowd together agreed that the priests should remain with them, and that they could perform everything that was consonant with the Christian mysteries without hindrance. And so the king left the assembly, directing his officer to

229

accompany the bishop's envoy to report the people's acceptance of what he proposed. The king was happy about this in every way, yet he could not give his full consent until another assembly had been held in another part of his kingdom to give the same report to the people who lived there ... When the date of that assembly arrived, the king's spokesman presented the lord bishop's mission and also described everything that had been said and done in the earlier assembly. So, by the grace of divine providence, the hearts of all were so united that they all approved the vote of the former assembly, announcing their readiness to agree to all these things too.

When this had taken place, the king called the lord bishop to him and related what had taken place. Thus, by the common agreement and assent of all, he ordered that churches should be built and priests accepted among them, and that anyone in the population who wanted to become Christian could do so without restraint.

# Envoi

Common sense from the Viking Age

A stupid man lies awake all night
Brooding over his troubles.
When morning breaks he's quite worn out
And things are as bad as ever.

. . .

A stupid man in company
Had better hold his tongue.
No-one will know how stupid he is
If he doesn't talk too much.
(Though a man who knows nothing cannot know
When he is talking too much).

. . .

Early to rise if you want to steal
Another man's money or his life.
The slumbering wolf misses his prey,
The sleeper the victory.

. . .

Early to rise if you have few helpers.
Set about the job yourself.
No future for the man who sleeps all morning.
Hard work is half the fortune.

. . .

Sensible men must question and answer
If they want to be thought wise.
Let one know your thoughts; not two.
If three, the whole world will know.

. . .

Now are the words of the High One spoken
In the High One's hall,
Most useful to the sons of men,
Useless to the sons of giants.
Good luck to the one who spoke them!
Good luck to the one who knows them!
Put them to good use, you who learn them!
Good luck to all who have heard them!

# List of texts quoted

I give here a list of the major texts quoted/translated with the editions used, and cross-references to the present book, (the latter in brackets). For the sagas of Icelanders, *Heimskringla, Íslendingabók, Knýtlinga saga, Landnámabók, Nóregs konunga tal* and *Orkneyingasaga*, I have used the 'standard' editions in the series *Íslenzk fornrit*. For poems of the Poetic Edda I have in general taken the convenient text of Gustav Neckel, 3rd ed. (Heidelberg, 1936) but for certain poems other editions noted below. On runic inscriptions I have consulted the standard corpora: Denmark and related territories in Lis Jacobsen & Erik Moltke, *Danmarks runeindskrifter*, 3 vols. (Copenhagen, 1941–2) (= DR); Norway in Magnus Olsen *et al., Norges innskrifter med de yngre runer* (Oslo 1941–, in progress) (= NIyR); Sweden in *Sveriges runinskrifter* (1900–, in progress), distributed among the Swedish regions, G(otland), Sm(åland), Sö(dermanland), U(ppland), V(äster)g(ötland), V(ä)s(tmanland), Ö(ster)g(ötland).

Alcuin, Anglo-Saxon scholar, letter to Bishop Higebald of Lindisfarne, 793 [ed. Colin Chase, *Two Alcuin letter-books*. Toronto, 1975, pp. 50–2] (p. 79).

*Anglo-Saxon Chronicle* [parallel versions ed. Benjamin Thorpe, Rolls Series. London, 1861, vol. 1] entries for 876 (p. 58); 878,

880 (p. 177); 991 (p. 178); 994 (p. 224); 1010–11 (p. 77); 1014–16 (p. 160); 1015–16 (p. 146); 1066 (p. 135).

Anglo-Saxon treaties [ed. F. Liebermann, *Die Gesetze der Angelsachsen*. Halle a.S., 1903–16, vol. 1] AGu, Alfred the Great and Guthrum, *c*.886 (p. 177); IIAtr, Æthelred the Unready and the Viking army, *c*.995 (p. 179).

*Annales Bertiniani* [Annals of St Bertin; ed. G. Waitz, Scriptores rerum Germanicarum in usum scholarum. Hanover, 1883] entry for 839 (p. 97).

*Atlakviða* [The song of Atli, ?C10; ed. Ursula Dronke, *The Poetic Edda*. Oxford, 1969–, vol. 1, pp. 3–74] (p. 118).

*Austrfararvísur* [Verses on the eastern journey, poem by Sigvat Thordarson, C11] (p. 49).

*Battle of Brunanburh*, Old English poem, *c*.940 [ed. Elliott van Kirk Dobbie, *The Anglo-Saxon minor poems*. ASPR 6. London & New York, 1942, pp. 16–20] (p. 136).

*Battle of Maldon*, Old English poem, *c*.995 [ed. Elliott van Kirk Dobbie, *The Anglo-Saxon minor poems*. ASPR 6. London & New York, 1942, pp. 7–16] (p. 134).

*Bersöglisvísur* [The plain-speaking verses, poem by Sigvat Thordarson, C11] (p. 162).

*De administrando imperio* [On administering

a realm, by Constantine Porphyrogenitos, *c*.944; ed. G. Moravcsik. Revised text Dumbarton Oaks, 1967] ch. 9 (p. 94).

*Egils saga Skalla-Grímssonar* [The tale of Egil Skalla-Grimsson, C13] ch. 57 (p. 24); ch. 60 (= Egil's 'Head ransom') (p. 21); ch. 77 (p. 28); ch. 78 (p. 215).

*Eiríksmál* [Funeral ode for Eirik Bloodaxe, C10] (p. 110).

*Encomium Emmae Reginae* [A book in praise of Queen Emma, *c*.1040; ed. Alistair Campbell. Camden Society, 3. Ser. 72. London, 1949] i §§3, 4 (p. 116); ii §4 (p. 117); §15 (p. 146).

*Eyrbyggiasaga* [The history of the people of Eyr, C13] ch. 4 (p. 29).

*Fagrskinna*: see *Norégs konunga tal*.

*Flateyiarbók*, compilation mainly of kings' sagas, C14 [ed. Guðbrandr Vigfusson & C. R. Unger. 3 vols. Kristiania, 1860–68) vol. 1 p. 328 (p. 22); vol. 2 p. 242 (p. 24); p. 377 (p. 23).

*Frostaþingslög* [Law of the Frostathing, from *c*.1260, but incorporating earlier material; ed. R. Keyser & P. A. Munch in *Norges gamle love indtil 1387*, I. Christiania, 1846, pp. 19–258] i §1 (p. 35); ix 1 (p. 180); 12 (p. 181).

*Gesta Hammaburgensis ecclesiae pontificum* [Activities of the prelates of the church at Hamburg, by Adam of Bremen, *c*.1075; ed. Bernhard Schmeidler, Scriptores rerum Germanicarum in usum scholarum. Hanover & Leipzig, 1917] iv §§1, 4–7 (p. 41); §21 (p. 36); §§21, 22 (p. 43); §§26–7 (p. 220); §§31–3 (p. 43); §38 (p. 92).

*Gesta regum Anglorum* [Exploits of the English kings, by William of Malmesbury, first half C12; ed. William Stubbs. 2 vols. Rolls Series. London, 1887–9] ii §228 (p. 135); iii §260 (p. 104).

*Hákonarmál* [Funeral ode for Hakon the Good, C10] (p. 111).

*Hávamál* [The words of the High One, Poetic Edda, ?date; ed. David A. H. Evans. Viking Society for Northern Research Text Series 7. London, 1986] vv. 1–5, 10–12 (p. 140); vv 19–21 (p. 142); vv. 23, 27 (p. 231); vv. 34, 39 (p. 171); vv. 35, 38 (p. 141); vv. 36–7, 61 (p. 142); vv. 41–7, 50–2 (p. 171) vv. 54–6 (p. 143); vv. 58–9, 63 (p. 231); vv. 66–7 (p. 39); vv. 70–1 (p. 141); vv. 76–7 (p. 138); v. 78 (p. 142); vv. 81, 84–94 (p. 143); vv. 95–110 (p. 191); vv. 138–41 (p. 194); vv. 146–63 (p. 213); v. 164 (p. 231).

*Heimskringla* [The world's circle, a collection of sagas of kings, by Snorri Sturluson, *c*.1230]:
Preface p. 5 (p. 17); p. 6 (p. 26).
*Ynglinga saga* [History of the Ynglings] ch. 6–7 (p. 212).
*Haralds saga ins hárfagra* [History of Harald Finehair] ch. 39–40 (p. 31).
*Hákonar saga góða* [History of Hakon the Good] ch. 11 (p. 34); ch. 28 (p. 18) ch. 31 (p. 111).
*Haralds saga gráfeldar* [History of Harald Greycloak] ch. 16 (p. 147).
*Óláf's saga helga* [History of St Olaf] ch. 71 (p. 54); ch. 91 (p. 48); ch. 160 (p. 22).
*Magnúss saga ins góða* [History of Magnus the Good] ch. 15–16, (p. 162).
*Haralds saga Sigurðarsonar* [History of Harald Sigurdarson] ch. 71 (p. 164).

*Helgakviða Hundingsbana I* [The first lay of Helgi, killer of Hunding, Poetic Edda, ?C11] (p. 127).

*Hrafnsmál* [The raven's tale, poem by ?Thorbiorn hornklofi, *c*.900] (p. 107).

*Íslendingabók* [The Icelanders' book, by Ari Thorgilsson, *c*.1130] ch. 1, 3 (p. 26); ch. 1, 3 (p. 59); ch. 2 (p. 173); ch. 4 (p. 175); ch. 5 (p. 176); ch. 6 (p. 92); ch. 7 (p. 225).

*Knútsdrápa* [Poem in praise of King Knut, by Ottar the Black] (p. 156).

*Knýtlinga saga* [The history of the descendants of Knut, C13] ch. 7–13 (p. 156).

*Landnámabók* [The book of the settlements, by Ari Thorgilsson and Kolskegg Asbiarnarson, C12, but existing only in later recensions, listed here as S, H] S5 (p. 61); S42 (p. 62); S64–5 (p. 27); S72 (p. 62); S95, 97–8, 110 (p. 64); S120 (p. 28); S145 (p. 66); S165 (p. 28); S194–6 (p. 66); S197 (p. 67); S198 (p. 28); S207 (p. 67); S215 (p. 68); S242 (p. 69); S270 (p. 70); S297 (p. 70); S327 (p. 28); S328–9 (p. 71); S355 (p. 71); S376 (p. 72); S377 (p. 73); S394 (p. 74); S399 (p. 223); H5 (p. 61); H63 (p. 63); H78 (p. 92); H223 (p. 69); H268 (p. 173); H276 (p. 70); H294 (p. 58).

*Λόγος νουθετητικος*, [A word of wisdom, by Kekaumenos, later C11; ed. B. Wassiliewsky & V. Jernstedt, *Cecaumeni Strategicon*. St Petersburg, 1896] *Προς Βασιλεα* §12 (p. 104).

*Lokasenna* [Loki speaks his mind, Poetic Edda, ?date] (p. 195).

*Nestor's chronicle:* see *Russian primary chronicle.*

Nikolas of Thvera, Icelandic traveller, C12, [ed. Kr.Kålund, *Alfræði íslensk*, I. Samfund til udgivelse af gammel nordisk litteratur 37. Copenhagen, 1908.] *Landafræði* §5 (p. 40).

*Norégs konunga tal* [The list of Norway's kings, *c.*1230) ch. 2 (p. 107); ch. 4 (p. 32); ch. 8 (p. 109); ch. 12 (p. 19); ch. 14 (p. 148); ch. 51 (p. 100).

*Old English Orosius* [Old English translation of Orosius's *Historia adversum paganos, c.*890; ed. Janet Bately. EETS SS 6. Oxford, 1980] i, §1 (p. 46).

*Orkneyingasaga* [History of the men of Orkney, *c.*1200] ch. 58, (p. 168).

*Povest':* see *Russian primary chronicle.*

*Prose Edda* [by Snorri Sturluson, *c.*1220; ed. Finnur Jónsson, 2nd ed. Copenhagen, 1926.] *Gylfaginning* §7 (p. 186), §50 (pp. 189, 190, 211), *Skáldskaparmál* §1 (p. 192).

*Rígspula* [The rhyme of Rig, Poetic Edda, date disputed] (p. 150).

Runic inscriptions:

Denmark: Hedeby 1 DR 1 (p. 167); Hedeby 3 DR 3 (pp. 90, 167); Jelling 2 DR 42 (p. 224); Hørning DR 58 (p. 170); Egå DR 107 (p. 169); Kolind DR 108 (p. 91); Gunderup DR 143 (p. 75); Glavendrup DR 209 (p. 174); Uppåkra DR 266 (p. 91); Sjörup DR 279 (p. 105); Sövestad 2 DR 291 (p. 10); Hällestad 1 DR 295 (p. 106); Hällestad 2 DR 296 (p. 106); Hällestad 3 DR 297 (p. 105); Valleberga DR 337 (p. 91); Vester Marie DR 387 (p. 145); Svenstrup in Erik Moltke, *Runes and their origin: Denmark and elsewhere.* Copenhagen, 1985. p. 312 (p. 146).

Norway: Alstad NIyR 62 (p. 91); Dynna NIyR 68 (p. 170); Galteland NIyR 184 (p. 91); Kuli NIyR 449 (p. 225); unknown place in Norway NIyR 541 (p. 11); Bergen in Aslak Liestøl, *Runer frå Bryggen.* Bergen, 1964, p. 37 (p. 223).

Sweden: Stenkumla G207 (p. 171); Timans G216 (p. 12); Transjö Sm5 (p. 86); Tuna Sm42 (p. 169); Sävsjö Sm76 (p. 169); Sävsjö Sm77 (p. 169); Glömsjö Sm100 (p. 56); Nöbbelesholm Sm101 (p. 87); Tjuvstigen Sö34–5 (p. 80); Åda Sö39 (p. 80); Bjudby Sö54 (p. 170); Bjudby Sö55 (p. 82); Djulefors Sö65 (p. 82); Kungshållet Sö106 (p. 82); Fagerlöt Sö126 (p. 81);

Lundby Sö131 (p. 89); Råby Sö160 (p. 82); Grinda Sö165 (p. 82); Grinda Sö166 (p. 82); Esta Sö171 (p. 81); Tystberga Sö173 (p. 89); Gripsholm Sö179 (p. 89); Mervalla Sö198 (p. 80); S. Betby Sö260 (p. 83); Turingevägen Sö311–12 (p. 56); Turinge Sö338 (p. 81); Hillersjö U29 (p. 75); Hansta U72, 73 (p. 76); S.Sätra U101 (p. 56); Ed U112 (p. 84); Runby U114A (p. 55); Nora U130 (p. 75); Broby U136 (p. 85); Täby U164–5 (p. 56); Väsby U194 (pp. 10, 86); Veda U209 (p. 83); Vallentuna U212 (p. 56); Vallentuna U214 (p. 83); Sälna U323 (p. 55); Yttergärde U343–4 (p. 85); Näs U347 (p. 55); Ängby U356 (p. 83); Skepptuna U358 (p. 84); Sigtuna U379 (p. 171); Steninge U439 (p. 88); Ubby U504 (p. 85); Husby-Lyhundra U539 (p. 85); Söderby-Karl U582 (p. 83); Stäket U605 (p. 85); Bro U617 (p. 169); Låddersta U636 (p. 84); Ekilla U644 (p. 88); Varpsund U654 (p. 89); Råby U661 (p. 89); Kålsta U668 (p. 86); Sjusta U687 (p. 83); Ågersta U729 (p. 168); Svinnegarn U778 (p. 88); Ulunda U792 (p. 84); Gryta U867 (p. 55); Söderby U954 (p. 145); Karberga U996 (p. 57); Fjuckby U1016 (p. 84); Årby U1033 (p. 55); Lövsta U1087 (p. 85); Tierp U1143 (p. 89); Norra Äsarp Vg181 (p. 87); Smula Vg184 (p. 87); Vist Vg187 (p. 88); Dalum Vg197 (p. 88); Berga Vs19 (p. 90); Högby Ög81 (p. 87); Harstad Ög94 (p. 87); Sylten Ög155 (p. 90); Kullerstad Ög162 (p. 56); Karlevi, Öland (= DR 411) (p. 15); Malsta, Hälsingland, in Sven B. F. Jansson, *Två runstenar i Hälsingland: Malsta och Sunnå*, Filologisk Arkiv 33. Kungl. Vitterhets Historie och Antikvitets Akademien, 1985. p. 25 (p. 75).

England: London (= DR 412) (p. 91).

Isle of Man: R. I. Page, 'The Manx runic inscriptions' in Christine Fell et al, *The Isle of Man in the Viking Age*, London, 1983, pp. 140–1: Andreas II (p. 222); Braddan II (p. 145); Braddan IV (p. 223); Bride (p. 223).

Russia: Berezan' in Aslak Liestøl, 'Runic inscriptions', *Varangian problems.* Scando-Slavica: supplementum 1, p. 126 (p. 97).

*Russian primary chronicle/Nestor's chronicle/Povest'* [The narrative of past times, 1111–13, but surviving only in later recensions, and incorporating earlier material; ed. Dmitrij Tschiževskij, Slavistische Studienbücher 6. Wiesbaden, 1969] entries for 907 (p. 98), 912, 945 (p. 99).

*Sonatorrek* [The grievous loss of my sons, poem by Egil Skalla-Grimsson, C10] (p. 217).

*Vafþrúðnismál* [What Vafthrudnir said, Poetic Edda, C10; ed. Tim William Machan. Durham Medieval Texts 6. 1988], p. 183.

*Vita Anskarii* [Life of St Ansgar, by Rimbert, *c.*870; ed. G. Waitz. Scriptores rerum Germanicarum in usum scholarum. Hanover, 1884] §§11–12 (p. 227); §§26–8 (p. 228).

*Völsunga saga* [The saga of the Volsungs, C13; ed. R. G. Finch. London, 1965] ch. 9 (p. 125).

*Völuspá* [The wise woman's prophecy, Poetic Edda, ?*c.*1000] (p. 205).

# Index

## A

Adam of Bremen, German historian 35–6, 41–5, 49, 92–3, 155, 220–1

Ægir, brewer of real ale 54, 195–7, 202, 220

Ælfheah, St, Archbishop of Canterbury 78–9

Æsir, race of gods 51, 188, 190, 203, 205–7, 209, 212

Æthelred the Unready, English king 98, 115, 156, 158, 160, 179, 224

Africa, Vikings in 101, *see also Serkland*

*álfablót*, elf-sacrifice 50–1

Alcuin, English scholar 79

Alfred the Great, English king 45–6, 98, 176–7

Althingi, Icelandic General Assembly 26, 175, 225–6

AM 748 4°, Icelandic manuscript containing Eddic poetry 12, 183

America, *see* Vinland

*Anglo-Saxon Chronicle* 30, 58, 77–9, 134, 135–6, 142, 146, 160–1, 176–8, 224–5

*Annales Bertiniani*, Annals of St Bertin 97

Ansgar, St, Apostle of the North 227–30

Ari Thorgilsson, Icelandic historian 25–7, 34, 59, 60, 175

Athelstan, English king 31–4, 110, 136

*Atlakviða*, the Song of Atli 118–24

*Austrfararvísur* 49–54

## B

Baldr, beloved god, killed by Loki's wiles 110, 191, 198, 203, 208–9, 211

bartering 148

*Battle of Brunanburh*, Old English poem 136–8

*Battle of Maldon*, Old English poem 133–5

*baugeiðr*, ring-oath 30, 174, 193

Berezan', island at the mouth of the Dnieper 94, 97, 167

*Bersöglisvísur, see* Plain-speaking verses

Birka, Swedish market town 220, 227–9

Book of the Icelanders, *see Íslendingabók*

Book of the Settlements, *see Landnámabók*

Bragi, minor god 110, 114, 195–7, 204

bridge-building 55–6, 85, 170

Byzantium, Constantinople, *Mikligarðr* 12, 36, 82, 94, 97–100

Byzantine empire, Greece 12, 76, 84–5, 87, 97–104

## C

calendar, reform of 175

causeways, *see* bridge-building

Christianity 9, 27, 30, 35, 42, 44, 55–7, 59, 62, 65, 81, 85, 89, 102, 111–12, 148–9, 155, 163, 177, 194, 204, 214, 220, 222–30

Cnut (Knut) the Great, King of Denmark and England 8, 10, 22, 85–6, 91, 115, 117, 146, 155–61, 222

Codex Regius, manuscript containing Eddic poems 12, 13, 118, 124, 183, 195, 204

common sense 141